The Most Glorious Crown

The Story of America's
Triple Crown Thoroughbreds
from Sir Barton to Affirmed

Marvin Drager

TRIUMPH
BOOKS
CHICAGO

Library of Congress Cataloging-in-Publication Data

Drager, Marvin.
    The most glorious crown : the story of America's Triple Crown Thoroughbreds from Sir Barton to Affirmed / Marvin Drager.
        p. cm.
    Originally published; New York : Winchester Press, [1975]
    Includes bibliographical references and index.
    ISBN 1-57243-724-3
    1. Triple Crown (U.S. horse racing) 2. Race horses—United States.   I. Title.

SF357.T74D7 2005
798.4'0092'9—dc22

                                                                2004059898

This book is available in quantity at special discounts for your group or organization. For further information, contact:

Triumph Books
601 South LaSalle Street
Suite 500
Chicago, Illinois 60605
(312) 939-3330
Fax (312) 663-3557

Printed in United States of America
ISBN 13: 978-1-57243-724-1
ISBN 10: 1-57243-724-3
Design by Patricia Frey

To

Lenore

and

Sharon, Laura, Iris

"The women in my life"

With love, thanks, and gratitude for the patience and equanimity

with which you endured oft-told horse tales.

Contents

Acknowledgments

Special thanks and recognition for their generous time, cooperation, and assistance to:

Bob Corran Jr.—The Jockey Club
John I. Day—Thoroughbred Racing Associations
Calvin S. Rainey—The Jockey Club
John Kennedy—The Jockey Club
Robert F. Kelley
Alfred G. Vanderbilt—New York Racing Association
William C. Steinkraus
Charles Hatton—*Daily Racing Form*
Cathy C. Schenck—Keeneland Library
Amelia K. Buckley—Keeneland Library
Phyllis Rogers—Keeneland Library
George Cassidy—New York Racing Association
Charles J. Lang—The Maryland Jockey Club (Pimlico Race Course)
Philip McAuley—Casper, Wyoming, *Star-Tribune*
Owen A. Frank—Casper, Wyoming, *Star-Tribune*
John A. Cypher Jr.—King Ranch
J. K. Northway, DVM—King Ranch
Dick Nash—Los Angeles Turf Club (Santa Anita Park)
George Lobris—Narragansett Racing Association (Narragansett Park)
Stan Bowker—Knights of Ak-Sar-Ben
Robert P. Benoit—Hollywood Turf Club (Hollywood Park)
Francis Dunne—New York State Racing Commission
Bud Hyland—The Jockey Club
Pat Lynch—New York Racing Association (Aqueduct, Belmont Park, Saratoga)
Thomas S. Rivera—Chicago Thoroughbred Enterprises (Arlington Park)
William J. (Buddy) Hirsch
H. A. (Jimmy) Jones—Monmouth Park Jockey Club
William Rudy—Churchill Downs
Alex Robb—New York State Breeders Service

Michael P. Sandler—*Daily Racing Form*
Fred Grossman—*Daily Racing Form*
Sam Siciliano—Pimlico Race Course
John Cooney—The Jockey Club
Martha Mischo—The Jockey Club
Marguerite Smithers—The Jockey Club
Jack Fletcher—United Press International
Mike LeTourneau—Wide World Photos
Marty Monroe—Wide World Photos
Humphrey Finney
Charlie Kenney—Stoner Creek Stud
Louis Weintraub—New York Racing Association
Steve Haskin—*Daily Racing Form*
Jennifer Lusk—*Daily Racing Form*
The New York Public Library
Columbia University Library
Kerry Cordero—New Video
John Lee—New York Racing Association

. . . and the many people in the United States, Canada, England, and France who were kind enough to take time out to respond to inquiries I made in the course of researching the book.

This book was prepared with a dedicated devotion to the accuracy of the information contained within its covers. Any errata which may crop up are purely unintentional, for which the author begs the reader's indulgence.

Introduction

A small red box with gold snap-lock and hinges sits atop a tall green safe in the posh offices of the Thoroughbred Racing Associations (TRA). It contains a triangular, three-sided, sterling silver vase approximately eight inches tall, which symbolizes the epitome of achievement for a three-year-old Thoroughbred. It is the Triple Crown of American turfdom.

Each side of the trophy represents one of the three races that a single horse must win in a single year to earn the title. Often referred to as the three "jewels" in the Triple Crown, they are the Kentucky Derby, the Preakness Stakes, and the Belmont Stakes, three of the oldest classics of America's king of sports.

From 1978 through 2004, every spring, the vase had been sent to its designer, Cartier, to be burnished to a painfully brilliant gloss in anticipation of the next winner of the trophy. On the second week of June, in each of these years, the vase was returned to its red box, which was returned to its perch atop the tall green safe in the posh offices of the TRA, as yet another season passed without a recipient.

The fact is, from 1875 through 2004, the years that all three races have been in existence simultaneously, only 11 horses have won the Triple Crown, making it the most elusive championship in all of sports. It was last won in 1978, and the members of this exclusive club of titleholders are: Sir Barton (1919), Gallant Fox (1930), Omaha (1935), War Admiral (1937), Whirlaway (1941), Count Fleet (1943), Assault (1946), Citation (1948), Secretariat (1973), Seattle Slew (1977), and Affirmed (1978).

In fairness to all Thoroughbreds, past and present, it should be duly noted that some extenuating circumstances ruled out at least eight possible winners.

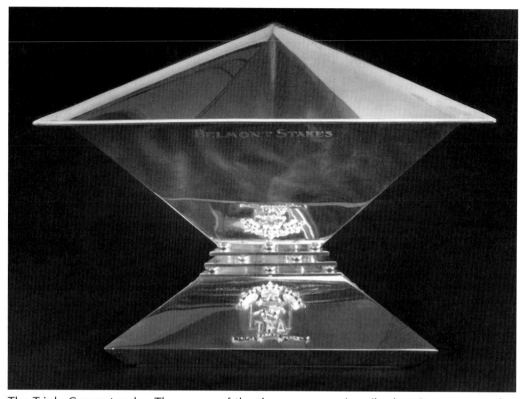

The Triple Crown trophy. The names of the three races are inscribed on it, one on each of the three sides.

In 1890, both the Preakness and the Belmont Stakes were raced on the same day; there was a three-year hiatus in the running of the Preakness, from 1891 to 1893; Governor Charles Evans Hughes of New York banned racing in the state during 1911 and 1912, which blacked out the Belmont Stakes; and both the Kentucky Derby and the Preakness were raced on the same day in 1917 and 1922.

Although the Kentucky Derby is the most famous of the three races, it is the youngest. It was first run in 1875 on land owned by John and Henry Churchill in Louisville, Kentucky. The tract eventually took on the name of Churchill Downs. Today, the race is presented on the first Saturday in May. Its official flower is the rose, which prompted sportswriter Bill Corum to coin the phrase "Run for the Roses." Perhaps its greatest importance lies in the fact that it is "the first race in which the best horses from one crop of foals meet at the accepted classic distance of a mile and a quarter," carrying 126 pounds.

The Preakness is raced two weeks later at Pimlico Race Course in Baltimore, Maryland. It was established in 1873 at Pimlico and was raced at Morris Park in the Bronx, New York, in 1890, and at Gravesend Course in Brooklyn, from 1894 to 1908. Finally it settled permanently thereafter back in Maryland. The distance is 1 3⁄16 miles, with 126 pounds, for a blanket of black-eyed Susans, the state's official flower.

Although it is the oldest of the three, the Belmont Stakes is perhaps the least popularly known. However, a combination of the heroics of Canonero II, New York City's new off-track betting system, worldwide satellite television coverage, and the largest crowd in New York racing history (81,036 people), gave the race a huge new measure of notoriety in 1971. It was founded in 1867 and is raced on the first Saturday in June at Belmont Park in Long Island, New York. The distance is 1½ miles, with 126 pounds, for chrysanthemums. To aficionados of the turf, this race offers a truer picture of the quality of the Thoroughbred. By the time it is run, the three-year-old has fully matured, and the field has been weeded out, so that only the very best of the crop are entered. That is why the field is usually the smallest of all three races. Also, the distance offers the sternest test for the entry, and any defect in the horse's breeding is most apt to show up. It is because of these factors that breeders, owners, and trainers would prefer

The Kentucky Derby trophy.

to win this one race over the other two. The stud value of a Belmont Stakes winner immediately soars simply because more horses have proved best in stud who have won the Belmont. This is also why turfmen call it "the Test of the Champion."

The Triple Crown title was formally proclaimed in December 1950, at the annual awards dinner of the Thoroughbred Racing Associations in New York. Because there had been no candidate that year, it was decided to present the trophy retroactively to the first winner, Sir Barton. This became an annual feature at the dinner for the next seven years, until they ran out of former winners. Then the turf nabobs could only hope for a newcomer to reach the hallowed winner's circle.

Credit for initiating the movement to proclaim a Triple Crown is given unofficially to Charles Hatton, the venerable columnist of the defunct

Morning Telegraph and present *Daily Racing Form*. It was in the early thirties that his copy began to include the phrase "triple crown," whenever he wrote about the Kentucky Derby, Preakness, and Belmont Stakes. As with many newsmen who eschewed the touch system of typing in favor of the two-finger hunt-and-peck method, Hatton tired of having to spell out the names of the races in his copy every spring. He evolved his own shortcut by referring to them collectively as the "triple crown" races. "It was rhetorically more acceptable," he claimed. In time, his fellow fourth-estaters picked up the cue, and the phrase became so popular that more and more owners began to point their horses toward winning the triad of races. By 1941, newspapers were hailing the feat with banner headlines, such as: "Triple Crown to Whirlaway: Easily Takes Belmont Stakes."

The Triple Crown is not an American racing innovation. Rather, it came to us from England. There are five British classic races for three-year-olds, dating back two centuries. They are the St. Leger (1778), the Oaks (1779), the Derby Stakes (1780), the Two Thousand Guineas (1809), and the One Thousand

Churchill Downs. This photograph was taken on May 7, 1946, the day Assault won the Kentucky Derby.

Guineas (1814). Because only fillies may run in the One Thousand Guineas and the Oaks Stakes, the other three races became major tests for all Thoroughbreds in England, and, in time, the winner of all three was classified as the Triple Crown champion. West Australian, in 1853, was Britain's first Triple Crown winner.

The Two Thousand Guineas is raced at Newmarket in May, at one mile. The Derby is run at Epsom Downs on the nearest Wednesday to June 1, at 1½ miles. The St. Leger takes place on the Town Moor at Doncaster, Yorkshire, in September, over a distance of one mile, six furlongs, 132 yards. It is generally conceded that the American triple is the more difficult and demanding because there is no long span of time between the races as there is in England.

The importance of the Triple Crown races grew apace with the evolution of the science of breeding Thoroughbred horses. After the Thoroughbred gained a foothold in England, an unending search began to improve the bloodlines and the swiftness afoot of these magnificent animals. Consequently, their performances in the classic races became a barometer for excellence in potential breeding stock. It follows, therefore, that in addition to the traditions of Thoroughbred racing, the British handed down to us the Thoroughbred as a species bred specifically for racing.

"The term 'Thoroughbred' as applied to the horse is universally accepted and recognized as applying specifically and limitedly to the equine strain which traces to the Arabian, Barb, or Turk," say the editors of *Call Me Horse*, a book that devotes itself to horse racing and breeding.

The Arabian, or what is referred to as the Southern Horse (hot-blood line) in the evolution of the horse, was indigenous to Asia Minor and the Middle East or to the neighboring lands of Persia, India, and Arabia. Its lineage was traced back for five thousand years to the wild horses Honshaba and Baz, which supposedly were captured by and belonged to Baz of Yemen, the great-great-grandson of Noah. A member of the modern species of horse, the Arabian was descended from an Asiatic ancestry and was one of two strains of this species that migrated westward from Central Asia. It had a sleek coat, beauty, speed, and stamina, and was extremely popular with sultans and kings, some of whom owned as many as forty thousand, as did King Bahram in 120 A.D. By 1290 A.D., fantastic prices were paid for select horses, such as the racing filly El Karta, who went for sixty-four

The Preakness Stakes trophy.

thousand Turkish pounds. Stakes races of sorts were also popular between the stables of rival emirs and sultans, the races often consisting of turning loose thirsty steeds trained to run to the nearest waterhole in the desert.

The Arabian became a favorite mount of the Turks, who, with the Roman legions, brought the horses to the Continent during their invasions. The horse also found its way across North Africa via Egypt to Barbary, or what is today Morocco and Algeria, where it was bred with the local stock, the new breed taking on the name of "Barb." From Africa, the Barb moved to the Continent with the Saracens, who introduced it into France to the Moors, who took it to Spain.

All of this migration resulted in the Southern Horse coming into contact with his counterpart, the Northern Horse (cold-blood line), a shaggy-haired, sturdy, vigorous beast. This second strain migrated westward from Central Asia and settled in the desolate northern part of Europe. By crossbreeding the two strains, the Romans found that they could produce excellent chargers. Consequently, in time the Arabian horse, although not noted for being a particularly good racer, became much sought after for breeding purposes. Its first appearance in England was the result of the Roman and Norman invasions.

At the outset in England, the emphasis was on producing a massive war charger capable of carrying the tremendous weight of a man in full armor. They overdid it. The load became so great, and the horse so big and slow, that by the end of the 16th century both horse and warrior came to a virtual standstill. To all practical purposes they were immobilized.

The need for a lighter horse with speed and dexterity was painfully evident during the Crusades when the great knights suddenly found themselves completely outsped and outmaneuvered by the swift, streamlined Arabian flyers. One battlefield report said: "The Infidels not being weighed down with heavy armour like our knights were always able to outstrip them in pace, were a constant trouble. When charged they are wont to fly, and their horses are more nimble than any others in the world; one may liken them to swallows for swiftness." Some of these flyers were brought back to England by the knights, but King Henry VIII would have nothing of them. He was a heavy-horse enthusiast, no doubt partly because of his own massive bulk, which needed all the support he could get under him. He was so fanatical about this that he even issued an edict

Aerial view of Pimlico Race Course.

The Belmont Stakes trophy.

calling for the slaughter of all light horses and compelling concentration on weight-carrying breeds. It was after his demise in 1547 that the turn-about came.

Although the first racehorses in England to be identified by name were the Arabian stallion Arundel and the mare Truncefice in 957 A.D., the sport of racing was introduced around 1174 during the reign of King Henry II. Horse fairs were held every Friday night outside the gates of London and were attended by earls, barons, and knights, with races run over the open fields. Except for the hiatus dictated by King Henry VIII and a brief interruption in 1654 by Oliver Cromwell, the sport was encouraged by succeeding monarchs, which eventually led to its being dubbed "the sport of kings." For example, James I favored Epsom Downs in the early 1600s; Charles II, called the "father of the British turf," established Newmarket as the headquarters for both racing and breeding in the middle 1600s; and Queen Anne gave Ascot its high distinction for racing between 1702 and 1714. Finally, in 1750, the establishment of the Jockey Club formalized the British Thoroughbred, as all of its breeding and racing activities were rigidly controlled by uniform rules and regulations.

During the reign of the Stuarts in the 1600s, Barbs, Arabs, and Turks were imported in great numbers. It was between 1688 and 1729 that three famous stallions arrived in England, from whom all modern Thoroughbreds trace their lineage. They were the Byerly Turk, Darley Arabian, and Godolphin Arabian or Barb. Their mating with British stock proved their supremacy to such a degree that the native breed of sires died out completely.

The Byerly Turk is thought to have been captured by Captain Robert Byerly in 1687, when he fought the Turks in Hungary, and brought back to Byerly's

Aerial view of Belmont Park.

home in Yorkshire. The Darley Arabian was foaled about 1702 and was shipped from Syria to Richard Darley, of Yorkshire, as a gift from his son. The Godolphin Arabian was foaled about 1724 and is said to have been a gift to King Louis XIV of France from the Emperor of Morocco. However, he was stolen from the king's stables and disappeared until Edward Coke spotted the horse pulling a water cart through the streets of Paris. Coke bought him for three pounds, imported him into England around 1730, and presented him to his friend Roger Williams, who in turn passed him on to the Earl of Godolphin.

Organized racing in America began with the British invasion of New Amsterdam in 1664. In addition to renaming the city "New York," Colonel Richard Nicolls, commander of the troops, established organized racing in the colonies by laying out a two-mile course on Long Island, calling it Newmarket, and offering a silver cup to the best horses in the spring and fall seasons. As the sport spread in popularity, efforts were made to breed better horses. Thoroughbreds were imported from England, the first of which was the Dutton Arabian in 1721. He was mated with the predominant native mustangs, but the results were disappointing half-breeds.

Thereafter, aristocratic planters in New York, Maryland, Virginia, the Carolinas, and Kentucky set about in earnest to produce a truly fine Thoroughbred strain in the United States. In the next 45 years, they imported some 113 stallions and 73 mares from England. At the same time, too, the pattern of American turfdom emerged, with New York becoming the center of racing, and Virginia, Maryland, and Kentucky the centers of breeding.

From the beginning, and continuing until the Civil War, racing in America was apparently influenced by the rugged pioneer spirit of the fledgling country. The hallmark of excellence for the American Thoroughbred was stamina, rather than speed. Races were long, as long as four miles, and involved several heats. For example, on October 13, 1832, at the Union Course on Long Island, a field of America's best mares ran a total of 20 miles in one afternoon before a winner was determined. It is also pertinent that racing had become the common man's sport, as evidenced by a turnout at the same track in 1842 of between fifty thousand and seventy-five thousand fans, who paid a $10 admission charge to watch a match race between the filly Boston and the colt Fashion. It is little wonder that the original appellation was eventually changed to "the king of sports."

After the Civil War, American racing went through a refining process. Speed became the goal and the British system the model. For one thing, distances were lowered to the classic 1½ miles, and then to the 1¼, and the mile. By the turn of the 20th century, stamina no longer was most important, and the most common distance was ¾ of a mile. Finally, two- and three-furlong dashes came into vogue for two-year-olds, raced at the beginning of the year, leading up to 1¹⁄₁₆ miles for the best of them by October. Jockey clubs sprang up in different states to regulate breeding and racing through uniform rules. Purses were increased, too, until special races, the handicaps and stakes, took on added significance.

The one major difference between American and British racing was the track. In England, all races are run on turf, which custom dates back to the early days when the nobility gallivanted over the countryside. In America virtually all races are held on oval, dirt tracks, most of which are one mile around.

Efforts to set up clusters of races along the lines of the British Triple Crown also began after the Civil War. In 1875, Colonel Louis M. Clark, the founder of Churchill Downs, tried to promote the Endurance Handicap, Kentucky Derby, and Key Derby. New York, around 1900, offered the Withers, Belmont Stakes, and Lawrence Realization. The efforts failed, although the individual races flourished. There was just too much provincialism among turfmen, with each group refusing to recognize the other, each insisting that its own track was preeminent. In fact, it was a long time before the socialites of the eastern states, who largely controlled the sport, would even allow their horses to run in the "West," at Churchill Downs. It was this stubborn attitude which impelled Samuel Riddle to keep the great Man o' War out of the Kentucky Derby in 1920, thereby denying him a sure-bet Triple Crown.

By the same token, it was the fierce, competitive spirit of a distinguished Canadian sportsman, Commander John Kenneth Levison Ross, who was most eager for his horses to run in the 1919 Derby that was, in some respects, the catalyst that brought East and West together. In fact, it was the dramatic victories of one of his Thoroughbreds in the Derby, Preakness, and Belmont that marked the beginning of a new turf tradition in America—the Triple Crown.

Sir Barton

Sir Barton
(chestnut colt)
{
  Star Shoot { Isinglass / Astrology
  Lady Sterling { Hanover / Aquila
}

Chapter 1

Sir Barton

~1919~

n the spring of 1971, the general opinion among turfmen was that Hoist the Flag would win the Kentucky Derby easily and could even take the Triple Crown. A few weeks before the Derby, however, he shattered a leg during a workout at Belmont Park, which ended his racing career. As a result, there was a mad scramble to enter horses in the Derby at the last moment, Thoroughbreds that otherwise never would have made the trip to Louisville. Suddenly, everyone began to have delusions of winning the "Run for the Roses," now that the favorite was gone.

A little more than a half century earlier in the spring of 1919, a rather diminutive, deep-chested colt, with an irregular blaze and richly burnished chestnut coat, was also entered in the Kentucky Derby at the last moment. He had an undistinguished track record and really had no business running the classic race. However, he had a specific purpose. He was to lose. But after the race, he rose from obscurity to the peak of success and, sadly, then returned to obscurity. This is the dramatic story of Sir Barton, America's first Triple Crown champion.

He was foaled on the vast Hamburg Place farm, just outside of Lexington, Kentucky, which was owned by John E. Madden, one of the foremost breeders of Thoroughbred horses at the time. The colt was by Star Shoot, out of Lady Sterling, a 17-year-old mare. His sire was the son of Isinglass, an English Triple Crown winner, and he was the half-brother of Sir Martin, who had been acclaimed the two-year-old champion of America in 1908. For all of his excellent lineage, he was plagued with soft, shelly hooves, which he inherited from his sire. His feet were so tender that shoeing was always an intricate process.

Piano felt was often inserted between the shoe and the foot, but he still walked in pain. Because of this condition, it was not unusual for him to lose his shoes in competition, and in one race later in his career, he lost all four of them.

Despite this physical problem, Madden liked the horse and kept him for his own colors. Sir Barton made his debut in the Tremont Stakes at Aqueduct in New York City as a two-year-old, finishing fifth. He next raced at Saratoga in August, in the Flash, U. S. Hotel, and Sanford Memorial classics for freshmen horses and lost in each race. Although his showing was rather dismal, he still displayed an ability for good speed.

Attending the Saratoga meeting that August was John Kenneth Levison Ross, a former commander of a World War I destroyer in the Royal Canadian Navy and the scion of a distinguished Dominion family that helped to found the Canadian Pacific Railway. He had started a stable in 1915. With him was his trainer, H. G. Bedwell, a former Oregon cowboy who had a reputation for restoring broken-down horses to winning form. Both men were looking over the year's crop. Madden knew of Ross' desire to add to his string and encouraged him to consider Sir Barton. Madden had become disenchanted by the horse's performances, but still felt that with the proper handling the colt had the ability to become a winner. By the end of August, Ross and Bedwell had arrived at the same conclusion. They paid $10,000 and went home with Sir Barton.

Their immediate objective was to prepare him to run in the Futurity Stakes at Belmont Park on September 14. In the meantime, he was used to help train the top horse of the Ross stable, Billy Kelly, another two-year-old who soon found it tough to keep pace with his new stablemate. The immortal Earl Sande, then just a youngster, rode Sir Barton in the Futurity. Although there was little hope that he would finish in the money as he went off at 15-1, the colt flashed across the finish line second to Dunboyne with a surging burst of speed, even though he had been boxed in until the last furlong. Nevertheless, the 1918 season ended with victory still eluding the chestnut colt.

All through the winter, Ross thought only of the Kentucky Derby and of how Billy Kelly could beat his archrival, Eternal, who had been the winner in a match race by the two at the Laurel Race Course in Maryland. When the time came to travel to Kentucky, it was decided at the last moment to send Sir Barton along as a running mate. Shortly thereafter, Ross and Bedwell evolved a strategy for the race, and Sir Barton was also entered in it. The plan was for Sir Barton to take the lead at the start and set a fast pace to kill off the top competition, Eternal and Under Fire. When they had been run into the ground, Billy

Kelly would then breeze by for the win. Earl Sande was given his choice of horses and naturally picked Billy Kelly. Johnny Loftus, who had won the Derby in 1916 on George Smith and was considered a master of pacing, was assigned to Sir Barton with the instructions to give him his head and let him run for as long as he could. But for the fact that he was paired with his stablemate, Sir Barton would have left the post at 50-1 instead of as a favorite. He was still a maiden in search of his first taste of victory.

Among other sportsman qualities, Ross was noted for his eagerness to accept a challenge, dare, or side bet. A few months before the Derby, he was seated with friends in a restaurant when he was approached by a "yeasty-faced little man" who started up a

Commander John Kenneth Levison Ross (right), owner of Sir Barton, with his trainer, H. G. Bedwell.

conversation on the forthcoming race. The man believed that Eternal would win it and desired to bet on the results. Ross' son recalled the incident in his book *Boots and Saddles*:

> My father, in his usual courteous manner and, I might say, with typically fast response to a dare, asked what amount the stranger wanted to bet. He told me later he expected an answer around or below $100.
> "Would fifty thousand suit you, Commander?"
> At first my father thought it was a joke, but he didn't hesitate to reply.
> "That would suit me well, sir. Provided you produce some guarantee of payment should you lose."

The stranger seemed insulted, which was understandable to Ross' friends, for they knew the stranger. He was Arnold Rothstein, the noted gambler, who had yet to make his reputation as one of the supposed principals behind baseball's infamous "Black Sox" World Series scandal in 1919. However, he did enjoy a good reputation in the underworld for paying off his debts. As a result, the wager was made, but with the understanding that it would be off if neither horse finished in the money.

Derby day found the track heavy from a night of rain. The race went according to plan for 1¼ miles. Sir Barton ran well out in front as the field thundered past the stands to the first turn. He was moving effortlessly and increased his lead to three lengths by the top of the stretch. At the ⅛ pole he was supposed to fade. Instead, he went to a five-length lead. "There was no Billy Kelly. But neither was there anybody else," wrote the younger Ross. "Sir Barton crossed the finish line with his ears pricked and with Loftus standing in the stirrups glancing over his shoulder wondering what happened to the rest."

Billy Kelly came in second, Under Fire third. It was the first time in the history of the Kentucky Derby that the one-two horses wore the same colors. It was also the first time that a maiden had won the Derby, and the racing world rubbed its eyes in disbelief. The mud and other excuses were cited for the poor showings of the favorites. Regardless of these, the knowledgeable railbirds conceded that the spectacular victory was of major consequence. The Derby, according to them, was "just another horse race" until Sir Barton put it on the map. The race also proved that Mr. Rothstein was a man of his word. A few days later, Commander Ross received payment.

The common judgment of Sir Barton's victory was that it was a freak happening, but wait until the Preakness. In 1919, winning both was no mean

Sir Barton leads Billy Kelly as he becomes the first maiden ever to win the Kentucky Derby.

trick because Pimlico staged its event just four days later, on May 14, leaving little time for training. There was also the risk of a horse developing shipping fever or being injured while moving from Louisville to Maryland at a time when transportation was a lot slower and full of risks for such a fragile commodity as a Thoroughbred horse.

Nevertheless, in the Preakness Sir Barton went off as a $1.40 to $1.00 favorite. His nearest and strongest competitors were Eternal, 9-to-1; Sweep On, 15-to-1; and Dunboyne, 4-to-1, in a field of 12.

This time, Ross and Bedwell had Earl Sande ride another stablemate, Milkmaid. The plan called for Sande to wheel in and break up the general alignment in as legitimate a fashion as would pass the inspection of the starter in order to allow Sir Barton to find a favorable position. Loftus, on the other hand, was merely told to "get out to the front as soon as possible and stay there." Unlike the Derby, the track was fast.

Once more, Sir Barton needed little urging. He swept out front at the start and was never headed or passed, winning over Eternal by four lengths. As for Milkmaid, a filly, she found too many colts around of more than passing interest for her to take the race seriously. The Preakness made many believers out of doubters: Sir Barton had arrived.

With the Kentucky Derby and the Preakness under their belts, Ross and Bedwell refused to ease up the pressure to keep their colt razor sharp. They entered him in the Withers at Belmont on May 24. Here it was decided to let Eternal take the lead into the stretch. The race at that time was run clockwise, and Bedwell, in training, had observed Eternal's tendency to bear out and away from the rail at the final turn. Loftus, therefore, trailed the horse until the homestretch and then moved Sir Barton inside Eternal to win by three lengths as he made up his lost distance with the maneuver.

This victory sent the fans stark raving mad for Sir Barton, and they looked forward to the Belmont Stakes on June 11 with excruciating impatience. The Belmont would be the true test for the colt, with nobody doubting that he would win, even though the distance would be longer than he had ever run. In 1919, the race was at 1⅜ miles instead of 1½ miles as it is today. So confident was the public that they established him a whopping 7-to-20 favorite.

By then, Sir Barton began to display a personality distinctly his own. Perhaps it was the assurance born of winning. The fact is, he made everyone aware of him in the stable. He had a nasty disposition, no doubt partly because of his sore feet. He ignored horses, despised humans, and hated pets. He preferred to remain

Sir Barton, with jockey Johnny Loftus up, is held by trainer H. G. Bedwell in the winner's circle after his upset victory in the 1919 Kentucky Derby.

Official Chart of the Kentucky Derby

42305 FIFTH RACE—1 1-4 Miles. (May 9, 1914—2:03⅗—3—114.) Forty-fifth Running KENTUCKY DERBY. $20,000 Added. 3-year-olds. Allowances. Net value to winner $20,825; second, $2,500; third, $1,000; fourth, $275.

Index	Horses	A	Wt	PP	St	¼	½	¾	Str	Fin	Jockeys	Owners	Equiv. Odds Str't
39683[2]	SIR BARTON	wb	112½	1	1	1^{2}	1½	1^{2}	1½	1^{5}	J Loftus	J K L Ross	†260-100
(42081)	BILLY KELLY	w	119	11	8	3½	3^{4}	2^{3}	2^{4}	2^{1}	E Sande	J K L Ross	†
42227[2]	UNDER FIRE	w	122	7	11	9½	9½	6½	3^{1}	3^{1}	M Garner	P Dunne	1915-100
42227	VULCANITE	w	110	6	10	10½	5^{h}	4½	4^{1}	4^{6}	C Howard	W F Polson	7000-100
42227[3]	SENNINGS PARK	wb	122	8	9	6^{2}	4½	5½	5^{1}	5^{1}	H Lunsf'rd	O A Bianchi	§1410-100
42222[3]	BE FRANK	w	119	2	6	7^{h}	7½	7½	6½	6½	J Butwell	C M Garrison	2745-100
(41177)	SAILOR	wb	119	10	12	12	10^{2}	10½	8½	7^{8}	J McIntyre	J W McClelland	‡210-100
42227	ST. BERNARD	w	119	4	2	5^{h}	6^{1}	9^{1}	7^{2}	8^{2}	E Pool	B J Brannon	§
(42227)	REGALO	w	117	9	7	8^{2}	$8^{1\frac{1}{2}}$	8^{1}	9^{2}	9^{4}	F Murphy	Gallaher Bros	605-100
(41798)	ETERNAL	w	122	5	3	2½	2½	3½	10^{5}	10^{10}	A Schu'g'r	J W McClelland	‡
38508	FROGTOWN	w	119	12	4	11^{2}	11½	11^{2}	11^{10}	11^{20}	J Morys	W S Kilmer	2245-100
(42137)	VINDEX	w	122	3	5	4^{nk}	12	12	12	12	W Knapp	H P Whitney	815-100

†Coupled in betting as J. K. L. Ross entry; ‡J. W. McClelland entry. §Mutuel field.

Time, 24⅕, 48⅖, 1:14, 1:41⅘, 2:09⅘. Track heavy.

$2 mutuels paid, J. K. L. Ross entry, $7.20 straight, $6.70 place, $6.00 show; Under Fire, $10.80 show.

Equivalent booking odds—J. K. L. Ross entry, 260 to 100 straight, 235 to 100 place, 200 to 100 show, Under Fire, 440 to 100 show.

Winner—Ch. c, by Star Shoot—Lady Sterling (trained by H. G. Bedwell; bred by Messrs. Madden & Gooch).

Went to post at 5:10. At post 4 minutes. Start good and slow. Won easily; second and third driving. SIR BARTON raced into the lead at once and, well ridden, led under restraint until reaching the stretch, where he was shaken up and easily held BILLY KELLY safe in the last eighth. BILLY KELLY held to his task well, was under restraint in the early running and finished gamely. UNDER FIRE gained steadily from a slow beginning and finished fast and gamely. VULCANITE ran well and finished close up. ETERNAL was done after going three-quarters. REGALO ran disappointingly. SENNINGS PARK tired in the stretch.

Scratched—(42257)Corson, 122; 42142[3]Clermont, 122.

Overweights—Sir Barton, 2½ pounds.

Official Chart of Preakness

42339 FOURTH RACE—1 1-8 Miles. (May 17, 1911—1:51—3—112.) Twelfth Running PREAKNESS STAKES. $25,000 Added. 3-year-olds. Allowances. Net value to winner $24,500; second, $3,000; third, $2,000; fourth, $1,000.

Index	Horses	A	Wt	PP	St	¼	½	¾	Str	Fin	Jockeys	Owners	Equiv. Odds Str't
(42305)	SIR BARTON	wB	126	8	3	1^1	1^1	1^2	1^6	1^4	J Loftus	J K L Ross	†140-100
42305	ETERNAL	w	126	2	1	$4^{1\frac{1}{2}}$	3^1	2^1	2^1	2^3	A Schu'g'r	J W McClelland	920-100
(42250)	SWEEP ON	wsB	126	3	2	3^2	$4^{1\frac{1}{2}}$	4^2	3^3	3^2	L McAtee	W R Coe	‡1555-100
42274^2	KING PLAUDIT	wB	114	9	4	2^1	$2\frac{1}{2}$	3^2	4^3	$4^{1\frac{1}{2}}$	L Lyke	Brookside Stable	5325-100
(42297)	OVER THERE	w	122	4	10	$8\frac{1}{2}$	8^3	7^3	7^6	5^{nk}	H Myers	W R Coe	‡
42291^2	ROUTLEDGE	w	122	12	5	5^1	$5\frac{1}{2}$	5^{nk}	$6\frac{1}{2}$	6^h	E Ambr'se	W M Jeffords	7080-100
42305	VULCANITE	w	114	1	7	7^1	7^h	8^1	8^3	$7^{1\frac{1}{2}}$	R Troxler	W F Polson	3945-100
42121^3	MILKMAID	w	109	6	6	6^{nk}	6^2	6^2	$5\frac{1}{2}$	8^3	E Sande	J K L Ross	†
42291	DRUMMOND	wB	114	7	9	$9\frac{1}{2}$	$9\frac{1}{2}$	9^2	9^1	$9\frac{1}{2}$	A Johnson	M Shea	14500-100
42222	YURUCARI	w	114	11	8	11	$10\frac{1}{2}$	10^5	10^8	10^{15}	T Rice	Quincy Stable	12540-100
42250	DUNBOYNE	w	126	5	11	10^2	11	11	11	11	L Ensor	P A Clark	420-100
42305	VINDEX	wB	115	10	Left at the post.						W Knapp	H P Whitney	365-100

†Coupled in betting as J. K. L. Ross entry; ‡W. R. Coe entry.

Time, 23⅖, 47⅕, 1:13, 1:39⅕, 1:53. Track fast.

$2 mutuels paid, J. K. L. Ross entry, $4.80 straight, $3.20 place, $2.70 show; Eternal, $7.50 place, $6.00 show; W. R. Coe entry, $5.00 show.

Equivalent booking odds—J. K. L. Ross entry, 140 to 100 straight, 60 to 100 place, 35 to 100 show; Eternal, 275 to 100 place, 200 to 100 show; W. R. Coe entry, 150 to 100 show.

Winner—Ch. c, by Star Shoot—Lady Sterling (trained by H. G. Bedwell; bred by Messrs. Madden & Gooch).

Went to post at 4:21. At post 5 minutes. Start good and slow. Won easily; second and third driving. SIR BARTON went to the front while rounding the turn into the backstretch and, setting a terrific pace, drew away into a long lead in the last quarter and was eased up at the finish. ETERNAL was a forward contender from the start, met with no mishaps and ran a game race. SWEEP ON was always prominent in the running, but was tiring at the end. DUNBOYNE began sideways in behind the other horses and had no chance. KING PLAUDIT ran a good race. OVER THERE made a fast finish. ROUTLEDGE and VULCANITE ran well.

Scratched—42221^3Terentia, 117; 42291^3Natural Bridge, 114; 42273^3Pride of India, 114.

Overweights—Vindex, 1 pound.

aloof and was a thorough snob. On top of this, he gave his trainer fits. In track parlance, he was not a "generous horse," and would extend himself only when he was made to believe that he was in a real race. As a result, Bedwell had to resort to the subterfuge of using fresh horses in relays to pace him, and was often heard to say ruefully: "To get him fit you have to half-kill him with work—and a lot of other horses as well." Ross' son tried to explain it another way: "Horsemen speak of Thoroughbreds with this faraway gaze as 'having the look of the eagle' and they believe that it is invariably the sign of greatness. Sir Barton was an irascible, exasperating creature. But he had the look of the eagle."

He proved his mettle in the Belmont Stakes, when he "pulverized" the opposition, winning in a canter by five lengths while setting a new American record of 2:17⅖. In the process of becoming the first Triple Crown winner, he also was the first colt to include the Withers in this victory skein, a feat that was not to be duplicated until 24 years later in 1943 by Count Fleet. Therefore, when 1919 came to a close, there was no question that he was the top horse of the year, having humbled most of the finest Thoroughbreds in the country. He had raced thirteen times and had won eight times. He had campaigned so much that Commander Ross seriously considered retiring him, rather than entering him in the grueling handicap schedule of 1920. His sore feet were the big question marks for the coming year.

The owner's reservations about his colt's performance in 1920 proved to be about 50 percent justified. Sir Barton had an on-and-off spring and, overall

Official Chart of Belmont Stakes

42784 FOURTH RACE—1 3-8 Miles. (June 16, 1917—2:17⅘—3—126.) Fifty-first Running BELMONT STAKES. Guaranteed Value $10,000. 3-year-olds. Weight-for-Age. Net value to winner $11,950; second, $1,500; third, $750.

Index	Horses	A	Wt	PP	St	¼	½	¾	Str	Fin	Jockeys	Owners	O	H	C	P	S
(42499)	SIR BARTON	wʙ	126	1	1	2²	2³	2⁵	1³	1⁵	J Loftus	J K L Ross		2-5	2-5	7-20	out—
42725²	SWEEP ON	wʙ	126	3	2	3	3	3	2½	2⁸	C F'b'ther	W R Coe		†2	12-5	12-5	out—
42751²	NATUR'L BRIDGE	w	126	2	3	1²	1⁸	1¹	3	3	L McAtee	W R Coe		†2	12-5	12-5	out—

†Coupled in betting; no separate place or show betting.
Time, 2:17⅘ (new American record). Track fast.
Winner—Ch. c, by Star Shoot—Lady Sterling (trained by H. G. Bedwell; bred by Messrs. Madden & Gooch).
Went to post at 4:09. At post 1 minute. Start poor and slow. Won easily; second and third driving. SIR BARTON, after beating the gate, indulged NATURAL BRIDGE with the lead over the Belmont course, then easily took the lead after entering the main course and, drawing away, was easing up at the end. SWEEP ON was saved under early restraint and made a vain challenge at the homestretch entrance, but tired near the end. NATURAL BRIDGE tired badly after pacemaking to the homestretch.
Scratched—42641²Pastoral Swain, 126; 42725 Over There, 126.

for the year, won only five of the thirteen races he started. He was alternately brilliant and mediocre. More significantly, his championship crown was challenged by a newcomer to the ranks of the American Thoroughbred, a colt whom many have called a superhorse, "the horse of the century," one whose influence is still felt to this day. He was Man o' War, and Sir Barton would have to reckon with him before the year was up.

It was March 29, 1917, at the Nursery Stud of Major August Belmont near Lexington, Kentucky, the year America entered World War I. A broodmare groom opened the foal book, made a routine entry, "chestnut colt, by Fair Play, out of Mahubah," and thereby commenced the dramatic story of "the greatest Thoroughbred of all time." The colt was a red chestnut, marked with a star and an indistinct, short, gray stripe on his forehead. It was Louis Feustel, his eventual trainer, who nicknamed him "Big Red." In setting down his early appraisal of the horse, he wrote: "Very tall and gangling . . . thin and so on the leg as to give the impression of ungainliness one gets in seeing a week-old foal." But he was high on the horse because he so admired his sire, Fair Play, the best stallion on the farm, even though Mahubah was an untried mare of English extraction.

In the spring of 1918, Major Belmont announced that because of his involvement in the war effort, he would sell his crop of 1918 yearlings. He offered the lot to Samuel Doyle Riddle for $42,000. Riddle was a 57-year-old textile magnate from Glen Riddle, Pennsylvania, who had been a horse enthusiast since childhood. By the time he was 21, his reputation as a fearless rider on the Pennsylvania-Maryland hunt circuit had been firmly established. He also began his racing stable at that time, subsequently building Glen Riddle Farm into one of the major breeding centers of American Thoroughbred racing.

When the offer was made, Feustel was training Riddle's small stable. He had been a youngster with the Belmont stable in the days of Fair Play and had

Man o' War

never lost his admiration for the horse. Therefore, he urged his employer to purchase a colt by Fair Play. As a result, Riddle sent the trainer and an assistant, Mike Daly, to Kentucky to look over the Belmont yearlings. On their return, they reported that the horses were rather undersized and the offer was turned down. Belmont finally shipped the yearlings to the Saratoga Sales in August, at which time Riddle and Feustel noticed the big-framed, long-legged colt, now tagged with the impressive name Man o' War courtesy of Mrs. Belmont.

"You said the yearlings were undersized," a puzzled Riddle said to his trainer. "Surely this colt is big enough."

"But we don't remember seeing the colt when the yearlings were shown to us in Kentucky," replied the equally puzzled trainer.

Riddle had been thoroughly schooled in the whys and wherefores of horse trading and, armed with the knowledge of Feustel's enthusiasm for the colt's sire, suspected that the major was apparently so taken with him that he wanted to hold him out of the sale. All of this made Riddle more determined to buy him at any price. Belmont, on the other hand, did in fact want to keep the horse, but feared that the sale of the other yearlings would suffer if he held onto him.

The auction took place on August 17, and the bidding for the horse reached $4,900, with some 15 persons reportedly willing to pay this sum. Riddle raised it $100, and the sale was completed. Interestingly enough, he at first never considered the colt for racing, rather figuring he would make a good hunter because of his size. It was Riddle's wife who persuaded him to leave this decision to Feustel.

At the very beginning, they ran into trouble with the colt. It was almost impossible to break him. "He fought like a tiger. He screamed with rage, and fought us so hard that it took several days before he could be handled with safety," recalled Riddle. After he was broken, though, he displayed a tremendous speed, the likes of which none of his handlers had ever seen. As a two-year-old in 1919, he scorched every racetrack he ran on, winning nine of the ten races he started. His only defeat was by Upset in the Sanford Memorial at Saratoga, a loss that has been charged by some to a bad ride by jockey Johnny Loftus, and by others to the starter, C. H. Pettingill, who allowed the race to get off while Man o' War was standing broadside to the barrier when the flag was dropped. The end of the year found him unquestionably the number one horse of his class with earnings of $83,325.

Between his two- and three-year-old forms, he emerged as a giant. He had the size and power of a sprinter, with the conformation of a stayer, and he struck fear into the hearts of all who opposed him. He was "muscled enormously, and full of the flowing spirit of the Fair Plays. His action was high and his courage matched it and when he had a horse to go with him, he did not run as much as hurtle," is the way turf historian Joe Palmer described him. He did everything with a flair, even when he ate, consuming 12 to 13 quarts of oats and all the hay they could give him in a day. He was so ravenous that they had to put a bit in his mouth while he was feeding to keep him from eating too fast.

In 1920, he won all 11 races in which he started, including the Preakness, Withers, Belmont, Stuyvesant Handicap, Dwyer, Miller, Travers, Lawrence Realization, Jockey Club Gold Cup, Potomac Handicap, and Kenilworth Gold Cup. He set five records on the way and wound up the year with winnings of $166,140, the first Thoroughbred to bring his total earnings to over $200,000. He had everything, in the view of turf writer C. W. Anderson: "blinding speed, stamina to go any distance and a love for running that is the heart and core of a fine horse. He smothered his opposition and overran his finishes by furlongs."

In all of the annals of Thoroughbred history, no other horse was ever compared to some of the greatest champions of sports the way "Big Red" was by the distinguished sportswriter Grantland Rice: "Man o' War was something different—something extra—as great a competitor as Ty Cobb, Jack Dempsey, Tommy Hitchcock, Ben Hogan, or anyone else . . . he had a furious desire to win." A classic example of this was the Lawrence Realization, in which all of

Samuel Riddle (right), owner of Man o' War, and his trainer, Louis Feustel.

the other competing horses were scratched. To avoid disappointing the crowd, the track sent in an entry, Hoodwink, with a 10-pound advantage. The result of the race was a foregone conclusion, but Man o' War's jockey, Clarence Kummer, was given instructions to hold him back and win by not too big of a margin. It was a tall order. At the end of a ¼ of a mile, Man o' War was 20 lengths ahead. Try as he might, Kummer just could not hold his horse in, and he won by a modestly estimated 100 lengths. It was an arbitrary measurement, as Hoodwink had been eased when hopelessly beaten. Still, the margin of victory was by nearly a ¼ of a mile, and in record time.

The spectacular success of Man o' War soon brought about the inevitable offers to purchase him. Riddle turned down all of these out of hand, with the exception of one from W. T. Waggoner. The wealthy Texan first suggested $500,000, then raised the figure to $1,000,000. When he was still turned down, he continued to persist, claiming that everything had a price. With that, he signed a blank check and told Riddle to fill in the numbers. The reply to this became a classic in racing lore: "You go to France and bring the sepulchre of Napoleon from Les Invalides. Then you go to England and buy the jewels from the crown. Then to India and buy the Taj Mahal. Then I'll put a price on Man o' War." Years later, the horse's devoted groom, Will Harbut, reported it another way: "A man came here and offered a million dollars for him, and Mr. Riddle said no, lots of men might have a million dollars, but only one man could have Man o' War."

As the 1920 racing season progressed into the Saratoga meet, it became evident that the one horse who bid well to steal some of the thunder from "Big Red" was the Triple Crown champion. Although Sir Barton's victories were far fewer in number, they were almost as impressive. In fact, Sir Barton was among the leaders of the year's handicap division. It was at Saratoga that the abilities of the two colts came into sharp focus. Their performances in several races were almost identical.

Man o' War had two distinguished victories, the Miller and the Travers Stakes. In the latter, he equaled the record for the 1¼-mile distance, which Sir Barton had set in the Saratoga Handicap. On the other hand, Sir Barton in the Merchants and Citizens Handicap covered the distance Man o' War had run in the Miller by a full second faster while carrying two extra pounds. The feats fed fuel to a public clamor for the two horses to meet in a match race, head to head, to determine the better of the two.

Pressure for the race became so intense that both Riddle and Ross relented and agreed to the meeting. They decided to accept the first $50,000 offer to

Man o' War, with Johnny Loftus in the irons, finishes second to Upset in the Sanford Memorial Stakes at Saratoga. This loss ranks as one of the most spectacular upsets in turf history. Coming in third is Golden Broom.

come along. It was made by A. M. Orpen, a Toronto promoter who controlled Kenilworth Park at Windsor, Ontario. Orpen then increased the purse to $75,000, plus a $5,000 gold cup. He knew that Colonel Matt Winn of Churchill Downs was also eager for the race and tried to head him off with an irresistible offer. Both owners accepted the proposal just a few hours before a telegram arrived from Winn with a $100,000 offer.

Thus, the first "race of the century" was set. It would be the best of America versus the best of Canada, a great international event to determine the top horse on the North American continent. It was a natural, one to excite any turf fan. The terms of the race were quite simple. Only the two colts would run, under weight-for-age conditions, the four-year-old Sir Barton to carry 126 pounds and the three-year-old Man o' War 120 pounds. The distance of the race would be 1¼ miles, and it would be run on October 12, 1920. It was also stipulated that if either horse failed to start, the other was to "walk over" for the gold trophy only. In other words, the horse need only to walk around the track and over the finish line to be declared the winner.

In actuality, neither owner was particularly in need of the purse. To Riddle, it was the means to the end of making "Big Red" the leading money-winning Thoroughbred, the first to top the $200,000 mark. For Ross, who had become one of the most popular figures in the American turf world, even described by some at the time as "the best sportsman Canada ever sent to this country," winning the race and the large purse would enhance his country's position as a leader in Thoroughbred racing.

Sir Barton arrived in Windsor from Laurel, Maryland, five days before the race and almost immediately was the target of a barrage of adverse newspaper stories. It was reported that he was training poorly, that trainer Bedwell was drinking, that the Kenilworth track was too hard for his sore feet. Bert E. Collyer of the *Chicago Evening Post*, for one, wrote in appraising the horse's last workout at Laurel: "Let it be said that he is a horse of moods and hard to train. Bedwell may be a wizard, but it is my firm conviction that his charge has been in better shape than he will be on Tuesday." Bedwell was quick to dispute this. "Sir Barton is doing all I have asked him in his work for the race," he told the press. "He is ready to run as fast as he has in the past and I look for him to render a brilliant account of himself. I am making no predictions, but I believe Sir Barton will not disgrace himself in the most pretentious effort of his successful turf career."

Sir Barton, ridden by Earl Sande, beats Exterminator in the Saratoga Handicap in record time for the 1¼ mile.

Earl Sande rides Sir Barton (on rail) to a win over Gnome in the Merchants and Citizens Handicap at Saratoga. He ran the 1³⁄₁₆ a full second faster than Man o' War's time for the same distance.

Actually, Ross and Bedwell were concerned with who their jockey would be. Clarence Kummer, who had ridden Sir Barton, was already set to mount Man o' War in the match race, while Johnny Loftus, who had also ridden Sir Barton, had had his license revoked and was out of racing. That left Earl Sande, then just 21 and a contract jockey for Ross. There was talk that he had a nervous stomach from dieting to keep his weight down, that he had displayed timidity in his riding of late, and that Bedwell feared he might get the jitters, the way he had when he rode Ross' Billy Kelly in a match race with Eternal two years prior and lost.

Both owner and trainer finally decided to wait until the day of the race to make up their minds. In the meantime, they snuck in a standby jockey, just in case. He was Frank Keogh, a veteran of the track who rode for Admiral C. T. Grayson and Samuel Ross, of Washington, D.C. The admiral was the personal physician of President Woodrow Wilson. Keogh merely was told to report to promoter Orpen at Kenilworth on October 11, without being advised why. The next morning, on the day of the race, Ross and Bedwell watched Sir Barton in a workout. The horse did not seem to be razor sharp, and Sande appeared to be in an extreme state of anxiety. It was at that moment that Ross made his decision to have Sande stand down. He broke the news to the young man in the jockey's room just about an hour before the race, and Sande sat down and cried. The owner then released a statement to the press. "I have determined to substitute Jockey Frank Keogh for Earl Sande on Sir Barton in today's race for the reason that my boy is not in good form, as his recent performances will show." He insisted that there was no prejudice toward Sande involved, that it was only for the good of the horse.

Man o' War also had a few anxious moments. He had struck himself in the Potomac Handicap at Havre de Grace, Maryland, and, according to trainer Feustel, started to bow a tendon. His leg also filled once while preparing for the special match race, but he surmounted this and was fit on the morning of the big race.

The net result of the prerace speculations and happenings was that Man o' War was made the overwhelming favorite at 5-to-100, and Sir Barton the underdog at 550-to-100. The match was the fourth race on the program of the day, and the bulging stands included many celebrities of the turf world, such as Joseph Widener, William Woodward, Major August Belmont, John E. Madden (who had bred both horses), and Enrico Caruso, the Metropolitan Opera star.

The jockeys had been given identical instructions—get to the front and stay there. Man o' War was fractious at the barrier, which was located at the near turn of the track. Sir Barton, on the rail, was more docile and broke first with the flag. His inside position gave him a temporary advantage as they moved into the stretch for the first sweep past the stands. The lead was short-lived, for Man o' War caught up quickly and went ahead to stay after they had traveled only 60 yards. "He actually galloped the Ross colt dizzy in the first mile and drew away so easily in the final quarter of a mile that he was never fully extended," reported the *New York Times*. Despite this, he won by seven lengths in 2:03, a new track record that clipped ⅗ of a second from the old mark.

It was a ridiculously easy victory, a race that the press labeled as a "farce," a "great spectacle, hardly a great race." Some critics blasted the race, saying it should never have been run, that Sir Barton should never have been allowed to race because of his sore feet. There was no doubt but that he had been completely outclassed and humbled. Ross was among the first to admit to the superiority of Man o' War, not only over his own horse but over any other one around, when he rushed over to Samuel Riddle's box to offer congratulations.

Man o' War follows the lead pony toward the starting line for his match race with Sir Barton in Canada. Jockey Clarence Kummer is up.

Man o' War races to a seven-length victory over Sir Barton. Frank Keogh is in the saddle of the Triple Crown champion.

The reporter for the *Times*, in assessing the talents of the horse after the race, wrote: "As it is, even with the scalp of Sir Barton dangling from his belt, Man o' War has yet to show just how fast he can run." Riddle himself could not provide the answer to this: "We don't know to this day how fast he was," he said, "as we were afraid to let him down; knowing his intense speed, we feared he might injure himself." He was even more expansive in his praise on his return to Glen Riddle two days later, when he told a cheering welcoming crowd: "The colt lived up to expectations at Windsor. He just caught Sir Barton and romped ahead of him at every step. The crowds went wild. Many believed that the advance reports about Man o' War were exaggerated, but when Kummer, his jockey, let him out, hats went up in the air, women shrieked, racetrack men who had never seen the colt before gasped in astonishment, and few of the thirty thousand persons who crowded every inch of the track went home without getting hoarse."

The race was not without a number of interesting sidelights. Its purse was the richest prize ever offered for a turf event on the North American continent. It drew the largest crowd ever at a Canadian track. The fans at the track bet $132,000 on Man o' War and only $14,000 on Sir Barton. It was also the first horse race to be filmed in its entirety over a circular track. The photographer was Eadweard Muybridge, who 40 years earlier had produced the first record on film of a running animal. At that time, he had used 20 cameras lined up at close intervals on a straight track with silk threads stretched across the track tripping the camera shutters as they were broken by the horse. This time, he used 14 cameras, and the film was later shown in a Broadway theater at reserved-seat prices.

Top news events manage to attract myths that, in later years, are accepted as fact. They add extra color and excitement to future descriptions of the action, even though there is not much truth in them. The match race of Sir Barton and Man o' War was no exception, and a recounting of it some 18 years later by Charles Farmer, in his book *For Gold and Glory*, is a case in point. It told of what happened when Man o' War caught up to Sir Barton just after the race started:

> They swept down the stretch, Man o' War fighting for his head. After a quarter-mile, Kummer's left stirrup broke from weight and pressure. The boy, in catching to hold on until he could get balanced again, had to give Man o' War his head. The latter ran the next 150 yards like a wild creature, opening a big gap between him and Sir Barton before Kummer could steady him. Sir Barton was never able to gain a foot, and the farther they ran the more he fell behind.

Another story, carried by *The Blood-Horse*, revealed that "Feustel said he found after the race that Man o' War's stirrup leathers had been cut, but the job had been done badly, and the straps had held." The fact is, neither account is accurate. Man o' War merely bounded forth with his tremendous sweep and power and he was not to be denied. There was no tampering with his tack before the race.

It has been said that Man o' War broke some of his opponents' hearts. Is this another myth? Obviously, there is no sure reply to the question. Nevertheless, it is true that America's first Triple Crown champion was never the same again after the match race. Ross did race him three more times in the fall of 1920, but he won none, though he finished second once and third twice. The fire seemed to be gone, and he was retired to stud.

It was all downhill thereafter, and the end of this great and colorful Thoroughbred's saga was sorrowful. Sir Barton began his first stud season in 1921, when a few mares were bred to him. The next year, Ross decided to sell him for $75,000 to B. B. and Montfort Jones, the owners of Audley Farm, near Berryville, Virginia. The brothers had sold off their oil holdings in Oklahoma and had gone into the even more speculative business of breeding and racing Thoroughbreds, eventually building their operation into one of the most productive centers in the country. The story is that Sir Barton was their first stallion, or one of their first, and that it was at the recommendation of John E. Madden, the man who had brought the horse into the world and had sold him to Ross, that they purchased him.

The record book indicates that he was unimpressive in stud. But, according to Hobson McGehee, former manager of Audley Farm, "He had a lot of winners. He was bred to good mares. His book was full most every year. Mr. Jones had so many good mares of his own, 90 to 100, at Audley that we didn't care particularly about attracting outside mares to breed to him. He was advertised at $1,000 stud fee, which was pretty good at the time." Sir Barton's best offspring was Easter Stockings, the filly who won the 1928 Kentucky Oaks and had purses totaling $85,310. The fact is, the most prominent racers of his get were fillies, according to the former manager of the farm. "I think you can say that it figured to be that way. Sir Barton, on his breeding, came from horses that stood out on the bottom side . . . Sir Barton's was a strong distaff line, more than his sire's side."

The stallion remained on the farm for 11 years, when he was turned over to a U.S. Remount Station near Front Royal, Virginia, in 1933, at the age of 17. A man named Colonel Wall was the commanding officer and apparently was a friend of the Jones brothers. Nobody seems to know why the horse was sent away, particularly since the Joneses held on to pensioners at Audley. The story is equally obscure in that Sir Barton is said to have also wound up at a U.S. Remount Station at Fort Robinson, Nebraska, that same year, with his stud fees reported to be between $5 and $10. Then, later in the year, he was purchased by Dr. J. R. Hylton of Douglas, Wyoming, who owned a string of racehorses.

Sir Barton grazes in his corral on the Wyoming ranch of Dr. J. R. Hylton in 1934. He died three years later at the age of 21.

The good doctor brought the Thoroughbred to his La Prele Creek Ranch in the foothills of the Laramie Mountains, some 18 miles from Douglas, where he lived out the rest of his years. Sir Barton, America's first Triple Crown champion, died on October 30, 1937, when he was 21 years old. He was buried near a paddock on the ranch in a plot enclosed by a picturesque post-and-rail fence, with a sandstone marker inscribed by the foreman's wife.

For more than 30 years, the famous racer reposed in quiet obscurity on the Hylton ranch, until in 1968, through a Jaycee-sponsored project, Sir Barton once again came into prominence. His remains, carefully exhumed from their original resting place, were put beneath a handsome equestrian statue in Washington Park at Douglas—a site that is one of the area's foremost tourist attractions today. It is only fitting that the horse was so honored, albeit the tribute was not without a bit of irony despite the good intentions of the Douglas citizenry. He did suffer one more indignity. It appears that the heroic statue is not a likeness of Sir Barton. Rather, it is a fiberglass replica of "a" horse, produced as a stock item by a Montana company whose specialty is life-sized models of large animals.

Man o' War also came to the end of his competitive days with the Kenilworth race. Samuel Riddle feared the weights that would be assigned to

The gravesite of Sir Barton in Douglas, Wyoming. The famous racer had originally been buried on the Hylton ranch.

Man o' War with his devoted groom, Will Harbut. More than 1,323,000 people visited the horse during his retirement.

him if he participated in the handicaps in his fourth year. He had had a sample of this earlier in 1920, when the horse was asked to carry as much as 138 pounds. Thus, he was retired to stud and wrote a new and glorious chapter to an already phenomenal career. His first foals reached the races in 1924. Out of his second crop came Crusader, the first of his offspring to exceed $200,000 in earnings. Man o' War, in 1926, headed the sire list, as his sons and daughters won a record-breaking $408,137. He became a headliner once again in 1937, when his son, War Admiral, captured the Triple Crown, and his grandson, Seabiscuit, became one of the turf's greatest campaigners and money-winners, and the two locked heads in one of the most exciting battles ever witnessed on an American racetrack.

Man o' War lived out his days on his owner's Faraway Farm in Kentucky, where more than 1,323,000 people visited him. He died in 1947. By a conservative estimate, the initial investment of $5,000 that Samuel Riddle made in purchasing him paid off more than $4 million in purses won by him and his progeny and from stud fees. His epitaph was a remark made by Will Harbut, his groom: "He wuz the mostest horse."

Gallant Fox

Gallant Fox
(bay colt)
{
  Sir Gallahad III {
    Teddy
    Plucky Liege
  }
  Marguerite {
    Celt
    Fairy Ray
  }
}

| Chapter 2 |

Gallant Fox

~1930~

Early in 1925, Arthur B. Hancock was faced with a pressing problem. The master of Claiborne Farm, one of the country's prime Thoroughbred breeding centers near Paris, Kentucky, had lost two sires and was sorely in need of a first-class stockhorse. The knotty matter was resolved before the year was out, but the breeder could hardly have envisaged the chain reaction of events that followed, which added brilliant pages to the history of Thoroughbred racing in America.

It was in March that his attention was first drawn to photographs of a French-bred colt, Sir Gallahad III, as he won the Lincolnshire Handicap in England in a gallop. Sometime later, he again saw pictures of the horse beating Epinard in a match race in Le Sport Universal in France. There was something about his bearing that grabbed Hancock. It was a hunch at first, but it nurtured into a strong desire when he learned the colt's impressive pedigree.

His sire, Teddy, of the Bend Or line through a chain of Ajax-Flying Fox-Orme-Ormonde, had been the outstanding stallion of 1923 in France and one of that country's best in 15 years. Plucky Liege, his dam, had dropped a whole cluster of distinguished sons and daughters, while Sir Gallahad III himself had chalked up an impressive skein of wins and purses in three years of campaigning before retiring to stud in 1925. The statistics had sufficient weight to warrant further investigation. Hancock therefore cabled the British Bloodstock Agency, requesting an inquiry to determine if Sir Gallahad III's owner and breeder, Captain Jefferson Davis Cohn, would consider selling him.

A favorable response was received. Accompanying it was an option on the horse until the last day in November and an invitation to visit the Normandy stud farm. Hancock would be allowed to inspect the stallion and the mares bred to him in the spring to confirm his fertility and good health. Encouraged by this, the Kentucky breeder next contacted three aristocrats of the American turf—banker and chairman of the Jockey Club William Woodward, department store tycoon Marshall Field, and Wall Street broker Robert A. Fairbairn. Hancock explained his plan and proposed that they form a syndicate with him to help finance the venture. The three agreed, but only if he recommended it after inspecting the horse.

Hancock sailed at once for France, landing in Cherbourg on November 24, 1925. He visited the farm the following day, met with Cohn at the Ritz in Paris the day after, and concluded the deal the next morning. The price was in the vicinity of $150,000, but that included all freight and insurance costs.

Little time was wasted thereafter in bringing the prize stallion to America, and in style too. He was shipped to Boulogne, then to London, and, finally, to the United States aboard the liner S.S. *Minnetonka* in special quarters prepared for him on one of the passenger decks. Upon his arrival in New York on December 15, he was met by a special float that transferred him to a private railway express car made available by Woodward for the trip to Kentucky. Sir Gallahad III finally reached Claiborne safe and sound to begin his first stud season on American soil in the spring of 1926; something like 40 mares were awaiting the pleasure of his company.

"It may be fitly said that he was destined to exercise a more potent influence upon the American breeding fabric than any other stallion imported for many years, and that this animal marked the beginning of a new development in our stud history," said noted turf historian John Hervey, who wrote under the pen name of "Salvator." His first issue came of racing age in 1929. They numbered 23, 15 of which went to the post, with 7 winning 15 races. All told, they earned a total of $47,947. However, the following year, with only two- and three-year-olds representing him at the track, Sir Gallahad III established a new world record when 16 of his get won 49 races and purses adding up to $422,200. It topped Man o' War's record from 1926, when 26 of his offspring won 49 races and earned $408,137.

One of the mares scheduled for a date with the French stallion in the breeding shed was William Woodward's Marguerite. He had purchased her in 1921 at Saratoga from a lot of yearlings put up for sale by Arthur Hancock. She was English-bred, and the banker paid $4,700 for her simply because he fancied the chestnut filly. She was broken at his Belair Farm in Prince George's

County, Maryland, after which she made her racing debut at Belmont on May 27, 1923. She went off at 15-1 and finished last. It was also her last race because she seemed to wrench her back, failed to respond in training, and was finally retired the following year. Her owner was not concerned because he had felt all along that she would do better as a broodmare.

Her first foal was a colt in 1925, followed by a filly the next year. Then, on March 23, 1927, to the cover of Sir Gallahad III, she dropped a bay colt with black points, a blaze face, and coronets marked with white. They named him

Trainer James "Sunny Jim" Fitzsimmons. This photograph was taken in 1938, after he had saddled two Triple Crown champions.

Gallant Fox, and it was largely because of his illustrious accomplishments in racing three years later that his sire, Sir Gallahad III, became the world's leading stallion.

William Woodward was a unique owner. He cared little for the two-year-old stakes races, such as the Futurity and the Hopeful. Rather, he looked forward to the classics—the Kentucky Derby, Preakness, and Belmont Stakes. Consequently, after the yearling Gallant Fox was weaned at the Belair Stud, he was shipped to the Belair stable at Aqueduct Race Track in New York to come under the care of the great trainer "Mr. Fitz," James "Sunny Jim" Fitzsimmons. He was to be brought along slowly for the rigors of the three-year-old campaign.

It was no surprise, therefore, that his two-year-old season was somewhat unimpressive, at least at the outset. He made his debut at Aqueduct on June 24, 1929, raced greenly, but finished a strong third behind the winner, Desert Light, in a field of 10. Five days later, he was out again in the six-furlong Tremont Stakes with 12 other horses. He finished eighth—the only time in his career he ever wound up out of the money. The result was no surprise to his trainer because he had become accustomed to an infuriatingly bad habit of the colt—curiosity. "The Fox" was simply nosy about all that was going on around him, which kept him from settling down to business. The Tremont was an example. Fitzsimmons claimed, "He was so interested in the others that he forgot to leave the barrier until he saw them running down the track away from him, when he started after them and did pass five of them."

Finally, on July 29, Gallant Fox broke his maiden, "closing like a lion" from third in the stretch to take the Flash Stakes at Saratoga by a length and a half. The win convinced Woodward and Fitzsimmons that they had a rather good horse in training. Nobody was particularly upset, therefore, when he lost the next three races, the U.S. Hotel Stakes, Futurity Trial Stakes, and Futurity Stakes. Each race found him running stronger. His final outing of the year was in the Junior Champion Stakes at Aqueduct, on September 28. He caught the leader, Desert Light, with ⅛ of a mile to go, wrote Neil Newman, the respected turf writer with the distinctive nom de plume "Roamer." "[Gallant Fox] swept past him as if he were anchored and won with his head on his chest by two lengths." That race stamped Gallant Fox as a high-class colt, and his name, from that time on, was mentioned in all discussions about the three-year-old classics of 1930.

So, as the colt prepared to spend the winter at Aqueduct, he did, indeed, become the talk of the turf. Before the year was up, both Whichone and

Boojum, the Harry Payne Whitney precocious speedsters, were withdrawn from the Kentucky Derby of 1930 because of leg problems. The only other horse that rated with the track fans was the Kentucky-bred Desert Light, and Gallant Fox had already beaten him. Reflecting in retrospect on the colt's sudden elevated status, Roamer commented: "As a two-year-old Gallant Fox was a first-class race-horse, but I doubt if any outside of his immediate circle, prior to the running of the Junior Champion Stakes the latter part of September, suspected that he was a potential champion and record maker." Whatever doubt existed evaporated progressively as the winter of 1929 eased into the spring of 1930.

A fusion of factors within a relatively short span early in the year virtually guaranteed a phenomenal racing season for Gallant Fox. First off, he weathered the rigors of a New York winter with ease, growing and developing into a handsome, powerful frame, an inch over 16 hands tall and weighing some 1,200 pounds. Then, after the snow had disappeared from the track, James Fitzsimmons laid out a grueling training campaign for him. Although he was not entered in any races until the Wood Memorial in April, he nevertheless trained as though he were preparing for an outing any day. The fact is, they had him sizzling through eight furlongs in 1:41 as early as March. Also, Gallant Fox seemed to have put to rest his insatiable curiosity about things around him and was all business. Finally, Earl Sande decided to come out of retirement and become the colt's regular jockey. They became the dream team of the year, one of the best of all time.

Sande had begun riding as an amateur in his hometown of American Falls, Idaho, at the age of 10. In 1918, he turned professional as an apprentice in New Orleans, from which point he rose to the top of his profession and was lionized with the same awe and admiration as was Babe Ruth in baseball. By 1923, he was the highest-paid rider, a far cry from the youngster with the nervous stomach who had been taken off Sir Barton for the match race with Man o' War. Sande finally retired in 1928, when making weight became something of a chore. He turned to training and owning his own string. The venture was anything but a success, and he eventually wound up $75,000 in debt. With the death of his wife, and still only 34 years old, he began to yearn for the track. He started working out to see if he could regain some of his old finesse. Then, as the important Wood Memorial on April 26 approached, he was prevailed upon to ride Gallant Fox in the colt's first race at age three. For the jockey, it was his first competitive ride since September 1928.

Earl Sande and Gallant Fox, the turf dream team of 1930. The colt's right eye had too much white around the pupil, giving it the appearance of walleye, which some said frightened his rivals.

"Sande has a spell to which horses seem unable to refuse response," reported Vernon Van Ness in *The New York Times*. "And most horsemen will tell you that Sande is the only real genius among jockeys they have ever seen." Going off at 8-5 in the mile-and-70-yards race, the Gallant Fox–Earl Sande duo romped to a four-length victory. At the outset, Crack Brigade jumped out to an early lead, as the rest of the field closed in and pinched off the Belair colt. Into the far turn, he was still boxed in on the rail, whereupon Sande eased him back and made a move around the field on the outside. As he came on, Desert Light challenged him, at the same time forcing him still farther away from the rail. The strategy failed, for Gallant Fox just kept going, reaching the leader at the ¼ pole and galloping home as he pleased, in 1:43⅗, carrying 120 pounds as if it were nothing.

Followers of the turf said the win created more excitement and enthusiasm with the twenty thousand fans at the track and throughout the racing world as to the horse's prospects in the upcoming Preakness and Kentucky Derby than had been shown in a horse in years, particularly because all of the horses who ran in the Wood were Derby candidates. Unfortunately for Desert Light, the second favorite of the race, he bowed a tendon and was lost for the season.

Thirteen days later, on May 9, it was Preakness time at Pimlico. This was one of the years when the race was run before the Kentucky Derby. A field of 11 Thoroughbreds went to the post, and once again Gallant Fox was in trouble at the outset. Running on the rail, he "lacked early footing," was passed, pocketed, and lost even more ground on the clubhouse turn. Moving into the backstretch next to last, Sande's golden touch with a horse became evident when he started what was described in the *Times'* account of the race as "the most electrifying dash that has been seen in Maryland in many a day. Finding a hole here and a gap there, Sande snaked his way through the field and was third at the far turn." Every other horse looked like it was on a treadmill.

Gallant Fox was second at the top of the stretch, at which point Sande gave his charging mount a breather before moving to within a head of the leader at the mile. A neck and neck battle for the lead was joined with Crack Brigade, who "couldn't stand the strain and gave just a little" 150 yards from the finish line, enough to wind up second by three-quarters of a length. The time was 2:00⅗, and the crowd of 51,925, including Vice President Charles Curtis, tried to figure out how the horse had pulled off the victory when he had appeared to be so hopelessly lost on the first pass of the grandstands.

The accolades tumbled forth in a gush. Bill Corum, in the *New York Journal-American*, crowed: "The squarest shooting kid that ever clucked in the ear of a race horse came back to the big time to give us as masterly an exhibition of horsemanship as ever he flashed when his name was a byword of the turf." Roamer wrote: "This race demonstrated that Gallant Fox did not have to have everything his own way during the race, and also proved that the experience of Sande was an invaluable asset to Gallant Fox's natural ability."

Sande was somewhat more laconic. "I didn't call on him until we hit the furlong pole. Then he came on with a rush and hung it on Crack Brigade." Mr. Fitz was equally matter-of-fact. He professed not to have been worried,

Gallant Fox, with Earl Sande up, drives down the homestretch to win the Preakness by three-quarters of a length over Crack Brigade.

Official Chart of Preakness

47354
May-9-30-Pim

FIFTH RACE—1 3-16 Miles. (Big Blaze, Nov. 13, 1924—1:58⅗—3—118.) Thirty-ninth Running PREAKNESS STAKES. $50,000 Added. 3-year-olds. Entire Colts and Fillies. Weight-for-Age. Net value to winner $51,925; second, $5,000; third, $3,000; fourth, $2,000.

Index	Horses	A	Wt	PP	St	½	¾	1	Str	Fin	Jockeys	Owners	Equiv. Odds Str't
(46944)	GALLANT FOX	wB	126	1	2	8^{nk}	3^{2}	2^{4}	1^{h}	1¾	E Sande	Belair Stud Stable	100-100
47197^{2}	CRACK BRIGADE	ws	126	8	3	$2^{1\frac{1}{2}}$	2^{h}	1^{h}	2^{8}	2^{6}	G Ellis	T M Cassidy	1145-100
47154^{3}	SNOWFLAKE	wB	121	2	1	6^{nk}	$8^{1\frac{1}{2}}$	4½	3^{h}	$3^{1\frac{1}{2}}$	A Rob'ts'n	W J Salmon	†900-100
47197^{3}	MICHIGAN BOY	w	126	6	9	10^{1}	7^{h}	5^{3}	4^{3}	$4^{1\frac{1}{2}}$	J Shelton	J L Pontius	1475-100
(47006)	GOLD BROOK	w	126	9	6	$4^{1\frac{1}{2}}$	4^{nk}	$3^{1\frac{1}{2}}$	5^{3}	5^{h}	J Maiben	Howe Stable	‡1675-100
47198	SWE'T SENTIMENT	w	126	7	4	3^{h}	5^{2}	6^{h}	6^{3}	6^{3}	F Col'letti	Seagram Stable	1175-100
(47197)	WOODCRAFT	w	126	5	11	11	10½	10^{1}	7^{h}	7^{nk}	E Ambr'se	Audley Farm Stable	1695-100
(47234)	ARMAGEDDON	w	126	11	8	$7^{1\frac{1}{2}}$	9^{1}	9^{3}	9^{2}	8^{h}	J Eaby	W M Jeffords	1205-100
(47071)	SWINFIELD	w	126	10	7	5^{h}	6^{h}	8^{1}	8^{3}	$9^{1\frac{1}{2}}$	L Schaefer	W J Salmon	†
46951^{3}	FULL DRESS	w	126	4	10	9^{h}	11	11	11	$10^{1\frac{1}{2}}$	J McCoy	Glen Riddle St'k F'm Sta	2030-100
(47062)	TETRARCHAL	w	126	3	5	1^{2}	1^{nk}	7^{1}	10½	11	W Kelsay	Howe Stable	‡

†Coupled as W. J. Salmon entry; ‡Howe Stable entry.

Time, :23⅗, :48, 1:13⅗, 1:39, 2:00⅗. Track fast.

	$2 DONATIONS PAID			EQUIVALENT BOOKING		
GALLANT FOX	$ 4.00	$ 4.30	$ 2.90	100—100	115—100	45—100
CRACK BRIGADE		7.20	4.60		260—100	130—100
W. J. SALMON ENTRY			3.70			85—100

Winner—B. c, by Sir Gallahad III.—Marguerite, by Celt (trained by J. Fitzsimmons; bred by Belair Stud).

WENT TO POST—5:02. AT POST—6½ minutes.

Start good out of machine. Won driving; second and third easily.

GALLANT FOX, in trouble on the first turn, went to the outside in the back stretch, caught the others with fine speed and, given a breathing spell when in contention, responded gamely to wear down CRACK BRIGADE and, ridden out, was drawing away at the end. CRACK BRIGADE forced a good pace and raced TETRARCHAL into submission and held on gamely after taking the lead. SNOWFLAKE, shuffled back at the half-mile post, recovered and finished gamely. MICHIGAN BOY improved his position slowly, but could not menace the leaders. GOLD BROOK offered a strong challenge on the turn, but tired at the end. SWEET SENTIMENT could not keep up. WOODCRAFT began slowly and was never a factor. TETRARCHAL showed fine speed for seven-eighths and quit badly.

that "when he got close to the leader, I knew it was all over." The day was a heady one, indeed, for the principals. Sande and Woodward savored their first Preakness victories, and the colt achieved status. According to Roamer, "Gallant Fox had now attained national prominence, and was affectionately referred to by his admirers as 'the Fox of Belair.'"

In a driving rain, sixty thousand fans turned out for the 56th running of the Kentucky Derby on May 17. There was a festive air despite the weather because of the presence of the 17th Earl of Derby, who had been invited to visit the United States by Joseph E. Widener, president of the Westchester Racing Association in New York. There were 15 starters, with the Fox favored at 11-10. Next in line was the Kentucky-bred Tannery. Roamer was hardly impressed with the field:

> When the list of his prospective rivals was canvassed, not one had credentials of a first-class horse. Yet local pride in Kentucky was so great, coupled with an animosity toward anything hailing from the East, that a locally owned horse called Tannery was heralded as a real menace to Gallant Fox and many loyal Kentuckians were firmly of the opinion that "Pritchard's horse" [Tannery] would win the honors. This belief was held by some horsemen who had spent their lives around racetracks, and can only be ascribed to the intense chauvinism that sways many "Hard Boots" in intersectional contests.

The race was almost a duplicate of the Preakness. Gallant Fox started slowly, in fifth position going past the grandstands after leaving the gate. However, as the field entered the backstretch, it was the beginning of the end, and the only question that remained was by how much he would win. Sande moved the Fox to the outside and "closed on the leaders with a show of power that made those who had seen his Preakness rush chuckle," marveled the *Times*' Bryan Field. For a moment, three horses raced together as a team—Gallant Knight, Tannery, and Gallant Fox. Then the Fox made his move, and when Crack Brigade tried to keep up with him, "Sande looked over his shoulder, slapped Gallant Fox once or twice, and Gallant Fox moved away and daylight grew between his heels and Crack Brigade's nose." In the stretch it was all too "clear that a horse running in hand with power in reserve was not going to be beaten by horses failing to gain when under the

Gallant Fox roars through driving rain to beat Gallant Knight in the 1930 Kentucky Derby. The victory was Sande's third Derby win.

Official Chart of the Kentucky Derby

47619 FIFTH RACE—1 1-4 Miles. (Track record: Woodtrap, May 21, 1921—2:03$\frac{1}{5}$—7—106. Derby record: Old Rosebud, May 9, 1914—2:03$\frac{2}{5}$—3—114.) Fifty-sixth Running KENTUCKY DERBY. $50,000 Added. 3-year-olds. Net value to winner $50,725 and gold cup valued at $5,000; second, $6,000; third, $3,000; fourth, $1,000.

May-17-30-C.D.

Index	Horses	A	Wt	PP	St	½	¾	1	Str	Fin	Jockeys	Owners	Equiv. Odds Str't
(47354)	GALLANT FOX	wB	126	7	8	4^1	1^1	1^2	1^2	1^2	E Sande	Belair Stud Stable	119-100
47396^3	GALLANT KNI'HT	wB	126	8	7	7^1	$6\frac{1}{2}$	3^3	$2^{1\frac{1}{2}}$	2^2	H Schutte	Audley Farm Stable	2273-100
47475^2	NED O.	w	126	3	3	$12^{1\frac{1}{2}}$	13^h	$9^{1\frac{1}{2}}$	4^h	3^1	J D M'ney	G W Foreman	2579-100
47260	GONE AWAY	wB	126	10	14	$14^{1\frac{1}{2}}$	$11^{1\frac{1}{2}}$	$7\frac{1}{2}$	5^2	4^4	M Garner	Wm Ziegler Jr	5292-100
47354^2	CRACK BRIGADE	ws	126	6	13	6^1	4^{nk}	2^h	3^h	$5\frac{1}{2}$	G Ellis	T M Cassidy	1662-100
47401	LONGUS	wB	126	1	15	15	14^4	10^h	7^1	6^2	R O'Brien	R C Stable	†1812-100
(47475)	UNCLE LUTHER	w	126	2	12	$8^{1\frac{1}{2}}$	8^h	$6^{1\frac{1}{2}}$	6^1	7^2	R Creese	L Stivers	†
(47169)	TANNERY	w	126	12	2	3^1	3^1	5^h	$8^{1\frac{1}{2}}$	8^h	W Garner	E F Prichard	312-100
47475	BR'DWAY LIM'T'D	wB	126	14	11	$10\frac{1}{2}$	$12^{1\frac{1}{2}}$	12^2	10^2	$9^{1\frac{1}{2}}$	P Walls	Three D's Stk Fm Sta	‡5043-100
(47520)	ALCIBIADES	w	121	4	4	1^2	$2\frac{1}{2}$	4^h	9^h	10^h	L Jones	H P Headley .	†
40366^2	KILKERRY	w	126	9	9	$11^{1\frac{1}{2}}$	10^h	$11\frac{1}{2}$	11^4	11^6	T May	Three D's Stk Fm Sta	‡
47169^2	BREEZING THRU	wB	126	13	6	13^1	9^2	14^h	13^1	12^5	J Smith	E R Bradley	§875-100
47169^3	BUCKEYE POET	wB	126	15	5	2^h	$5^{1\frac{1}{2}}$	$8^{1\frac{1}{2}}$	12^2	13^1	E Legere	E R Bradley	§
47396	HIGH FOOT	w	126	5	1	5^h	7^1	$13\frac{1}{2}$	14^8	14^8	C Meyer	Valley Lake Stable	2288-100
47475	DICK O'HARA	w	126	11	10	9^2	15	15	15	15	N Barrett	P H Joyce	†

†Mutuel field. ‡Coupled as Three D's Stock Farm Stable entry; §E. R. Bradley entry.

Time, :23$\frac{3}{5}$, :47$\frac{4}{5}$, 1:14, 1:40$\frac{4}{5}$, 2:07$\frac{3}{5}$. Track good.

	$2 MUTUELS PAID			EQUIVAL'NT BOOKING ODDS		
GALLANT FOX	$ 4.38	$ 3.76	$ 3.42	119—100	88—100	71—100
GALLANT KNIGHT		14.60	8.78		630—100	339—100
NED O.			10.14			407—100

Winner—B. c, by Sir Gallahad III.—Marguerite, by Celt (trained by J. Fitzsimmons; bred by Belair Stud).

WENT TO POST—5:00. AT POST—2$\frac{1}{2}$ minutes.

Start good out of machine. Won easily; second and third driving.

GALLANT FOX, in extremely close quarters for the first three-eighths, raced into the lead on the outside after straightening out in the back stretch, held command under restraint thereafter and won with something in reserve. GALLANT KNIGHT began slowly, worked his way up with a big loss of ground, offered a mild challenge entering the final eighth, but tired badly near the end. NED O. began improving his position after five-eighths, lost ground on the last turn, but finished resolutely. GONE AWAY, on the extreme outside throughout, moved up fast on the stretch turn, but quit in the final eighth. CRACK BRIGADE, sent up with a rush after five-eighths, loomed up menacingly on the stretch turn, then quit. LONGUS came from far back in the stretch. TANNERY tired badly after racing prominently for seven-eighths. HIGH FOOT and ALCIBIADES tired. KILKERRY pulled up sore. BUCKEYE POET had early speed.

Scratched—47396 Busy, 126.

bat." At the wire, he was just coasting, coming in two lengths in front of Gallant Knight, in 2:07⅗.

The victory inspired Damon Runyon to lead off his story on the race with a verse that read in part:

> Why it's that handy
> Guy named Sande,
> Bootin' a winner in!

"Why it wasn't even close," Runyon wrote. "Gallant Fox, pride of the East, with the old mastermind of the horseman sitting his saddle as easily as if he were in a rocking chair on a shady veranda, galloped off with the $50,000 Kentucky Derby." Even Lord Derby was convinced early. Watching the colt move into the stretch out in front, he turned to William Woodward, said a terse, "Fine stuff," and looked for the route to the winner's circle for the presentation

The overhead view of the winner's circle as Gallant Fox, Earl Sande, William Woodward, and Lord Derby participate in the 1930 Derby victory ceremonies.

ceremonies. The crowd erupted with a tremendous roar when Gallant Fox returned from the track, cheering as much, or more, for Sande.

Some interesting facts showed up in news accounts later on. The victory, for example, was Sande's third in the Derby, his others being with Zev in 1923 and Flying Ebony in 1925. He thus became the first modern jockey and first white man to accomplish this, because the black jockey Isaac Murphy set the standard in the 19th century. William Woodward's investment in Sir Gallahad III paid off for him with his first Derby win. On the other hand, Gallant Fox rewarded his backers with a modest $4.38 for $2.00, or about 4-5, the shortest price in the classic since Old Rosebud won it in 1914. CBS radio, over a network of 70 stations with Ted Husing as the announcer, and NBC radio, with 50 stations and Graham McNamee and Clem McCarthy at the microphones, broadcast the race from trackside. One filly, Alcibiades, ran in the Derby that year and came in 10th. Celebrities were in ample supply among the crowd, causing one reporter to note that "Clem McCarthy . . . who dotes on notables when chatting with his audience, ran himself bowlegged collecting names." It was the first time that stall gates were used at the start in a Derby. The pari-mutuel figures showed that $582,384 was bet on the race, of which $207,706 was placed on the Fox. He picked up a tidy purse of $50,725, plus a $5,000 gold cup, which brought his total earnings, including the $19,890 in 1929 and the purses from the Wood and Preakness, to a very respectable $132,690.

Excitement among racing fans now began to inch up, reaching a fever pitch by June 7, 1930, the day of the Belmont Stakes. The race would see the first meeting of Gallant Fox and Whichone, regarded by many as perhaps the greatest juvenile in many a year in 1929. He had beaten Gallant Fox in the Futurity and had earned more than $100,000 to become the top two-year-old money-winner. However, he had been withdrawn from racing toward the end of the year when he developed bad knees, but had been pointed, ever since, toward a second meeting with Gallant Fox in the Belmont. He came up to the race in excellent condition following a fine victory in the Withers Stakes. His jockey, too, was the extremely capable Raymond "Sonny" Workman.

Respect for the two outstanding colts was obvious when only two other horses, Questionnaire and Swinfield, dared to face them. Furthermore, the capacity crowd of forty thousand sent the Fox off at 8-5 and Whichone at 4-5. "The classes preferred Whichone, the masses Gallant Fox," said Roamer. "It is the fashion of the so-called experts to favor a champion until he is beaten and tradition was adhered to in this instance to the letter." There still was doubt that the Belair colt had beaten much, despite his wins in three major races.

A drizzle was in the air when the four horses marched to the starting gate. Earl Sande shot the Fox of Belair to the front right off. Sonny Workman preferred to hold back. The Harry Payne Whitney colt, Whichone, "was sawing wood in last place," seemingly trying to conserve energy. Sande moved Gallant Fox out from the rail for better footing, giving up ground in the process and enabling Whichone to gain somewhat. The crowd was tense with excitement. "They were seeing a seemingly invincible horse held even by a colt which was supposed to have beaten only mediocre opposition in the Preakness and Kentucky Derby," the *Times* reported. They also saw Sande hand-ride his mount and still draw away, while Workman went to the whip in vain, losing by three lengths. The time was 2:31⅗, topping Crusader's 1926 record by ⅗ second, but behind Man o' War's track record for the mile and a half at 2:28⅘.

Damon Runyon had kept his eyes glued on the red-hooded Woodward colt, almost mesmerized. "Through the leaden-grey mist of a rainy Long Island afternoon, 'that red-headed horse,' Gallant Fox . . . galloped to his greatest triumph in winning the Belmont Stakes . . . the horse hadn't gone a hundred yards when

Gallant Fox becomes America's second Triple Crown champion as he crosses the finish line four lengths in front of Whichone in the 1930 Belmont Stakes.

Proud owner William Woodward leads Gallant Fox to the winner's circle.

Official Chart of Belmont Stakes

48551
June-7-30-Bel

FIFTH RACE—1 1-2 Miles. (Man o' War, Sept. 11, 1920—2:28⅘—3—118.) Sixty-second Running BELMONT STAKES. $25,000 Added. 3-year-olds. Net value to winner $66,040; second, $7,500; third, $3,000; fourth, $1,000.

Index	Horses	A Wt	PP	St	½	¾	1	Str	Fin	Jockeys	Owners	O	H	C	P	S
(47619)	GALLANT FOX	wB 126	1	2	1^{2}	1^{1}	1^{2}	1^{1}	1^{3}	E Sande	Belair St'd St	8-5	8-5	8-5	1-4	out
(48190)	WHICHONE	wB 126	3	3	4	4	3^{3}	3^{10}	2^{3}	R W'kman	H P Whitney	4-5	1	7-10	1-6	out
(48325)	QUESTIONNAIRE	wB 126	4	4	2^{2}	2^{h}	$2^{1\frac{1}{2}}$	2^{h}	3^{20}	A Rob'ts'n	J Butler	8	10	10	2	1-4
48190[2]	SWINFIELD	w 126	2	1	3^{1}	3^{3}	4	4	4	L Schaefer	W J Salmon	30	30	30	4	1

Time, :23⅘, :37⅗, :50⅕, 1:03⅗, 1:16, 1:28⅗, 1:41, 1:54, 2:07, 2:31⅗. Track good.

Winner—B. c, by Sir Gallahad III.—Marguerite, by Celt (trained by J. Fitzsimmons; bred by Belair Stud).

WENT TO POST—4:24. AT POST—1 minute.

Start good and slow. Won easily; second and third the same.

GALLANT FOX was rushed into the lead at the start, was rated along under restraint and, given a breathing spell passing the half-mile post and again on the far turn, drew away when called upon and then came wide entering the stretch, finishing with speed in reserve. WHICHONE was taken under restraint in the early stages, but did not stride freely in the greasy going, responded when called upon on the far turn and finished gamely on the inside of the winner. QUESTIONNAIRE, close up throughout, saved much ground turning for home, but could not menace the leaders. SWINFIELD made a determined effort when called upon, but quit badly and was eased up at the end.

Scratched—48399 Flying Gal, 121.

Sande's heels drummed vigorously at Gallant Fox's satin sides and the bright hood shot out to the front. And there it stayed." It was a rather easy victory for the new Triple Crown champion, the first since Sir Barton. The race was also the richest Belmont, worth $66,040 to Gallant Fox. This brought his total earnings to $198,730 and established him as the eighth leading money-winner. Subsequently, it was revealed that Sande rode despite being patched up following a car accident. There was just no way he would allow himself to be replaced. As the day came to a close, hardly anyone was prepared to bet that Gallant Fox would ever be beaten again.

The next two races appeared to confirm this. Three weeks later, on June 28, he waltzed in by three lengths in the Dwyer Stakes at Aqueduct. In Roamer's opinion, "The horse knew he was master of the situation and refused to exert himself unnecessarily." As a result, his stature leaped. He became the first horse to win five great three-year-old stakes: the Wood Memorial, Preakness, Derby, Belmont, and Dwyer. He also picked up an additional $11,500, which carried his earnings past the $200,000 mark, thereby moving him to the top spot as the leading money-winner of the year. Once again, Sande was a doubtful starter, having injured a leg a fortnight prior when he was unseated by a horse. Then, in Chicago on July 12, 1930, Gallant Fox took the Arlington Classic, winning by just a neck after a head-and-head duel with Gallant Knight down the stretch. It was his sixth consecutive win, and no horse in the history of the American turf had ever won the big races in the order that he had, all within just 60 days.

Gallant Fox beats Xenofol in the Dwyer to continue his spectacular streak of stakes victories.

To some, he was unquestionably America's "greatest horse since Man o' War." John "Salvator" Hervey saw him as a heroic figure: "His head is clean and hawklike with quick, nervous eyes. . . . To the eye he looked a bit high off the ground when in training, he stood on his feet with the poise of an athlete and there was about him an air of intense, almost flowing, vitality and dynamic force." Bryan Field ranked him with a "kingly host": "Gallant Fox is a horse of individuality and magnetism, and thus far has behaved in the opposite manner to the tempestuous Man o' War, who was a devil to break and a big, raw colt to handle and train as a two-year-old. He gives the impression of unusual grace and distinction and his symmetry and harmony have attracted thousands of admirers, as did Man o' War's effervescent temperament." It was as if he knew he was king, Field continued, for he was contemptuous of training workouts, refusing to extend himself. Mr. Fitz had to use relays of horses to counter this to keep his speed keyed—shades of Sir Barton. There were no other horses in the barn who could keep up with him.

There was even talk of an "evil eye," which threw fright into his rivals when he looked at them. Both of his eyes were bright and flashing, but one had too much white around the pupil, giving it the appearance of a "walleye," and the horse the impression of having a wild, staring expression. They even said he was something of a rogue because he raced with blinkers. Jim Fitzsimmons, however, cleared up this canard. The trainer refused to remove the blinkers because he was a superstitious sort. The colt had won his first race wearing them, and Mr. Fitz did not want to change his luck. Instead, he merely cut away most of the blinkers because he was afraid that Gallant Fox would risk defeat by easing up if he moved too far in front of the field and failed to see any of his opponents. "He seems to know he's a racehorse and he knows what's going on," said Fitzsimmons. "I let him run his own races pretty much and that's one reason Sande makes an ideal jockey for him." Bryan Field concurred: Sande had good hands and a good seat and understood horses. Field wrote, "But when he lays in behind a horse's ears and croons to him something happens with that horse which does not happen with other horses."

So it was, coming up to the prestigious Travers Stakes on August 16, the oldest race in America, dating back to 1864. It shaped up to be a piece de résistance of the Saratoga season because it marked the third impending meeting between Gallant Fox and Whichone, who by then had claimed victories in the Ballot Handicap, Saranac, Withers, and Whitney stakes races. Only two other horses, Sun Falcon and Jim Dandy, were entered. The Fox was favored at 1-2, and Whichone was 8-5. An indication of the value of the others was the 100-1 price on Jim Dandy. *The New York Times'* John Kieran reasoned that the fans were willing "to back the Flying Earl any time he goes to the barrier on anything faster than a clotheshorse."

The weather was extremely uncooperative. A heavy downpour the night before left the track in horrible shape. It was in such bad condition on the morning of the race that track officials, in a desperate effort to dry it out, placed "dogs," or 40-foot wooden beams, at right angles to the inside rail around the track, to prevent horses from exercising in that area. Consequently, the middle area was pretty well cut up by post time.

At the outset, it was virtually a match race between the Fox of Belair and Whitney Stable's Whichone. Going into the clubhouse turn, they were battling tooth and nail, head and head, and remained locked that way until they entered the homestretch.

The instructions to Sonny Workman on Whichone had been to take the lead immediately and run Gallant Fox off his feet. Figuring the middle of the track had better footing, Workman ran his race there, some 30 feet or more away from the rail, with Gallant Fox on his outside. The other two horses chose to stay on the rail. As they hit the near turn, Whichone bore out even more, carrying the Fox with him. It was at this point, explained Roamer, that Workman's colt broke down; his near foreleg gave way and "he naturally flinched away to his right and, as the Fox of Belair was lapped upon him, he too was carried out." Jim Dandy, meanwhile, still hugging the rail, saving lengths thereby and staying close to the leaders, suddenly shot forward past the floundering two, moving from third to first within 100 yards. Sande saw what had happened, tried to rouse his colt, but realized all too late that the duel with Whichone in the sticky mud had sapped his horse's strength, making it impossible to give chase. Therefore, he eased Gallant Fox and was content to come in second, six lengths behind the leader.

"It was like a transformation scene in a stage spectacle and left the entire assemblage, one of the largest in the history of racing at Saratoga, gasping in amazement," wrote John Hervey. "The famous favorites, to [all] intents and purposes, stuck in the mud," is the way John Kieran saw it. The result supported, once again, the axiom of backstretch people and track aficionados that Saratoga is "the graveyard of favorites." It also marked the end of a brilliant career for the crippled Whichone, and only the third win in 30 starts for

The 100-1 shot Jim Dandy stuns the Saratoga throng with an upset victory over Gallant Fox in the Travers Stakes. It was only the third win in 30 starts for the California colt.

the Californian, Jim Dandy. Moving out of the park, a fan was heard to mutter to himself: "I know that Jim Dandy. He did the same thing last year in the Grand Union," when he was only 50-1.

The Fox, showing no lasting effects from the loss, came out two weeks later and won the Saratoga Cup as he pleased, negotiating the 1¾ miles in 2:56, just a second slower than Reigh Count's 1928 record. He reaffirmed his prowess on September 6, 1930, when he ran what is considered the greatest race of his career in the Lawrence Realization at Belmont Park. "When it was over, turf veterans who have seen many champions in thrilling finishes lowered their glasses, still trembling with excitement," said Bryan Field. Only four horses were entered, and this time Sonny Workman was gunning for Gallant Fox aboard Questionnaire, an outstanding colt who, after finishing third in the Belmont Stakes, had won seven straight races and had never allowed a horse to come from behind and pass him. Gallant Fox was rated at 3-5, carrying 126 pounds, and Questionnaire was at 8-5 under 123 pounds.

Workman used the same strategy as in the Travers. He moved out front and stayed there, trailed furiously by Gallant Fox, until they reached the stretch. "Workman waited until Sande and Gallant Fox were at his saddle girth on the outside and then he bore out—bore out so far that he left a hole along the rail through which a couple of hay wagons could be driven," said Bryan Field. When they straightened out, however, Sande moved to the rail to pick up momentum from the slight inward sloping of the track and to shut off any of the other horses that might have designs on slipping through. There would be no Jim Dandy this time to steal a race. The Fox came on and ran head-to-head with Questionnaire just a nose in front. Both jockeys went to the whip, Workman reputedly the best with the bat, Sande the worst. "Then Sande dropped his bat and put up one of the hand rides that made him the kingpin on the American turf," said Bryan Field. In a bitter, fighting struggle in the last 200 yards, Gallant Fox won by a head.

There were statistics galore to gloat over after the race. The time for the 1⅝–mile race was 2:41⅕, only ⅖ second behind Man o' War's world's record, which never before had been so nearly reached. They ran the 1½ miles in 2:28⅗, surpassing the American record for that distance by ⅕ second. Gallant Fox won $29,610, which made him the country's greatest winning horse, with a total of $317,865, surpassing Zev's mark of $313,639. He was now second in world

Earl Sande rides Gallant Fox to a bitter, hard-fought victory by only a head over Questionnaire (barely seen on the rail) in the Lawrence Realization, which was considered the greatest race of his career.

ranks only to the French horse Ksar, who had earned $335,340. In summation, Roamer wrote of Gallant Fox: "He coupled the speed of a Thoroughbred with the heart of a lion. After this race it was the general opinion that he was the best horse bred in this country since Man o' War."

All was anticlimactic from there on. In the two-mile Jockey Club Gold Cup at Belmont on September 16, only the three-year-old maiden Yarn came out against him. "A battle between these two was like a battle between a spurred cock and a new-hatched chick," said Roamer. Therefore, in a wan effort to reduce the ridiculous, Belair Farm also sent out their Frisius, and the entry was rated at 1-30. But Frisius showed up heavily bandaged and looking like he was on the verge of a breakdown. He was taken in hand after one mile, and just did manage to hobble over the finish line. Gallant Fox, in the easiest win of all his races, came in three lengths to the good with the rather slow time of 3:24⅖. He won $10,300 to push his total to $328,165 and his earnings for just 1930 to $308,275—the first time a Thoroughbred had ever won more than $300,000 in a single year.

The Fox suddenly developed a fever and cough after the race. Therefore, William Woodward, who had all the money he needed and all of the glory he could expect from a horse, announced that he was retiring his horse to stud. The colt arrived at Claiborne Farm on October 28, 1930. His stud fee was set at $3,000 with no return if a foal was not produced, and his book was filled for his first season as a stallion in the spring of 1931. Woodward, in a show of pride, also arranged for Gallant Fox's measurements to be authenticated by the New York Museum of Natural History and to be preserved on a plaque that was placed next to the skeleton of the great Sysonby that was on display in the venerable institution.

The stud career of the Fox of Belair was short. He was successful for only a few years, siring the next Triple Crown champion, Omaha, and Flares and Granville, both of whom won the Ascot Gold Cup in England. In 20 years, from 1934 to 1953, his get earned $1,788,648 in North America and £25,957 in England. One reason attributed to the poor showing in stud is that there were so few good mares sent to him that he had little chance to gain a place among the leading sires. He was finally retired from stud in 1952.

Death came to Gallant Fox at about 1:00 P.M. on November 13, 1954, at the age of 27, an hour before the running of two important stakes races whose names reflected his fame. They were the Gallant Fox Handicap at Jamaica in New York, and the Marguerite Stakes at Pimlico in Baltimore. He was buried alongside his sire and dam on a hill overlooking the stallion barns at Claiborne Farm. A comment by Roamer was his epitaph:

> Since the retirement of Man o' War no horse has captured the imagination of the American public as has Gallant Fox. After a relatively light campaign as a two-year-old, he swept like a meteor across the racing sky in 1930 and when he was retired for all times after his bloodless triumph in the Jockey Club Gold Cup he was more than a racehorse—he was an institution.

Omaha

Omaha
(chestnut colt) {
  Gallant Fox {
    Sir Gallahad III
    Marguerite
  Flambino {
    Wrack
    Flambette
}

| Chapter 3 |

Omaha

~1935~

The career of the third horse to wear the Triple Crown in the United States could best be summed up, in a word, as "erratic." For every soaring peak that it reached, there was a valley of despair into which it plummeted. It was a thoroughly frustrating experience for his owner, William Woodward, his trainer, "Sunny Jim" Fitzsimmons, and the fans who backed him with hard-earned cash at the betting windows.

Woodward was the master of Belair Stud in Maryland and had long espoused the theory that excellent breeding results could be attained through a blending of the best French and American Thoroughbred blood strains. A notable example of this, of course, was Gallant Fox, whose sire had been imported from France by a syndicate that Woodward helped to form. It was with understandable anticipation, therefore, that he awaited the first crop of Gallant Fox in 1932. On March 24, at Arthur Hancock's Claiborne Stud, one was foaled out of the mare Flambino. He was a bright golden chestnut colt slashed with a blaze, and he was named Omaha.

It was soon apparent that Omaha had inherited his sire's early lazy racing habits, for he, too, was a slow starter. He made his debut as a two-year-old on June 18, 1934, at Aqueduct and finished second by a nose to Sir Lamorah among a field of maidens. Five days later, be broke his maiden in a five-furlong dash, which was his last win for the rest of the year. He started in seven more races, failing to win any. However, he ran well, coming in second in the Sanford Memorial, Champagne, and Junior Champion stakes, and displayed sufficient talent to convince many that he was a potential three-year-old champion.

"That Omaha was a comparatively unpretentious two-year-old," recorded John Salvator Hervey, "was largely due to the fact that he was so big, lathy [sic], and as yet needing time to develop and grow together." He did just that, for as a three-year-old he was built on heroic lines, standing 16½ hands tall and very long. Coming out of his winter at Aqueduct in April 1935, he won his first race easily, an allowance event of one mile and 70 yards. The following week, Omaha had his first big test in the Wood Memorial. Although he finished third, he ran strong at the end, which convinced his owner and trainer that he was a Kentucky Derby prospect.

The public took to him as well, and made him a prerace choice until May 4, 1935, dawned. Churchill Downs was enshrouded in a steady drizzle that turned the track into a sea of mud and made an estimated fifty thousand spectators miserable as they waited impatiently for the march to the post. Suddenly, the odds swung away from Omaha to the filly Nellie Flag, who became the favorite of the 18-horse field at nearly 4-to-1.

St. Bernard took the early lead, followed closely by Shut Eye and Nellie Flag. Jockey Willie Saunders bided his time until the backstretch, where he guided Omaha to the outside and charged into the lead. They were ahead by two lengths at the top of the homestretch, as a challenge by Roman Soldier materialized. It was short-lived, for, despite the heavy footing, Omaha closed fast in the last half-mile to beat out Roman Soldier by a length and a half in 2:05.

For some reason, the victory failed to impress the railbirds, a situation that had also confronted Sir Barton and Gallant Fox. The win, nevertheless, was not without a significant sidelight to intrigue turf historians. It was only the third time in 61 Derbies that a father-son double had been completed—Gallant Fox and Omaha. The others were Halma in 1895 and Alan-a-Dale in 1902, and Bubbling Over in 1926 and Burgoo King in 1932.

There were an estimated forty-five thousand fans at Pimlico one week later on Saturday, May 11, 1935, the largest crowd in the history of the track, as Omaha went up against seven other starters in the Preakness at less than even money. This time the track was lightning fast. Once again, Saunders lay back until they reached the backstretch, at which point he gave the horse his head on the outside. It was no contest thereafter, for Omaha "completely smothered his field," stifled any potential threat, and coasted home to a six-length victory. Actually, his cruise around the track was nothing more than a workout for the "Belair Bullet." In taking the race, he became only the fourth

Willie Saunders rides Omaha through the mud of Churchill Downs to a length-and-a-half win over Roman Soldier in the 1935 Kentucky Derby. It was only the third time in Derby history that a father-son double had been completed (Gallant Fox and Omaha).

Official Chart of the Kentucky Derby

SIXTH RACE
09640
May-4-35-C.D

1 1-4 MILES (Out of Chute). (Twenty Grand, May 16, 1931—2:01⅘—3—126.) Sixty-First Running KENTUCKY DERBY. $40,000 Added. 3-year-olds.
Net value to winner **$39,525**; second, **$6,000**; third, **$3,000**; fourth, **$1,000**.

Index	Horses	Eq't A Wt	PP	St	½	¾	1	Str	Fin	Jockeys	Owners	Equiv. Odds Str't
09312^3	OMAHA	wB 126	10	12	$9\frac{1}{2}$	5^1	1^2	$1^{1\frac{1}{2}}$	$1^{1\frac{1}{2}}$	SaundersW	Belair Stud Stable	400-100
(09170)	ROMAN SOLDIER	wB 126	3	10	11^1	$8^{1\frac{1}{2}}$	4^h	2^2	2^4	BalaskiL	Sachsenmaier & Reuter	620-100
(09434)	WHISKOLO	w 126	8	15	$12\frac{1}{2}$	$10^{1\frac{1}{2}}$	2^1	3^2	$3^{1\frac{1}{2}}$	WrightWD	Milky Way Farms Stable	†840-100
(09328)	NELLIE FLAG	w 121	9	1	$8^{1\frac{1}{2}}$	$7\frac{1}{2}$	5^3	4^3	4^h	ArcaroE	Calumet Farm Stable	380-100
09327^2	BLACKBIRDER	wB 126	13	14	14^1	11^1	11^2	5^1	5^2	GarnerW	Mrs C Hainsworth	†
09312	PSYCHIC BID	wB 126	7	11	4^h	4^1	7^1	6^3	6^4	JonesR	Brookmeade Stable	4920-100
09312	MORPLUCK	wsB 126	11	16	16^1	13^2	12^2	7^h	7^h	GarnerM	J H Louchheim	†
09312^2	PLAT EYE	w 126	15	4	$1\frac{1}{2}$	$1\frac{1}{2}$	3^1	8^1	8^1	CoucciS	Greentree Stable	1640-100
09170	McCARTHY	wB 126	4	18	18	15^1	14^4	14^1	9^3	FinnertyR	Morrison & Keating	†
09163^3	COMMONWEALTH	wB 126	17	17	17^4	12^1	9^h	10^2	10^2	WoolfG	Mrs W M Jeffords	950-100
09163^2	SUN FAIRPLAY	wB 126	5	3	10^1	$9^{1\frac{1}{2}}$	13^3	11^1	11^3	RenickJ	Fair Fields Stable	5230-100
(09312)	TODAY	wB 126	16	6	6^1	$6\frac{1}{2}$	8^1	9^2	12^6	Workm'nR	C V Whitney	840-100
09434^3	WHOPPER	wsB 126	2	9	$5\frac{1}{2}$	$3\frac{1}{2}$	$6\frac{1}{2}$	12^1	$13^{1\frac{1}{2}}$	LandoltC	H P Headley	†
09434	BLUEBEARD	wB 126	6	2	7^1	$14^{1\frac{1}{2}}$	15^1	15^1	$14^{1\frac{1}{2}}$	SchutteH	Mrs R B Fairbanks	†
09318	TUTTICURIO	wB 126	18	13	13^h	16^4	16^3	16^4	15^1	CorbettC	Brandon Stable	†
02596	BOXTHORN	wB 126	12	8	$3^{1\frac{1}{2}}$	2^1	10^h	13^1	16^2	MeadeD	E R Bradley	500-100
01724	ST. BERNARD	w 126	1	5	2^h	18	18	18	$17\frac{1}{2}$	KeesterP	E G Shaffer	†
09434	WESTON	wB 126	14	7	15^h	17^1	17^1	17^1	18	YoungS	Braedalbane Stable	†

†Mutuel field. Time, :23, :47⅗. 1:13⅖, 1:38⅗, 2:05. Track good.

	—$2 MUTUELS PAID—			—OFFICIAL BOOKING ODDS—		
OMAHA	$10.00	$ 5.00	$ 3.80	400—100	150—100	90—100
ROMAN SOLDIER		6.40	4.20		220—100	110—100
WHISKOLO (Field)			3.40			70—100

Winner—Ch. c, by Gallant Fox—Flambino, by Wrack (trained by J. Fitzsimmons; bred by Belair Stud).

WENT TO POST—5:13. AT POST—2½ minutes.

Start good and slow. Won easily; second and third driving.

OMAHA, much the best but lucky to escape interference in the early crowding, was taken to the outside after the first quarter, raced to the lead gradually after reaching the half-mile post and, upon taking command, held sway easily thereafter, winning with something left. ROMAN SOLDIER also enjoyed room in the early stages, worked his way to the outside after reaching the back stretch, responded well when called upon and stood severe pressure gamely in the final quarter, but could not menace the winner. WHISKOLO raced to a contending position with a rush, lost ground on the far turn and tired in the last three-sixteenths, but held the others safe. NELLIE FLAG suffered sharp interference from PLAT EYE soon after the start, was again impeded on the first turn, lacked room throughout the back stretch run and could not improve her position when clear in the last five-sixteenths. BLACKBIRDER came from far back and finished boldly. PSYCHIC BID raced well. MORPLUCK also showed good form. PLAT EYE caused much interference soon after the start, had speed, but quit badly after a mile. McCARTHY made up ground. COMMONWEALTH was never prominent, failing to respond to pressure. TODAY was in close quarters on the back stretch, but failed to respond when clear and tired in the stretch. BOXTHORN quit badly. ST. BERNARD was cut off after reaching the back stretch.

Scratched—02435 Color Bearer, 126; 09478³Chanceview, 126; 09434 Prince Splendor, 126; 09434 Calumet Dick, 126.

Omaha smothers the field as he coasts to a six-length victory over Roman Soldier in the Preakness Stakes.

Official Chart of Preakness

SIXTH RACE
09965
May-11-35-Pim

1 3-16 MILES. (Gallant Knight, May 7, 1932—1:58—5—121.) Forty-Fifth Running PREAKNESS STAKES. $25,000 Added. 3-year-olds. Scale-weights.

Net value to winner $25,325; second, $2,500; third, $1,500; fourth, $500.

Index	Horses	Eq't A Wt	PP	St	½	¾	1	Str	Fin	Jockeys	Owners	Equiv. Odds Str t
(09640)	OMAHA	WB 126	6	6	6^5	4^5	$1\frac{1}{2}$	1^6	1^6	SaundersW	Belair Stud Stable	95-100
(09702)	FIRETHORN	W 126	5	8	7^6	7^{12}	4^1	2^2	2^6	WrightWD	W M Jeffords	†355-100
09640	PSYCHIC BID	WB 126	7	4	3^4	3^2	2^3	3^4	3^2	WoolfG	Brookmeade Stable	1985-100
09312	MANTAGNA	W 126	3	5	5^h	$6\frac{1}{2}$	6^2	4^4	4^5	McCrossenC	Maemere Farm Stable	2460-100
09640	COMMONWEALTH	WB 126	1	7	8	8	8	6^h	5^1	Ros'gart'nC	Mrs W M Jeffords	†
09383³	BRANNON	W 126	8	1	1^2	1^3	3^h	$5^1\frac{1}{2}$	6^{nk}	MerrittR	Mrs C S Bromley	8400-100
09640	NELLIE FLAG	WB 121	2	3	$4^1\frac{1}{2}$	$5\frac{1}{2}$	7^5	7^2	7^5	ArcaroE	Calumet Farm Stable	495-100
09640	BOXTHORN	WB 126	4	2	$2^1\frac{1}{2}$	2^h	$5^1\frac{1}{2}$	8	8	WorkmanR	E R Bradley	925-100

†Coupled as Mr. and Mrs. W. M. Jeffords entry.

Time, :23⅖, :47⅗, 1:12⅖, 1:38, 1:58⅖. Track fast.

	—$2 MUTUELS PAID—			—OFFICIAL BOOKING ODDS—		
OMAHA	$3.90	$3.10	$2.60	95—100	55—100	30—100
MR. AND MRS. W. M. JEFFORDS						
ENTRY		3.40	2.80		70—100	40—100
PSYCHIC BID			4.60			130—100

Winner—Ch. c, by Gallant Fox—Flambino, by Wrack (trained by J. Fitzsimmons; bred by Belair Stud).
WENT TO POST—5:56. AT POST—3½ minutes.
Start good and slow. Won easily; second and third driving.
OMAHA, kept clear going to the first turn, bettered his position readily after going seven-eighths, swung to the outside of the leaders when moving to the front midway of the final turn, then drew out at will during the stretch drive to win with much to spare. FIRETHORN, placed to a determined drive in the last five-eighths, was forced to circle his field when reaching contention, then closed willingly in the final drive. PSYCHIC BID raced strongly in the early running on the outside of the leaders, saved much ground during the stretch drive, but tired steadily. MANTAGNA raced under pressure from the beginning and passed tiring horses during the closing stages. COMMONWEALTH dropped far out of contention and was unable to threaten. BRANNON had much speed while setting the pace, but was unable to hold command when vigorously urged. NELLIE FLAG had clear racing room from the beginning, but failed to rally at any stage of the journey. BOXTHORN raced strongly for seven-eighths, then tired.
Scratched—09702³Furfiber, 126; 09702 Legume, 126; (09318)Bloodroot, 121.

horse in history to win both the Kentucky Derby and the Preakness. As a result, he regained some hesitant fans and a bit more respect. It is also notable that he would be the first Triple Crown winner to be sired by a horse that had won the three classic races, Gallant Fox.

Then, on May 25, he lost the Withers by a length and a half after going off as a 1-2 favorite. The reaction was bitter, and he lost favor once more by

48

Omaha passes Firethorn in a duel down the homestretch on a gray, rainy day on a sloppy track to take the Belmont Stakes.

Official Chart of Belmont Stakes

FIFTH RACE **11843** June-8-35-Bel

1 1-2 MILES. (Man o' War, Sept. 11, 1920—2:28⅘—3—118.) Sixty-Seventh Running BELMONT STAKES. $25,000 Added. 3-year-olds. Scale weights.

Net value to winner **$35,480**; second, **$5,000**; third, **$2,500**; fourth, **$1,000**.

Index	Horses	Eq't A Wt	PP	St	½	¾	1	Str	Fin	Jockeys	Owners	O	H	C	P	S
10733^{2}	OMAHA	wB 126	3	5	$3_{\frac{1}{2}}$	3^{1}	4^{12}	2^{4}	$1^{1\frac{1}{2}}$	S'undersW	Belair Stud S	†4-5	4-5	7-10	1-6	out
09965^{2}	FIRETHORN	wB 126	2	2	$2^{1\frac{1}{2}}$	2^{h}	$3_{\frac{1}{2}}$	1^{nk}	2^{8}	WorkmanR	W M Jeffords	5	6	6	7-5	1-4
(10733)	ROSEMONT	wB 126	5	3	5	4^{4}	2^{h}	3^{2}	3^{1}	WrightWD	Foxcatcher F S	13-5	14-5	13-5	1-2	out
11072^{3}	COLD SHOULDER	wB 126	1	1	1^{3}	1^{5}	1^{3}	4^{15}	4^{15}	RenickS	A G Vanderbilt	8	10	10	$2_{\frac{1}{2}}$	4-5
11072	SIR BEVERLEY	w 126	4	4	4^{2}	5	5	5	5	MalleyT	Belair S Sta	†4-5	4-5	7-10	1-6	out

†Coupled as Belair Stud Stable entry.

Time, :24⅕, :48⅖, 1:13⅗, 1:39, 1:52, 2:05, 2:18, 2:30⅗. Track sloppy.

Winner—Ch. c, by Gallant Fox—Flambino, by Wrack (trained by J. Fitzsimmons; bred by Belair Stud).

WENT TO POST—4:22. AT POST—1 minute.

Start good and slow. Won easily; second and third the same.

OMAHA was shuffled back after the break, recovered quickly and, allowed to settle in his stride, came to the outside of the leaders entering the stretch, finished fast and was drawing away at the end. FIRETHORN was rated along steadily, saved ground entering the stretch and finished well. ROSEMONT was forced wide rounding the first turn and dropped back. He moved up stoutly on the back stretch when called upon, but faltered badly in the stretch run. COLD SHOULDER was rushed into command going to the first turn, was rated along steadily and had no mishaps. SIR BEVERLEY was not persevered with when he faltered.

Scratched—(11394)Gold Foam. 126.

the time June 8 rolled around for the Belmont Stakes. It was a rainy day, the track was sloppy, there were five starters, and he came in for a rough battle. It was not until he reached the turn into the homestretch that he caught up with the leader, Firethorn, who was running a strong race on the rail. The two engaged in a duel down the stretch until Omaha proved his class by drawing away to a one-and-a-half-length dramatic victory and the Triple Crown.

The smiles were back until he came in third to Discovery and King Saxon in the Brooklyn Handicap, but he rebounded to take the Dwyer Handicap on June 29, to equal Man o' War's record time in the process: 1:49⅕ for the 1⅛ miles.

By that time, Omaha had the public coming and going with his up-and-down performances. Consequently, he was written off as just the best of a bad three-year-old lot. Omaha, however, had a big surprise in store for everyone. On July 20, he flashed away from the starting barrier in the esteemed Arlington Classic in Chicago, carrying scale weight of 126 pounds, and clocked the fastest 1¼ miles ever run by a three-year-old in the country. The time was 2:01⅗. It was an electrifying win that made him a national hero as he traveled east to prepare for the Travers and Saratoga Cup races.

The joy was temporary, however, for soon after his arrival at the upstate New York track, the racing world was stunned by an announcement that Omaha had come up lame. Although the ailment subsided quickly, the champion was withdrawn from further competition for the balance of the year as a precautionary measure. There was no way of foretelling it then, but

Omaha blazes to an electrifying, record-breaking victory in the Arlington Classic. The time of 2:01⅗ was the fastest 1¼ miles ever run by a three-year-old in the country. St. Bernard finishes second, Bloodroot third. The race was the last in the United States for the "Belair Bullet."

Omaha had run his last race in the United States. "It was like the extinction of a great light," wrote Salvator.

William Woodward was not that easily discouraged. He had an interesting notion. Coincident with his theory of breeding foreign and native horses, he nurtured the hope of developing an American Thoroughbred that could cross the Atlantic and take on the English classics, notably the Ascot Gold Cup. Why not Omaha? There were compelling reasons that he could be the horse to do it. First, he had recovered rather well from his lameness. Second, his obvious strength suggested that he might well be suited for coping with racing on turf. Finally, the records showed that after his juvenile season, the Triple Crown champion had never won except at distances beyond a mile, and because all of the major classics in Britain were between 1½ and 2½ miles, they might just be his cup of tea.

After his resolve was firmed up, Woodward proceeded to make sure of the colt's condition for turf racing. He brought Captain Cecil Boyd-Rochfort, one

Omaha is led aboard the liner *Aquitania* on January 8, 1936, for the voyage to England to race in the Ascot Gold Cup.

The filly Quashed (left) nosed out Omaha at the finish line of the 1936 Ascot Gold Cup classic after a head-to-head duel in the uphill stretch.

of the most successful of English trainers, to America to pass judgment on the horse. It was favorable, and on January 8, 1936, Omaha was shipped out aboard the *Aquitania*, arriving in England seven days later. He sailed with everyone's good wishes, including a former worthy adversary, who sent him the following telegram:

> Roll on, roll on, O Omaha the great.
> Be sure you make the British late,
> And I will try to fill your place.
> You'll bet they'll know they had a race.
>   Signed: FIRETHORN

He made his English debut in the spring on May 9, 1936, in the Victor Wild Stakes at Kempton Park, Middlesex, just 14 miles from London. His reputation had preceded him, for he was soon the focal point of interest and popularity with the English racing fans. Omaha carried 129 pounds and won the 1½-mile race. On May 30, he took the Queens Plate by a neck at the same distance, carrying 130 pounds. Both races were tune-ups for the Ascot Gold Cup on June 18.

It was the 125th running of the race, and an estimated one hundred fifty thousand excited fans jammed the Royal Ascot Track. Nine horses started, with Omaha rated the favorite at 11-8. The track was very heavy from rain, and he lost to the filly Quashed, to whom he had given a sex allowance of 3 pounds, at 123. It was a thrilling battle over the 2½-mile course, reported *The Blood-Horse*. "The two had engaged each other a half-mile from the finish, at the bottom of the uphill stretch, and had run head-to-head to the finish line, where the filly got the decision by a nose."

Omaha raced once more in England in the 1½-mile Prince of Wales Stakes at Newmarket. He carried the top weight of 138 pounds under severe conditions: the track was rain-soaked. He seemed ill at ease, sweated profusely in the paddock, and, as one reporter was heard to say, must have lost seven pounds before going out on the course. Nevertheless, he was up with the leaders throughout the race. In the last quarter of a mile, he battled eye to eye with Taj Akbar, who carried only 120 pounds, and lost to the three-year-old by a neck. It was disappointing, but many blamed the loss on his handling by the

Omaha, at age 25, stands in the pasture of the Nebraska City farm of Grove Porter, the Nebraska racing commissioner. With him is Porter's son, Morton. The Triple Crown champion died two years later in 1959.

jockey in the last moments of the race. It was also his last race of the season. Yet, in spite of the losses in the two stakes events, Omaha had captured the hearts of the British race fans. The thrilling battles that he had put up caused them to proclaim him one of the best horses seen in England in years.

Woodward decided to keep him in the country for another crack at the Ascot Gold Cup in 1937. However, in mid-June he injured a tendon of the left foreleg and was returned to the United States. Once again, a valley had replaced a golden peak. This time, there was no recourse but to retire him to Claiborne Farm, where he had been foaled. This time, there were to be no more peaks to reach.

The final resting place for Omaha at the Ak-Sar-Ben Race Track near Omaha, Nebraska.

By 1943, it became obvious that the colt was unsuccessful as a stallion. At least, he was not likely to produce anything approaching his own class. As a result, his owner leased him to the Jockey Club's Lookover Stallion Station at Avon in upstate New York. He remained there until 1950, when he was passed on to a group of breeders in Omaha, Nebraska.

The colt finally stood in retirement at the Grove Porter Farm in Nebraska City, where he also was a popular tourist attraction. In the meantime, a monument in his honor, as a fitting tribute to the fame he had brought to the city and state, was erected at Ak-Sar-Ben, near Omaha, site of the racetrack and world-famous annual fair of that name. It was there that he was buried after his death in 1959.

Omaha's record was not the most distinguished of the Triple Crown winners. In his three seasons, he came in first in only nine of twenty-two starts, second in seven, and third in two. He had won a total of $154,755. But he had been something to behold on the track. "In action he was a glorious sight; few thoroughbreds have exhibited such a magnificent, sweeping, space-annihilating stride, or carried it with such strength and precision. His place is among the Titans of the American turf," was Salvator's final tribute to him.

War Admiral

and jockey Charley Kurtsinger

War Admiral
(brown colt) { Man o' War { Fair Play

Mahubah

Brushup { Sweep

Annette K.

| Chapter 4 |

War Admiral

~1937~

A fan will be hard-pressed to name two back-to-back years in American Thoroughbred racing that produced more absorbing drama and color than did 1937 and 1938. These were the years of the "Admiral" and the "Biscuit," two magnificent colts who streaked across the racing spectrum in a shower of speed, stamina, courage, and color. War Admiral was the fourth Triple Crown champion and Horse of the Year in 1937, a dynamic horse with an inbred spirit to win. Seabiscuit held the handicap champion title and was the leading money-winner of 1937 and Horse of the Year in 1938, one of the greatest campaigners who crisscrossed the country to race any and all comers. It was inevitable that these two fantastic steeds should clash in head-to-head combat. When they did, the race captured the attention of the public to such an extent that it even compelled the president of the United States to pause in his day's work to tune in to the action.

The careers of both horses also brought into the brilliant spotlight of publicity some of the most important figures of the turf at that time. First, there was Man o' War, the "giant stallion" who had made it all possible. He looked on with justifiable paternal pride from his Kentucky retirement farm at the accomplishments of his son, War Admiral, his most distinguished get, and his grandson, Seabiscuit. Then there were Samuel D. Riddle, owner of both Man o' War and War Admiral, who had already been to the well of success with a champion horse; Charles S. Howard, a San Francisco auto magnate and owner of Seabiscuit, who was making his first heady trip there; Cornelius V. "Sonny" Whitney, principal stockholder of Belmont Park and vice president of the Westchester Racing Association; Herbert Bayard Swope, chairman of the New

Handlers have War Admiral practice race starts in an effort to break his aversion to the stall gate.

York State Racing Commission; Joseph E. Widener, president of Belmont Park, which was owned by the Westchester Racing Association; William Woodward, chairman of the Jockey Club; and Alfred G. Vanderbilt, president of Pimlico Race Course.

War Admiral was foaled at Riddle's Faraway Farm, near Lexington, Kentucky, in 1934. He was out of Brushup, and it could be said that in many respects he was a mama's boy. He was on the small side, reaching a maximum growth of 15.3 hands, one hand shorter than his sire, and was brown, rather than red chestnut. When it came to racing, though, he took after his sire without question. Like his Triple Crown predecessors, he too was a late bloomer. His brief two-year-old season was promising: three wins in six starts and never out of the money. At the end of the year he was sent to the Glen Riddle Farm in Maryland for the winter and then shipped to Havre de Grace Track in the spring of 1937. His first race then was the 1 1/16-mile Chesapeake Stakes, which he won with ease. Because of that win, Riddle was motivated to make an unprecedented decision.

For years, he had had a phobia against entering any of his horses in the Kentucky Derby. It was his contention that the race was only an interloper trying to crack the orbit of renown of the Eastern turf centers. He also detested racing in the "West," as he considered Churchill Downs, because it was away from the stomping grounds of high society. Finally—and perhaps his most cogent reason—he felt that the Derby came too early in the year, before a Thoroughbred had developed to his full maturity. All of these reasons had kept the great Man o' War from the Triple Crown in 1920.

However, in 1937 Riddle decided to let War Admiral take a shot at the Derby and sent him to Churchill Downs late in April to prepare for it. On May 4, the colt was given a full-blown tryout at the 1¼-mile distance in an allowance race. It was only four days before the Derby, and the Admiral breezed home in front in 2:08⅗, an exhibition that immediately sent tremors through his opposition and caused him to become a strong favorite for the Run for the Roses.

Churchill Downs, on May 8, saw one of the biggest crowds ever in attendance, seventy-five thousand, which included "princes and paupers, movie

War Admiral, out in front wire to wire, wins the 1937 Kentucky Derby by almost two lengths over Pompoon.

Official Chart of the Kentucky Derby

SIXTH RACE **40796** May-8-37-C.D

1 1-4 MILES. (Twenty Grand, May 16, 1931—2:01$\frac{3}{5}$—3—126.) Sixty-third Running KENTUCKY DERBY. $50,000 Added. 3-year-olds. Scale weights.

Net value to winner **$52,050**; second, **$6,000**; third, **$3,000**; fourth, **$1,000**.

Index	Horses	Eq't	A	Wt	PP	St	½	¾	1	Str	Fin	Jockeys	Owners	Equiv. Odds Str't
(40297)	WAR ADMIRAL	w		126	1	2	$1^{1\frac{1}{2}}$	1^{1}	$1^{1\frac{1}{2}}$	1^{3}	$1^{1\frac{3}{4}}$	Kurts'gerC	Glen Riddle Farms	160-100
40490	POMPOON	w		126	14	6	5^{2}	4^{1}	2^{2}	2^{5}	2^{8}	RichardsH	J H Louchheim	800-100
40614^{2}	REAPING REWARD	wB		126	17	7	$8\frac{1}{2}$	$6\frac{1}{2}$	8^{3}	5^{3}	3^{3}	Rob'tsonA	Milky Way Farm	‡460-100
(40490)	MELODIST	w		126	3	10	6^{h}	5^{1}	5^{h}	4^{h}	4^{1}	LongdenJ	Wheatley Stable	1510-100
(38966)	SCENESHIFTER	wB		126	12	13	$10\frac{1}{2}$	$12\frac{1}{2}$	11^{h}	$7^{1\frac{1}{2}}$	5^{2}	StoutJ	M Howard	§1120-100
40127^{2}	HEELFLY	w		126	10	1	$3^{1\frac{1}{2}}$	$2\frac{1}{2}$	3^{3}	$3\frac{1}{2}$	6^{h}	WrightWD	Three D's Stock Farm	1620-100
(40614)	DELLOR	wB		126	2	4	$7^{1\frac{1}{2}}$	$9\frac{1}{2}$	$6\frac{1}{2}$	$6\frac{1}{2}$	$7\frac{1}{2}$	JamesB	J W Parrish	1370-100
(40282)	BURNING STAR	wB		126	15	15	14^{1}	13^{1}	13^{1}	10^{1}	8^{h}	ParkeC	Shandon Farm	†930-100
40297^{2}	COURT SCANDAL	wB		126	6	11	$12\frac{1}{2}$	8^{h}	9^{3}	12^{1}	9^{1}	SteffenE	T B Martin	†
40490	CLODION	wB		126	13	14	13^{2}	$14\frac{1}{2}$	12^{2}	9^{h}	10^{1}	AndersonI	W A Carter	†
40297	FAIRY HILL	wB		126	4	3	$2^{1\frac{1}{2}}$	3^{3}	$4\frac{1}{2}$	$8^{1\frac{1}{2}}$	$11^{1\frac{1}{2}}$	PetersM	Foxcatcher Farms	4460-100
40490	MERRY MAKER	wB		126	7	19	17^{2}	11^{1}	$10\frac{1}{2}$	$11\frac{1}{2}$	$12\frac{1}{2}$	DabsonH	Miss E G Rand	†
40614	NO SIR	wB		126	19	17	16^{h}	17^{1}	$17\frac{1}{2}$	$13^{1\frac{1}{2}}$	13^{h}	LeBlancH	Miss M Hirsch	†
40349^{3}	GREY GOLD	wB		126	11	18	19^{2}	$19^{1\frac{1}{2}}$	18^{1}	$14\frac{1}{2}$	14^{1}	RosenJ	E W Duffy	†
40614	MILITARY	wsB		126	5	9	$15^{1\frac{1}{2}}$	15^{1}	15^{1}	15^{1}	$15\frac{1}{2}$	CorbettC	Milky Way Farm	‡
(39858)	SUNSET TRAIL II.	wB		126	18	20	20	20	20	$16^{1\frac{1}{2}}$	16^{2}	DotterR	R Walsh	†
(40445)	FENCING	wsB		126	8	12	$9\frac{1}{2}$	$10\frac{1}{2}$	16^{h}	17^{2}	17^{5}	WestropeJ	M Howard	§
40614^{3}	BERNARD F.	w		126	16	16	18^{5}	18^{3}	$19\frac{1}{2}$	18^{3}	18^{1}	HardyL	I J Collins	†
40490^{2}	SIR DAMION	wB		126	20	8	$11\frac{1}{2}$	16^{h}	14^{3}	19^{4}	19^{12}	YagerE	Marshall Field	†
40445^{2}	BILLIONAIRE	wB		126	9	5	4^{h}	$7\frac{1}{2}$	7^{2}	20	20	WoolfG	E R Bradley	1650-100

†Mutuel field. ‡Coupled as Milky Way Farm entry; §M. Howard entry.

Time, :23$\frac{1}{5}$, :46$\frac{4}{5}$, 1:12$\frac{2}{5}$, 1:37$\frac{2}{5}$, 2:03$\frac{1}{5}$. Track fast.

	$2 MUTUELS PAID			OFFICIAL BOOKING ODDS		
WAR ADMIRAL	$ 5.20	$ 4.20	$ 3.40	160—100	110—100	70—100
POMPOON		9.40	6.00		370—100	200—100
MILKY WAY FARM ENTRY			3.80			90—100

Winner—Br. c, by Man o' War—Brushup, by Sweep (trained by G. Conway; bred by Mr. S. D. Riddle)

WENT TO POST—4:42. AT POST—8½ minutes.

Start good and slow. Won easily; second and third driving.

WAR ADMIRAL, fractious at the post but away fast and sent clear of his company under brisk urging, was taken under steadying restraint after racing a quarter mile, set the pace easily to the final half mile, increased his advantage gradually following a brisk shaking up on the stretch turn and, continuing well to the end, won in hand. POMPOON, forced wide throughout and a contender from the start, was reserved off the pace, offered good response when called upon and held on with fine courage, though he did not seriously threaten the winner. REAPING REWARD, in close quarters briefly approaching the first turn, dropped back slightly on the stretch turn, but came again, only to tire in the late stakes. MELODIST, a factor from the start, tired when the real test came. SCENESHIFTER, jostled about on the first turn and eased back in several futile atempts to secure racing room between horses, lost much ground on the final turn, then closed well in a splendid effort. HEELFLY, fractious at the post but away fast, had to be taken back slightly on the first turn as FAIRY HILL came over, saved ground during the final three-quarters, but tired in the stretch. DELLOR lost ground much of the race. BURNING STAR could not get up. COURT SCANDAL tired. CLODION was in close quarters on the inside in the back stretch. FAIRY HILL had speed, but was through after racing a mile. MILITARY was far back throughout. FENCING quit. BILLIONAIRE was through early.

queens, captains of industry, statesmen-leaders from all walks of life." The weather was pleasant, the track good, even though it had been muddy all week. A field of 20 started, with War Admiral at 8-to-5. His strongest competition was Pompoon, the horse his handlers feared the most. The race was held up for eight minutes when the Admiral acted up in a display of his aversion to the starting gate. It was a trait that could not be broken throughout his career.

War Admiral shot out from his number one position at the start, with jockey Charley Kurtsinger in the irons, and was in front immediately. He stayed there, wire to wire. He won by almost two lengths, came out of the race in excellent shape, and was shipped that same night to Baltimore to prepare for the Preakness the following Saturday.

The second leg of the Triple Crown, on May 15, was a race of another sort. Pompoon was not easily denied, and it turned out to be the most exciting race of the year. The two horses took charge from the top. The Pimlico track is noted for its sharp turns, and the Admiral went wide on each of them. As they approached the last turn, with Pompoon a length and a half behind but gaining, War Admiral bore out once more and jockey Wayne Wright shot Pompoon to the rail and into the lead, working hard and whipping his horse. Kurtsinger "sat tight and never did more with his whip than wave it once or twice alongside [his mount's] eyes." It was as stirring a stretch duel as had ever been witnessed on an American track, with the outcome in doubt to the very end, when the Admiral won by a nose. Although the track was not fast, War Admiral won in the excellent time of 1:58⅖, within ⅕ second of the 1934 record time of High Quest.

There were three weeks to go until the Belmont Stakes on June 5, and both horses were saved, being held out of the Withers or any other races. Once again War Admiral was favored, at 4-to-5, and once again he had trouble at the post, breaking out and delaying the start for five minutes. He even almost ruined himself as the race got under way, for he stumbled and, according to Robert Kelley, chronicler for the Jockey Club, "grabbed himself badly, shearing off a piece of the wall of his right forefoot. . . . He recovered with the agility of a dancer, however, and blazed the first quarter in :24 flat, to be nearly three lengths on top." A couple of horses made a go at him, but he would have nothing of that, finishing the 1½ miles completely alone in 2:28⅗, the new Triple Crown champion.

His time was outstanding in that it was ⅕ second faster than Man o' War's 1920 track record and equaled Handy Mandy's 1927 American record. The fact is, the Belmont was the Admiral's easiest of his three "jewel" victories, but it also was almost disastrous. He trailed blood from his injury on the way to the winner's circle and wound up out of action until October. Still, he had made his own indelible mark on racing. No other three-year-old had caused so much talk since Man o' War. Here was a horse who loved to run, and "once away from the hated gate, seemed to enjoy himself."

It was in autumn of the year that a new excitement arose. Suddenly, every track fan began to stir in anticipation of a meeting between War Admiral and Seabiscuit, when it was learned that both had been named for

In the most exciting race of the year, War Admiral (on the outside), beats Pompoon by a nose in the 1937 Preakness Stakes.

Official Chart of Preakness

SIXTH RACE
41058
May-15-37-Pim

1 3-16 MILES. (Dark Hope, May 9, 1936—1:58—7—113.) Forty-seventh Running PREAKNESS STAKES. $50,000 Added. 3-year-olds. Scale weights.
Net value to winner **$45,600**; second, **$5,000**; third, **$3,000**; fourth, **$2,000**.

Index	Horses	Eq't	A	Wt	PP	St	½	¾	1	Str	Fin	Jockeys	Owners	Equiv. Odds Str't
(40796)	WAR ADMIRAL	w		126	1	2	1^1	1^1	$1^{1\frac{1}{2}}$	1^h	1^h	Kurts'gerC	Glen Riddle Farms	35-100
40796^2	POMPOON	w		126	7	3	5^3	2^1	2^2	2^2	2^8	WrightWD	J H Louchheim	480-100
(40583)	FLYING SCOT	w		126	3	5	$2^{\frac{1}{2}}$	3^h	3^h	$3^{\frac{1}{2}}$	3^2	GilbertJ	J H Whitney	3830-100
(40421)	MOSAWTRE	wB		126	8	4	$4^{\frac{1}{2}}$	5^2	4^2	4^2	4^1	LeBlancH	J M Loft	4995-100
40297^3	OVER THE TOP	wB		126	5	6	6^h	7^1	5^h	5^1	5^2	WestropeJ	Mrs W H Furst	5895-100
(40726)	MATEY	wB		126	4	8	7^2	6^h	6^1	6^1	6^2	RichardsH	W M Jeffords	1395-100
40796	MERRY MAKER	wB		126	6	7	8	8	8	7^2	7^6	WoolfG	Miss E G Rand	2635-100
40490^3	JEWELL DORSETT	wB		121	2	1	$3^{\frac{1}{2}}$	4^1	7^1	8	8	DuboisD	J W Brown	11935-100

Time, :23⅕, :47, 1:12⅖, 1:37⅗, 1:58⅖. Track good.

	$2 MUTUELS PAID			OFFICIAL BOOKING ODDS		
WAR ADMIRAL	**$ 2.70**	**$ 2.30**	**$ 2.40**	**35—100**	**15—100**	**20—100**
POMPOON		**2.40**	**2.70**		**20—100**	**35—100**
FLYING SCOT			**6.00**			**200—100**

Winner—Br. c, by Man o' War—Brushup, by Sweep (trained by G. Conway; bred by Mr. S. D. Riddle).
WENT TO POST—5:25. AT POST—3½ minutes.
Start good and slow. Won driving; second and third the same.

WAR ADMIRAL, fractious as usual at the post, broke forwardly to take command in the opening eighth, was permitted to drift out after getting to the front, took a wide course at the first turn, then settled into his stride on reaching the back stretch, was steadied out in the firmer footing, rallied to a severe drive when POMPOON came to him on the inside entering the stretch, withstood a long drive willingly and was holding his own at the end. POMPOON stole through between horses after being slightly bothered at the break when MOSAWTRE came over, rallied strongly to engage the winner at the stretch turn, came through on the inside and fought it out determinedly after getting on even terms with the winner in the last sixteenth. FLYING SCOT held a forward position under good handling, made his challenge in the last five-sixteenths and continued gamely to prove best of the others. MOSAWTRE broke swiftly and toward the inside at the start, was straightened out quickly to follow close up on the outside, but failed to engage the leaders when the real test came. OVER THE TOP was kept under strong urging after getting into his best stride, but failed to enter contention. MATEY began slowly, saved ground, but could not reach a forward position. MERRY MAKER was outrun. JEWELL DORSETT showed speed for the first three-quarters, then retired.

War Admiral (bottom) stumbles at the start of the Belmont Stakes, injuring his right forefoot.

"The Admiral" cruises to an easy victory and wins the Triple Crown as he beats Sceneshifter. A foot injury in this June race put him out of action until October.

Trainer George Conway leads War Admiral and Charley Kurtsinger to the winner's circle.

Official Chart of Belmont Stakes

FIFTH RACE
42410
June-5-37-Bel

1 1-2 MILES. (Man o' War, Sept. 11, 1920—2:28⅘—3—118.) Sixty-ninth Running BELMONT STAKES. $25,000 Added. 3-year-olds. Scale weights.

Net value to winner **$38,020**; second, **$5,000**; third, **$2,500**; fourth, **$1,000**.

Index	Horses	Eq't	A	Wt	PP	St	¾	1⅛	1¼	Str	Fin	Jockeys	Owners	O	H	C	P	S
(41058)	WAR ADMIRAL	w		126	7	2	1^3	1^4	1^4	1^3	1^3	Kurts'gerC	Glen Riddle Fms	4-5	1	9-10	1-3	1-8
(41486)	SCENESHIFTER	w		126	6	7	3^4	2^2	2^5	2^5	2^{10}	StoutJ	M Howard	8	10	8	2½	1
41409	VAMOOSE	wB		126	1	5	4^4	4^1	$3^{1\frac{1}{2}}$	3^3	3^2	WorkmanR	Falaise Stable	60	100	60	20	10
40445³	BROOKLYN	wB		126	4	4	7	5^h	6^6	4^h	4^3	WrightWD	E R Bradley	6	7	6	2	1
(41409)	FLYING SCOT	w		126	5	1	2^h	3^3	$5^{1\frac{1}{2}}$	6^{10}	5^h	GilbertJ	J H Whitney	12	15	12	4	7-5
41058²	POMPOON	w		126	3	3	$5^{1\frac{1}{2}}$	6^4	4^{nk}	5^1	6^{12}	RichardsH	J H Louchheim	3	18-5	3½	4-5	1-3
41814	MELODIST	wB		126	2	6	6½	7	7	7	7	LongdenJ	Wheatley Stable	30	30	20	7	3

Time, **:24, :48, 1:12⅕, 1:37⅕, 1:49⅘, 2:02⅕, 2:15⅖, 2:28⅗** (new track record; equals American record) Track fast.

Winner—Br. c, by Man o' War—Brushup, by Sweep (trained by G. Conway; bred by Mr. S. D. Riddle)
WENT TO POST—4:22. AT POST—7½ minutes.

Start good and slow. Won easily; second and third the same.

WAR ADMIRAL, fractious at the post, began fast and, moving into command with a rush, was rated along steadily while saving ground and won with speed to spare. SCENESHIFTER raced forwardly from the start, was placed under severe pressure in the stretch, but was not good enough. VAMOOSE was restrained when outrun early, then moved up fast under urging in the stretch and held BROOKLYN safe. The latter was outrun early, but moved up gamely on the far turn, only to tire, but came again near the end. FLYING SCOT broke well and raced under restraint the first part, he was placed under pressure nearing the far turn, but could not menace the leaders and tired badly thereafter. POMPOON, sluggish in the early stages, failed to improve his position when called upon and tired. MELODIST was outrun and was never a factor.

the Washington Handicap in Laurel, Maryland, on October 30, 1937. While the Admiral had been busy reeling off one victory after the other in the three-year-old classics, the Biscuit had been defying the norm for Thoroughbreds by first coming into his own in his fourth year and racking up the handicaps.

Seabiscuit was bred in 1933 at the Claiborne Farm by Mrs. Henry Carnegie Phipps and her statesman-financier brother, Ogden Mills. He was by Hard Tack, owned by Mrs. Phipps, out of Swing On. Because his sire was a son of Man o' War, that made him a grandson of "Big Red." The Biscuit, like the Admiral, also took after his dam. He was a bay and on the small side, unlike his sire, who more closely resembled Grandpa. When fully grown, he topped out at a fraction over 15 hands, three inches. Size, though, was misleading, for he was a sturdy horse. When the time came, he was put in the care of Sunny Jim Fitzsimmons, who was then somewhat more preoccupied with the training of a rather more promising colt, Omaha.

Seabiscuit made his two-year-old debut at Hialeah Park in Florida on January 19, 1935, and finished fourth. The consensus was that, although not striking, Seabiscuit could still be a useful performer. From then through November he made 35 starts to wind up with the unimpressive record of five wins, failing to place in 18 and earning only $12,510. His three-year-old season was equally inauspicious, commencing in April at Jamaica. Perhaps all of this racing and attendant failure was getting to the horse, because early in the year he became careless, even lazy. It was no surprise, therefore, that by August, at the end of the Saratoga meet and after some 46 uninspired races spread over two years, his owners gave up and entered him in a claiming race for $6,000. He won the event, only to suffer the indignity of not being claimed by anyone.

Seated in the stands was a relatively new face in Thoroughbred racing, Charles S. Howard, a millionaire Buick distributor from San Francisco who hoped to establish racing on a grand scale on the West Coast. He was looking to add to his string. With him was his trainer, Tom Smith, a former cattle rancher, bronco buster, rodeo rider, and blacksmith who had a penchant and skill for rejuvenating discarded horses. Both men were attracted to Seabiscuit, possibly by the tremendous strength he seemed to possess, judging from the number of times he had raced in the past two years. Smith even discounted a left knee that was dangerously sprung. He had first seen the colt run at Suffolk Downs in June. After watching him take the Mohawk Claiming Stakes at

Saratoga, Smith urged his employer to buy Seabiscuit for the $7,500 asking price.

Seabiscuit then made the first of a number of cross-country trips. After some preliminary training by Smith in California, the colt began to race. He seemed to come alive suddenly and began to finish in the money. By the year's end, he had raced 23 times, scored nine wins, and earned $28,995, most of which winnings came in the last few months under the Howard colors.

In 1937, he became a "consistent and frequently brilliant performer." It was a rare occasion when he had to inhale the dust of front-runners. After two preliminary races, he was entered in the Santa Anita Handicap on February 27, at the time the world's richest race with a purse of $100,000. He was caught at the wire by Rosemont, losing by a nose. On March 6, he won the San Juan Capistrano at the same track, then polished off six more consecutive wins at California's Tanforan and Bay Meadows and New York's Aqueduct and Empire City tracks. His attempt to equal Discovery's record of eight straight wins was thwarted when he finished third in the Narragansett Special on September 11, 1937, on a sloppy track. The race proved conclusively that the Biscuit had developed a distaste for mud, so from then on his handlers avoided the goo whenever possible. The loss did not interfere with the colt's winning ways; he came back with three straight wins.

These set the stage for the big confrontation. It was October, and the leading three-year-old and the leading four-year-old were named for the Washington Handicap, a weight-for-age event. War Admiral was assigned 126 pounds and Seabiscuit 130. The tension rose acutely as the date approached, for it obviously had to be the race of the year—or years. "During 1937," wrote John Salvator Hervey, "the American public was privileged to behold in action two of the most remarkable Thoroughbreds that have ornamented the turf in recent times."

Unfortunately, the race was not to be. Rain began to fall during the week of the race, causing the track to be heavy. It interfered with Seabiscuit's work-outs, so he was withdrawn. War Admiral, on the other hand, stayed in and won handily. The racing fans were sadly disappointed, and their clamor for a meeting of the two horses continued at an octave higher and several decibels louder.

As the year finally drew to a close, both horses were in a struggle of another sort. Which of them would be the top money winner of 1937? The final result was in doubt until the last weeks, when Seabiscuit took the honors with a total of $168,580 after 15 starts that included 11 firsts, two seconds, and two thirds. War Admiral earned $166,500 from eight wins out of eight starts, six of which were in stakes. It was the first time since 1915 that an older horse had beat out a three-year-old.

In another respect, both horses did well for their owners. Seabiscuit enabled the Howard stable to be the leader in money won with $212,859, while the Triple Crown champion War Admiral helped to raise the Glen Riddle Farm to third place, with earnings of $176,140. It was truly a good year for all concerned.

January 1938 rolled around and the public's call for a meeting of the two horses continued apace. At the time, though, the prospects seemed somewhat dim. War Admiral had been shipped to Hialeah from the Riddle Farm in Berlin, Maryland, for the Widener Handicap in February. Seabiscuit was three thousand miles away, preparing for his second shot at the Santa Anita Handicap, also in February. There had been some speculation that the Admiral would be entered in the Santa Anita race, but Riddle quickly scotched this.

The "Mighty Atom"—another appellation hung on Man o' War's son—continued to show his class with an easy win of the McLennon Memorial Handicap on February 19, in a tune-up for the Widener. In fact, jockey Charley Kurtsinger was so confident of the result that he did not carry a whip. A week later, on February 26, both the Admiral and the Biscuit were in action on the same day. War Admiral, carrying top weight of 130 pounds, which caused Riddle to erupt in anger at the racing secretaries for setting such a heavy load on such a small horse, waltzed to his 10th consecutive victory in the Widener. Seabiscuit, on the other hand, lost by a nose to Aneroid in the San Antonio Handicap. He was nosed out again on March 5 by Stagehand in the Santa Anita Handicap—his second loss of the big race by a nose.

Of more importance to the owners, the three races pushed the earnings of both horses over the $200,000 mark. War Admiral thus became the second son of Man o' War to reach this goal, the other having been Crusader. Taking it back a generation further, Fair Play could boast of five descendants who had hit the figure: his sons Man o' War and Display and Crusader, War Admiral, and Seabiscuit.

When Seabiscuit won the Agua Caliente Handicap on March 27, also carrying the top weight of 130 pounds, the die was cast, and there was no getting away from a match race with War Admiral. Unbeknownst to the public, however, the wheels had started to move slowly toward one. One afternoon early in March in New York, Herbert Swope and Charles Howard discussed the idea for the race. The New York State Racing Commission chairman suggested that the horses be entered in the Suburban Handicap of the Belmont Park spring meeting. He also said that he would try to have the added value of the race increased from $20,000 to $50,000.

Howard voiced a desire for a match race "so that there would be no other horses to cause interference." He also preferred the autumn, obviously aware of the fact that in September the scale weights for the four-year-old War Admiral and the five-year-old Seabiscuit would be the same—126 pounds. Finally, he asked for a purse of $100,000, saying that a Western track was willing to go that high, and that "Belmont Park, the country's leading race track, although not the most prosperous because of the sporting way in which it is run, should be willing at least to meet that figure."

It could be said that the tail was wagging the dog. Howard was a newcomer in racing circles, and he was bucking the conservative, ultradignified, Eastern establishment. They needed him, he felt, and so he could lay down his conditions. Finally, in early April, Swope wired Howard that he thought something could be worked out. Although Howard still acted somewhat standoffish, he was anxious for the race to come off. He called Swope to say that he was amenable to the meeting. As a result, the press was advised on April 5 that the race was in the offing and that plans were proceeding to set a specific date. Joseph Widener, on behalf of the Westchester Racing Association, informed the commission that he would take immediate steps to arrange for the purse and the other details. The announcement was greeted immediately with loud hurrahs and a torrent of telegrams to the commission from appreciative fans all over the country. Riddle also wired in to say that he would make a special trip to New York in a few days after he had supervised the shipment of War Admiral and seven vanloads of his horses to Belmont for the spring season.

The newspaper columnists, in the meantime, began to warm up to the subject with a little acid in their typewriters. They had been championing the event for the better part of a year and were tired of the slow pace at which things were moving. On April 7, David Alexander wrote in the *Morning Telegraph*: "There is about as much chance of China and Japan agreeing, or Franco and the Loyalists agreeing, as there is of Howard and Riddle agreeing in the matter of weight." That same day, Bill Corum opined sarcastically in the *New York*

Journal-American: "If War Admiral had been a prizefighter and Seabiscuit had been a prizefighter, [boxing promoter] Mike Jacobs would have had them fighting in Yankee Stadium last September."

Things really came to a boil when, suddenly, John D. Hertz, chairman of Arlington Park and the Arlington Park Jockey Club, offered to put up $100,000 if the race was held in Chicago in July. His deal, though, called for a three-horse event that would include Stagehand, who had beaten Seabiscuit in the Santa Anita Handicap and was favored to win the Kentucky Derby. Riddle greeted this with his own facetious suggestion, that of holding two match races, one in New York and the other in Chicago, so that everyone would be pleased.

Swope, in the meantime, was having problems. Widener was ill in Palm Beach, but authorized him to negotiate with Riddle. However, Cornelius V. "Sonny" Whitney, whose approval would be needed before the Westchester Racing Association could authorize the $100,000 purse, was at sea fishing and could not be reached. Still, it was reported that New York had the veto power over the race and that no other city would be allowed to move in on it. "This race was originally our idea," boasted Swope, "regardless of what the Chicago people claim. Belmont is the cradle of American racing. Where else does such a race belong?" The following day, April 7, he reported that the proposed race had attracted so much worldwide interest that William S. Paley, head of the Columbia Broadcasting System, had offered to broadcast it internationally as well as in America.

Any doubts about New York's self-esteem in the racing world were set to rest when Mr. Swope further stated that "a meeting of the two horses in New York would give the occurrence added importance, as foreign turf bodies, notably the English Jockey Club, recognized only the New York Jockey Club as the governing body in this country." He went on to say that "Mr. Whitney has always been in favor of those steps which benefit New York racing and which bring honor to the Thoroughbred horse." It was all there. No intruders would be allowed to move in on what already was being hailed as "the race of the century."

On April 8, Riddle finally met with the racing chairman to work out the details. When the conference was over, the race was virtually set, to the amazement of most of the reporters. Normally a very obstinate man, Riddle gave in to almost all of Howard's conditions. He agreed to the scale weights of 126 pounds, the distance of 1¼ miles, and postponement if the track was

Seabiscuit and jockey Red Pollard.

not fast or if muddy, and he even offered the post position to Seabiscuit. His only demand was that there should be a walkup start because "War Admiral has never taken kindly to the stall gate," but he even relented on this. He agreed with Howard on a $100,000 purse, largely because each was eager for his horse to surpass Sun Beau as the greatest money-winner in the world. It was William Woodward of the Jockey Club who approved of the suggestion to use scale weights because it "would lend a classic touch to the event."

Chicago was definitely ruled out. Aside from New York's control over the matter, neither owner was particularly keen to run in the blistering heat usually forecast in Chicago in July. Furthermore, War Admiral had already been entered in the $50,000 Massachusetts Handicap at Suffolk Downs, and Seabiscuit in the Hollywood Gold Cup in Inglewood, California, both of which occurred at that time. The owners even ruled out a last-minute proposal by

Charles F. Adams, chairman of the board of Suffolk Downs in Boston, to stage a $100,000 race. This would have included six to twelve starters—winners of the Kentucky Derby, Preakness, and Massachusetts Handicap, as well as outstanding older horses to be selected by a board of leading handicappers and racing secretaries.

The press was advised, on April 10, that Howard had sent in his acceptance of the conditions for the race. All that remained was receipt of approval from Whitney, who was known to be against match races with big purses because they tended to commercialize Thoroughbred racing. Two days later, Whitney arrived for the board meeting of the Westchester Racing Association, and the vote was unanimous in favor of the race and the purse. However, they insisted that it be held on Memorial Day, May 30, rejecting a fall date on the grounds that there was no assurance of the physical condition of either horse then, that the possibility existed that one or the other might be defeated in other races which would reduce the value of the match race, and, most important, that they did not wish to detract from other traditional stakes races during the year. Whitney summed it up when he said: "We are offering this race because public interest is high and the two horses are sound and at the top of their form." He then added pointedly: "Why wait for one of them to break down?"

A few days later, both Riddle and Howard put the icing on the cake by agreeing that the winner would take the whole purse. This, in effect, would make it the largest purse ever offered in any race in the world.

Almost immediately, the experts began to send out a stream of assessments of the respective horses. The supposition seemed to be that War Admiral would outrun Seabiscuit and grind him to pieces, as he had done to his other opponents. For example, David Alexander, in the *Morning Telegraph*, checked the records and found that Seabiscuit had never won at 1¼ miles. Alexander also reasoned that because he had lost by a nose twice at Santa Anita at that distance, his "nose isn't long enough to win." *The New York Times'* Bryan Field said: "The race seems likely to develop into an East-West controversy as to the respective merits of the horses, as there appears one corporal's guard in this area willing to concede Seabiscuit any chance. From Herbert Bayard Swope through the ranks of officials who desired not to be quoted, and down to the ordinary horse player, there was a surprising unanimity for War Admiral."

Charley Kurtsinger, War Admiral's jockey, was very confident: "It won't be close. How can Seabiscuit get close to War Admiral?" John "Red" Pollard,

Seabiscuit's jockey, on the other hand, had some interesting observations: "If the race comes off, and somehow I'm skeptical about it coming off, I think the Biscuit will fool 'em all by showing as much early speed as the Admiral. From what I've seen of the Admiral, he's a horse that wins his races in the first ⅛ of a mile. When he takes his first step out of the gate he's already in stride. But what would you say if I told you that all I have to do is give Seabiscuit a couple of whacks on the flanks at the start to make him run the first ⅜ in :33?" At the time, the world's record for an official ⅜ of a mile was :32⅘.

His statement was remarkable, for it proved to be prophetic on both counts. Seabiscuit gave added dimension to the words a few days later when he won the Bay Meadows Handicap in San Mateo, California, carrying 133 pounds "as lightly as a feather" for the mile and a furlong in the track-record time of 1:49. It was a performance sufficiently impressive to impel an imaginative Associated Press sportswriter to call him the "black bullet of the American turf." After the race, George Woolf, who rode him, was quoted as saying: "He hasn't a single bad habit. Riding Seabiscuit is just as easy as resting in a cradle." This was hotly disputed by Joe Palmer in *The Blood-Horse*:

> Seabiscuit has a perfectly maddening habit of having his nose just behind Rosemont or Aneroid or Stagehand or Esposa at the finish of important races. The record further shows that War Admiral does not have this habit or anything resembling it. Seabiscuit is unquestionably a very high-class horse, and there have not been a dozen like him in the last 20 years. But how many years has it been since we have had a genuine stayer who did his staying from two to three lengths in front of his field? If you don't remember, Man o' War was retired after his race with Sir Barton at Kenilworth Park, October 12, 1920.

The tension mounted with the arrival of Seabiscuit at Belmont Park on April 25, after his train trip from California. He arrived in excellent condition, which was no surprise to Murray Tynan of the *New York Herald Tribune* because the Biscuit was "an accomplished traveler, who has made almost as many trips from coast to coast as the average film star." War Admiral was already at the track, and the sportswriters continued to size up the colts. Burris Jenkins Jr., the noted cartoonist of the *New York Journal-American*, captioned his drawings of the two with:

Like Dempsey, the Admiral is fiery, nervous, eager, emotional—a flaming, fighting spirit that wants to let everything go from the start. Like Tunney, the Biscuit is steady, quiet, determined, intelligent, courageous—"races with his head" and has a bulldog tenacity. The Admiral would run his eyes out in the first furlong if Kurtsinger gave him his head or his temper. While the Admiral is a bad boy at the barrier, the Biscuit is a scholarly gentleman who never neglects his lessons.

The bomb dropped on May 24. Charles Howard called the race off because Seabiscuit's legs were bothering him; they looked sore and puffy. There were reports that "Seabiscuit was high in flesh and wobbly in the knees." To experienced turfmen, the announcement came as no surprise because they had wondered all along about the horse's lack of speed in his workouts. Furthermore, the early odds indicated an easy win for War Admiral, which added to the suspicion. The disappointment was tremendous, but accepted in good faith. According to Joe Williams in the *New York World-Telegram*: ". . . the 'Race of the Century' turned out to be the 'Sporting Gesture of the Century.' For once the public got a break. All parties concerned got together and decided this would not be fair. If it couldn't be a real good race, there would be no race at all." Samuel Riddle came up with another sporting gesture when he announced that War Admiral would start in the Suburban Handicap on May 28, against his old rival, Pompoon, to ease the disappointment and enable New York track fans to see the Mighty Atom in action once more.

The second bomb dropped on the day of that race when War Admiral was scratched at the last moment. The reason given was the condition of the track, but the sportswriters disputed this, reporting that it was fast. More realistically, they wrote, it was because the Admiral was being asked to carry 4 more pounds than was Pompoon, 132 to 128, which was too much in view of the fact that Pompoon had won his last 10 races. "Riddle repeatedly had declared," wrote Bill Corum, "that his champion would never carry more than 130 pounds." The net result was extreme anger by the twenty-five thousand fans present, who hissed and booed and jeered the announcement for several minutes, and the mortification of track officials. Whitney called it an outrage. When asked about setting up another match race, he exploded: "Not if I could buy them for a dime a dozen . . . I'll never again consent to such a thing."

The public assumed Riddle was afraid to run War Admiral and had backed out as soon as a tough race came up and was furious with Riddle for wanting everything letter-perfect. There was even speculation that this was why War Admiral had such a fine track record. As Murray Tynan put it, "The turf believes there was only one reason War Admiral was scratched. It feels certain that the Riddle stables feared a defeat and simply could not take it." A defeat, it was assumed, might lessen War Admiral's importance as a sire.

Within one week in May 1938, the king of sports had suffered two successive black eyes. While the first had been tolerable at the outset, it took on a different significance with the advent of the second. *Newsweek* magazine wrote: "Turf fans soured on their sport last week. What promised to be one of the most glorious events in horse-racing history faded to mediocrity, then to washout."

Ironically, Riddle's concern about the outcome of the Suburban was ill-founded. The joke was really on him, for Pompoon lost by a nose to Snark, a 6-to-1 outsider who ran the race in record time, 2:01⅗. So, the big excitement subsided going into the summer racing season.

There was another flurry in July, when both War Admiral and Seabiscuit were entered in the Massachusetts Handicap at Suffolk Downs, but the Biscuit was withdrawn a half-hour before post time with a "fever-wracked tendon" in his leg. The track was also muddy. War Admiral finished a bad fourth after having cut his right forefoot by a sharp edge of his rear hoof plate. He had also given away 23 pounds to the winner, Mellow. The race proved, too, that he was not a particularly good mudder. It was his first loss in 12 starts and the first time that he had ever finished out of the money. Thereafter, in July, August, and into September, Seabiscuit campaigned in California, while War Admiral continued to race in the East. It looked for sure as though the two would never meet.

In mid-September, Seabiscuit returned to New York to run in the Manhattan Handicap at Belmont Park for his first appearance there since he was withdrawn from the match race. It was at this juncture that a new racing personality entered the picture in the history of the two horses. He was Alfred G. Vanderbilt, the 26-year-old scion of a distinguished family. His father had lost his life in the sinking of the RMS *Lusitania* and, at the age of 21, Vanderbilt took over the management of the family estate. It included his mother's Sagamore Stable of horses and the 400-acre Sagamore Farm, near Glyndon, Maryland. By 1935, he had become America's leading money-winning owner, with a total of

$303,605 and a top horse, Discovery. Two years later, he acquired a large interest in the Pimlico Race Course, was elected a director of the Maryland Jockey Club, and shortly thereafter was named president of the track. Early in 1938, while racing at Santa Anita, he was introduced by Charles Howard to his wife's niece, Malluela Maria Hudson. The chance meeting blossomed into a romance, and the two were married during the summer. It was in September, after returning from his honeymoon, that Vanderbilt caught up with War Admiral and Seabiscuit.

The Pimlico track in 1938 was a poor business risk. It was drawing weak attendance and losing money. Something was desperately needed to instill new life and interest in it. Why not the match race between War Admiral and Seabiscuit? After all, the public would still like to see it come off, and it was the opportune time, what with both horses racing in the East. So, much against the advice of his elders, who said it was an impossible dream, and with the zeal and fearless determination of youth, Vanderbilt tackled both owners in New York late in September. It took two weeks of endless telephone calls, meetings, cajoling, flattering, and reasoning before he was able to work out a viable agreement. First, he got both owners to agree in principle to the race. With Howard, he pressed the point that this would be the last chance for Seabiscuit to meet War Admiral because the year was coming to a close and Riddle had already announced plans to retire his horse to stud. With Riddle, he voiced confidence that War Admiral would have no trouble in beating the Western colt, playing up to the elderly gent's enjoyment at hearing nice things said about his horses. Vanderbilt then recommended a purse of only $15,000, plus a gold cup, winner take all, as a concrete gesture to the turf fans that this would be strictly a sporting venture by the owners and not a money-making deal. As further proof that they meant business, he even asked each to put up a $5,000 forfeit bond in case of a "no show." This, too, would indicate to the fans that every effort was being made to avoid a repetition of the previous fiasco.

November 1, 1938, was selected as the date of the race, with November 3 the alternate date in the event of rain, and the track would have to be judged fast on the morning of the race. The distance of 1³⁄₁₆ miles was deemed to be acceptable because War Admiral had won the Preakness and Seabiscuit had run the distance in winning the Riggs Handicap, also at Pimlico, the previous year. The proposed terms were acceptable to both owners, and then Riddle added a few of his own. He insisted on his own starter, George Cassidy, from

New York's tracks, in place of Pimlico's Jim Milton, with whom he apparently had a disagreement. Riddle demanded a walk-up start with the drop of a flag and the ringing of a bell. Finally, each horse would carry 120 pounds instead of the 126-pound scale weight.

Vanderbilt relayed this to Howard with bated breath, but the Westerner did not demur. He even signed a contract stipulating all of the terms. The young track executive then made a mad taxi dash through midtown Manhattan to Pennsylvania Station, where he caught up with Riddle as he prepared to board a train for Philadelphia. Shoving the contract into Riddle's hands, Vanderbilt refused to let him board the train until he had signed it. The following day, October 5, a formal announcement of the race was made to the press. It was regarded as a turf coup to rival all others on record.

At 8:00 A.M., November 1, a brilliant sun was rising in a cloudless sky, giving promise of a beautiful Indian-summer day. Two lonely figures walked slowly on the dirt of the Pimlico track, carefully examining the surface and underlying soil. One was Maryland State Racing Commission chairman Jervis Spencer Jr., and the other was Pimlico steward A. G. Weston. They made a complete circle of the track in half an hour, after which they joined Alfred Vanderbilt at the winner's circle. Spencer nodded and Vanderbilt stepped to a microphone and said: "In my opinion, there is no question but that the track will be fast this afternoon. The race is on." The gates were opened to the public at 10:00, and more than forty thousand people swarmed in—ten thousand alone standing in the infield. It was the largest crowd in the history of the track.

There was no turning back now. The two titans of the turf were on the threshold of their long-sought, much-discussed adventure. It could truly be the race of the century, pitting two Thoroughbreds with distinctly different styles of racing against each other. The Admiral liked to start with a burst of speed, sustain it until the end, and kill off his opposition early. Seabiscuit, the more phlegmatic of the two, preferred to come from behind, charging down the stretch with a terrific rush, frequently winning races at the wire. Their records attested to their phenomenal success. War Admiral, four years old and Triple Crown champion of 1937, had been in twenty-two starts, winning eighteen and finishing second in two, third in one, and out of the money once. His total earnings to date were $257,050, surpassing those of his great sire, Man o' War. Seabiscuit, five years old and Handicap Champion of 1937, had raced 83 times, winning 31, coming in second in 12 and third in 13, and winning $331,405.

Theirs was the seventh race on the program. War Admiral was a 1-to-4 favorite; Seabiscuit was at 22-to-10. The fans poured out $78,811 in bets on the race. The Admiral won the toss and pole position, and as recounted by Salvator, came out on the track first at 4:00 P.M., his seal-brown satin coat "gleaming and shimmering in sunlight." Charley Kurtsinger was his jockey. The Biscuit followed, his hard bay coat with black points also glistening as his "full-made coat of flesh . . . gave him an almost gladiatorial aspect . . . [in] contrast to the Admiral's slim elegance." George Woolf was up in place of Red Pollard, who had broken a leg while exercising a horse as a favor for a friend. It had happened at Narragansett Park in Rhode Island, when the horse bolted.

Two false starts kept the multitude on edge. First War Admiral broke, and then Seabiscuit. On the third try, George Cassidy sent them off and running for keeps. At the drop of the flag, Woolf whacked the Biscuit hard on his flanks, and he shot out in front with a great burst of speed as he was guided to the rail in front of the Admiral. They passed the stands, with Seabiscuit leading by an open length after 1/16 of a mile. "He was running cheerfully and boldly," wrote Salvator, "with his legs and feet well under him and his stride in perfect control. War Admiral, following directly in his wake, was also under a snug hold . . ."

It was an unexpected development that shocked the crowd, which had come to expect the Admiral to be in front at this stage of the race. Murray Tynan reported:

> They raced around the turn with Seabiscuit nicely in front and the
> stage was set for one of the most thrilling scenes ever enacted in
> racing. Kurtsinger called on the Admiral and in a half-dozen jumps
> he was at the Biscuit's head. . . . For a delicious half-mile the two
> went on as a team. No quarter was asked and certainly none was
> given. One heart had to break, one horse had to give up. As they
> rounded the turn still locked together, matching stride for stride,
> Kurtsinger brought his whip down sharply. The crowd knew that he
> was finished. If he needed the whip, then he couldn't last much
> longer. He didn't. The Biscuit was cracking him then and he split
> him wide open when they reached the stretch. War Admiral was
> losing ground slightly when they straightened out for the terrific run

War Admiral (No. 1), with Charley Kurtsinger up, leads Seabiscuit (No. 2), ridden by George Woolf, in the march to the starting line for their match race at Pimlico.

Seabiscuit (on the outside) leaps into the lead at the start of the race.

"The Biscuit" widens his lead as the horses pass the second turn.

War Admiral (on the outside) moves up on Seabiscuit as they round the third turn.

Heading into the stretch, Seabiscuit pours it on and begins to move away from War Admiral.

Seabiscuit relentlessly drives to the finish line in a four-length win over War Admiral in what is regarded as the greatest race of the 20th century.

to the finish, but he was still in hot contention. If he had it this was his golden opportunity. Kurtsinger lashed him savagely, but the Admiral was through. As he began to wilt, the relentless Seabiscuit went on, seemingly faster. Racing was never presented a finer sight than Seabiscuit charging down the stretch to his clean-cut victory.

Seabiscuit won by four lengths, in 1:56⅜, beating Pompoon's track record by ⅕ second.

A whole chorus of top turf correspondents waxed enthusiastic over the race. Bill Corum called it "undoubtedly the greatest match race of all times" and went on to say, "Seabiscuit proved himself the champion race horse of America . . . the grand old veteran from over the Rockies made the vaunted little horse walk the plank every step of the furious mile and three-sixteenths. . . . Men will grow old and their beards will be longer than the bearded lady's in the circus before they see another such race as this." As to the furious backstretch duel, he wrote: "Foot by foot, War Admiral cut down the distance. He caught the leader and, for a few strides as they moved by the regular half-mile post, the Riddle colt was in front. The pair ran the next furlong like two wrestlers locked together, but War Admiral couldn't get by, couldn't wrest the advantage from the other." The horses then turned into the homestretch. Corum wrote:

> Kurtsinger SOS'd the first faint signal of doubt and probably sent a tremor of fear through the hearts of the Admiral's backers, when he reached back and cut sharply at the brown colt's straining flank. It was only one swipe and it produced no result. . . . As Woolf swung the pacemaker into the home lane, he also plied the lash vigorously. Then, as he glanced fearfully back over his shoulders, the Montana cowboy caught a fleeting glimpse of the little Admiral's eyes. "All I could see was white," George said afterward, "and I knew the race was over. I stuck my bat in my boot, and set down to ride my horse out with my hands, hoping we might break the record. You see, I knew we had been going pretty fast all the way round."

Grantland Rice, in the *Baltimore Sun*, reported: " A little horse with the heart of a lion and the flying feet of a gazelle proved his place as the gamest Thoroughbred that ever raced over an American track. . . . The Admiral looked

Seabiscuit in the eye at the three-quarters—but Seabiscuit never got the look." Red Pollard, Seabiscuit's regular jockey and the man who had predicted the result as early as the previous May, exulted: "Once a horse gives Seabiscuit the old look in the eye, he begins to run to parts unknown. He might loaf sometimes when he's in front and think he's got the race in the bag. But he gets gamer and gamer the tougher it gets."

After the race, some interesting sidelights became known: George Cassidy, the starter, had to pay his way into the track. Somebody had failed to notify the guard at the jockey gate. He did not know Cassidy and refused to let him enter. The crowd at the paddock was so great before the start of the race that NBC's famous race announcer, Clem McCarthy, was unable to get back to the broadcast booth and wound up calling the action while roosting on the fence at the finish line. The bell used to start the race was the one Seabiscuit's trainer, Tom Smith, had used during practice sessions. Smith had made it himself, and offered it for the race when no other bell was available. It was reported that Tom Smith had trained his horse secretly at getting away to a fast start. Smith had trained quarter horses in the West, and that is the way they usually start a race. Both Howard and Smith had settled on the strategy of trying to beat the Admiral at his own game by sending the Biscuit off with a flying start. Mrs. Henry Carnegie Phipps, the original owner of Seabiscuit, was present, as was actor Pat O'Brien, making his second cross-country trip from Hollywood for the race. He had also come east in May. President Franklin D. Roosevelt arrived a few minutes late for a White House press conference; he explained to the reporters that he had been listening to the race on the radio. Mrs. Howard, a devout Catholic, pinned a medal of St. Christopher, the patron saint of travelers, on the saddle blanket of Seabiscuit before the race. A month earlier, Commander R. B. Irving had docked the mammoth liner RMS *Queen Mary* in New York Harbor without assistance from tugs because of a strike. He credited his success for the unprecedented feat on the St. Christopher medal he carried, causing a boom in the market for the lucky piece. Howard increased his colt's insurance from $100,000 to $200,000 after the victory. Vanderbilt had scheduled the race for a Tuesday because he feared the track could not handle a Saturday crowd. Charles Hatton, in the *Morning Telegraph*, gave Seabiscuit perhaps the kindest bow of all when he said: "From a rather cheaply held stallion, he had become fashionable."

The race saw the curtain descending on a spectacular career for America's fourth Triple Crown champion. War Admiral ran once more that year, 11 days

Left to right: owner Charles Howard, jockey George Woolf, trainer Tom Smith, and Pimlico president Alfred Vanderbilt hold the winner's cup after Seabiscuit's victory over War Admiral.

later, when he won the Rhode Island Handicap, and once as a five-year-old before he was retired to stud. As a sire, he again showed his Thoroughbred class. In 1945, his progeny made him the leading stallion of the year, with 20 winners piling up purses amounting to $591,352. His stakes-winner get included Busher, War Jeep, Blue Peter, Busonda, and Navy Page. War Admiral died in 1959.

Seabiscuit, on the other hand, did not race again in 1938, but his victory over War Admiral earned for him Horse of the Year honors. He returned to the West Coast to rest before running once in 1939 at Santa Anita. He bowed a tendon and was retired to stud at the Howard Ridgewood Ranch, some 200 miles north of San Francisco. The Biscuit's stud record was not particularly good. Through 1946, his get won $261,313. Actually, Howard refused to ship him to a stud farm in Kentucky, where he might have had a better stud record, because he wanted to keep him "at home."

Seabiscuit came out of retirement on February 9, 1940, just short of a year after his last race. There was one more goal to attain—the Santa Anita Handicap, which he had lost twice by a nose. On his third try, he prevailed, winning in the record time of 2:01⅕, the second-fastest 1¼ miles ever run in American turf history. The win boosted his earnings to $437,730, the most ever won by a Thoroughbred anywhere in the world. In six years, he had been in 89 races, and he had won 33 of them. On May 17, 1947, he died in his stall of a heart attack.

Whirlaway

Whirlaway
(chestnut colt) {
  Blenheim II {
    Blandford
    Malva
  }
  Dustwhirl {
    Sweep
    Ormonda
  }
}

| Chapter 5 |

Whirlaway

~1941~

He was colorful. He was controversial. He generated more charisma than is likely to be found in a whole herd of thundering Thoroughbreds, much of it due to some rather unique traits. To begin with, he had an inordinately long tail, reaching to just about an inch from the ground. Naturally, it became a focal point for imaginative sportswriters, who promptly nicknamed him "Mr. Longtail" and "the Flying Tail." Sportswriter David Alexander commented sardonically that he was "a horse with a tail that resembled the beard of the Smith Brother on the right-hand side of the cough drop box." Conversely, he was middle-sized, a modest 15.2 hands tall. Nevertheless, he was a graceful, powerful, courageous racer who drove his fans into frenzies with a pulse-quickening propensity for coming from behind to win in the last ¼ mile.

He was also one of the fittest Thoroughbreds ever to campaign in America. In a little more than three years on the track, he started in 60 races and failed to finish in the money in only four of them. This remarkable feat of stamina made it all too obvious halfway through his career that he was on a collision course with a record set by Seabiscuit, who was winding up his illustrious turf days as the greatest money-winning horse in the world the very same year the young chestnut colt was embarking on his own spectacular racing career.

The other side of the coin presented a somewhat less heroic picture of the colt. Dumb, half-witted, willful, knuckleheaded, stubborn, unmanageable—these and similar adjectives were sprinkled in the reams of copy written about him. But for his winning ways, it was difficult to dispute the barbs. At one time or another during his career, each could be applied with some justification, and it is a wonder that he ever made it to the track, let alone won the Triple Crown. This study in contrasts is what makes the story of Whirlaway one of the most fascinating chapters in American turf lore.

Warren Wright Sr., in the late twenties, inherited two thriving enterprises. One was the Calumet Baking Powder Company of Chicago, and the other was the Calumet Farm in Lexington, Kentucky. His father had purchased the one thousand–acre spread in 1924 to raise Standardbred horses (trotters). When he died, his son converted the facility for breeding Thoroughbreds. Wright's first horses raced in 1932, and within the next quarter-century, the Calumet colors were carried across the finish line by some of America's greatest equine stars.

It was on July 7,1936, that a syndicate of 10 breeders, formed by Wright, consummated a deal in London for the purchase of a nine-year-old stallion, Blenheim II, from His Highness Prince Aga Khan. During his racing days, the horse had won the Epsom Derby and later had sired the Derby winner Mahmoud. In stud, he was reported as perhaps the best revenue producer among European stallions. His price tag was in the neighborhood of $250,000, and he arrived in America from the Aga Khan's stud farm, Marly la Ville, near Paris, on July 21, aboard the liner *Berengaria*. He was immediately shipped to the Claiborne Farm in Kentucky, where his stud mate was Sir Gallahad III, sire of the great Gallant Fox.

One of the Calumet mares sent to Blenheim II in the mating shed at Claiborne was the 12-year-old Dustwhirl. She had been bred by Joseph E. Widener and had shown good speed. However, according to *The Blood-Horse*, she was "marked by a distinct willfullness, which may have been the cause of her failure to race and for her retirement to stud as a three-year-old." As a broodmare, though, she was eminently more successful, producing stakes winners Feudal Lord for Widener and Reaping Reward for Arthur B. Hancock, her next owner, before she was sold to Wright in 1936. Then on April 2, 1938, at Calumet Farm, she dropped a blaze-faced chestnut colt who was named Whirlaway. His lineage was indeed one from which champions are made. Not only could he draw from the racing prowess of his sire, but his dam had a fine bloodline. She was a daughter of Sweep, who had sired Brushup, the dam of War Admiral, who, in turn, was a son of Man o' War.

In his second year, Whirlaway was turned over to the talented Ben Jones for training and made his successful racing debut on June 3, 1940, at Lincoln Fields, winning by a nose over Beau Brannon. The next five races produced one victory and four defeats, ranging from a fourth-place finish to a loss by a neck.

More significant than the outcomes for trainer and racing fan, however, were the colt's long tail and his peculiar style of racing, both of which became conversation pieces. He displayed a great kick in the stretch, but also a zany habit of running out from the rail on the turn into the stretch. It was only his remarkable speed that saved him from disastrous defeats. Consequently, his performance in the six-furlong, winner-take-all Saratoga Special on August 10 seemed to cast the die on what could be expected from the colt in the future. Although he was the favorite, he almost went down at the start and ran last in a field of eight at the far turn. According to Arthur Daley of *The New York Times*, it was Whirlaway's supreme race as a two-year-old, "where he was at his knuckleheaded worst." He was running so hard that he never did make the turn but, instead, ran straight into the outside rail. By the time jockey Johnny Longdon straightened him out, he was in last place. "Did he win? Don't be silly," exclaimed Daley. "Of course he won. He came like the whirlwind he was to triumph in the very last 25 yards" by a length over New World.

The story was out: Whirlaway, at age two, had become acutely unmanageable. At times it took several men to saddle him. "He jumped, he reared, he developed a habit of bearing out on the track as if headed for the rail. It was feared he might become an 'outlaw' or go completely to pieces and never be able to race again," was Anita Brenner's analysis of him in *The New York Times Sunday Magazine*. It was as though the genes of his equally temperamental dam had taken control over his personality and senses. His behavior caused his exasperated trainer, Ben Jones, to expostulate at one point: "Dumbest horse I've ever trained." He claimed that the colt learned everything very slowly and that he would "have to give him plenty of races" to try to get the message through. His performances for the rest of the year were virtually carbon copies of each other. He lost his next race, the Grand Union Stakes, and then smashed to a smart win in the Hopeful Stakes in the mud, each finding him trailing at first and making up the distance at the very end. By September 28, with the advent of the prestigious Belmont Futurity, he was one of the leading money-winners among the two-year-olds, which gave him stature among his peers. They included King Cole, New World, Attention, Swain, Porter's Cap, and Bushwacker, in a field of 13 colts and one filly. The race was likely to determine the champion of the juveniles.

Whirlaway was in trouble from the start. He shuffled back as was his wont, and the crowd anticipated his late rush. Jockey Eddie Arcaro on Our Boots thought otherwise and kept his mount moving. As a result, Whirlaway "cracked and King Cole put him away near the 16th pole." The chestnut colt with the long tail wound up third.

He brushed off the defeat to take the Breeder's Futurity at Keeneland, Kentucky, in the last 70 yards, but failed in the Pimlico Futurity on November 2, when he bore out in the stretch and blew a race he, seemingly, had sewn up. With all of his ups and downs, he kept piling up purse money, so that by the time he ran his last race of the year, the Walden Stakes on November 14, he was breathing down the neck of the earnings leader, Our Boots. Whirlaway took care of that when jockey George Woolf rode him to victory and pushed his earnings to a handsome $77,275, or about $5,000 ahead of the year's total for Our Boots.

All in all, therefore, despite his problems the colt had had a rather successful year, with wins in three stakes events, the Saratoga Special, the Hopeful Stakes, and the Breeder's Futurity. The sportswriters acknowledged this by voting him Best Two-Year-Old, 425 votes to 345 over Our Boots. It marked the first time in the history of the poll that a horse beaten in the Belmont Futurity had been chosen leader of the two-year-old colts. He also was the first of Blenheim II's offspring to win an American stakes race.

Whirlaway's first start as a three-year-old, in 1941, was on February 8, in an allowance race at Hialeah. Ridden by Wendell Eads, he continued to display his old tendency to run in the middle of the track, as well as his ability to "run down his field" in the final ¼ mile as he won the race by a head. Then, he finished third in his next race, was held off until March, and came in third and second by a neck in two events at Tropical Park. His first real pre-Derby test was in the Blue Grass Stakes on April 24, at Keeneland. In fact, it was the first important challenge of the year for him. The evil habit continued to plague him, however. He ran so far out that he had to make up too much ground in the stretch, weakened, and lost to Our Boots by six lengths.

With each race, it appeared that Whirlaway's Derby chances grew dimmer. The final test was the Derby Trial on April 29. He began slowly, in fifth position, for the first ½ mile, at which point he was sent with a rush around the far turn, a drive that some track buffs said was the fastest they had ever seen. He was leading by a half-length going into the stretch but bore out. Before Eads could get him straightened out, Blue Pair caught him and went on to win by three-quarters of a length.

The spring had turned into a nightmare for Ben Jones. He was at his wit's end. How to cure this miserable habit was the big question. The sportswriters

Trainer Ben Jones, on the white horse, rides slowly down the track at Hialeah Park next to Whirlaway, ridden by exercise boy Pinky Brown, in an attempt to help lessen the colt's fears on the track.

were hardly helpful. Early in the season, the eminent Grantland Rice had needled the trainer. "They tell me that your horse is a halfwit," he said. "I don't know about that," replied Jones, "but he's making a halfwit out of me." Jones' patience was shored up only by an abiding faith in Whirlaway. "Plain Ben loved Whirly just as a father grows to love a child who almost drives him to distraction. That's what Mr. Longtail did to Jones," is the way another writer saw it.

The trainer was convinced that Whirlaway would be a great horse if only he could smooth out the things that were bothering him. Jones realized the horse was filled with fears and tried to dissolve them. He spent most of the day with him, riding alongside of him on his white pony. Over and over Jones exposed the horse to things that appeared to excite him at the track, but under quiet, reassuring conditions. Jones even worked out a sort of therapy routine. One day he would have the colt run as fast as he could, and on another he would keep him on grass. Some days the colt was saddled and unsaddled over and over again. Groups of people were even moved around him, in an effort to make him feel comfortable in a crowd. It was, indeed, a rather unorthodox training program for a Thoroughbred.

Only two other people had the same confidence in the horse as did Jones, reported Frank Graham in the *New York Journal-American*. One was Pinky Brown, his exercise boy, a "mild-mannered feller" who would "kill anybody that harmed Whirlaway," and who "believed that his darling, with whom he lived day and night, could beat anything on four legs." The other was columnist Bill Corum, who in July 1940, at Arlington Park, had made the rash prediction that Whirlaway would win the Hopeful, Futurity, and Triple Crown. As of then, Corum was batting .500.

Just four days remained before the Kentucky Derby, and Jones made a last-ditch effort to resolve Whirlaway's problems. Following the defeats in the Blue Grass Stakes and Derby Trial, he reasoned that Wendell Eads was not the jockey for Whirlaway in the big race. Once before he had made a similar decision, in Florida, when he put Eads up in place of Basil James. Now, Jones went for hard experience, for a man he hoped would be able to control his horse and keep him on course. It was Eddie Arcaro, the "Kentucky Italian," who happened to be without a Derby mount. Arcaro had been riding for 10 years, had been in eight thousand races, and was known as a strong jockey with a light touch— "good hands." This was important because Whirlaway was known to have an extremely sensitive mouth. Furthermore, the jockey had won his first Derby with Lawrin in 1938 for Jones, so they understood each other.

The trainer then planned another special exercise. He would sit on his white pony at the bend of the track, leaving just enough room for a horse to get through on the rail, and would have Arcaro drive the colt into this narrow opening. It was a somewhat hairy maneuver, but the jockey was not one to question the wisdom of the boss. Finally, after one such workout, when the horse still veered out, Jones stomped toward him, pulled a knife out, and muttered, "I'll get that so-and-so." Arcaro blanched for a moment at what he thought was about to happen, but calmed down as he saw the trainer cut away the inside blinker on the horse, leaving him with a broader vision out of his left eye. He hoped this would help keep the colt's attention drawn to the inner part of the track.

The 67th running of the Kentucky Derby took place on May 3, 1941, on a bright day and a fast track. A crowd of one hundred thousand turned out—the first time the attendance had reached that figure at Churchill Downs. The horses also contributed to a record that day, as each horse entered required that more money be added to the pot. And a field of 11 horses went to the post, making it the richest running of the classic, worth $61,275 to the winner.

Except for the losses in the Blue Grass and Derby Trial, Whirlaway should have been quoted at the shortest odds. "What was going on in Whirlaway's head and whether 'something' was hurting him became matters for nationwide speculation," *The Blood-Horse* reported on the race. Yet, for all his straying problems, he was still the public's choice, albeit a lukewarm choice, with Porter's Cap and Our Boots next in line.

Starting from the fourth stall in the gate, the chestnut Flying Tail got off slowly, but Arcaro was in no hurry as he moved quickly to the inside and let Whirlaway take his time to the first turn. The colt was still among the tail-enders at the ¾ pole, when he began to plow through the pack. With only a ¼ mile to go, he had moved up to fourth place behind the pacesetter, Dispose. It was then that the one-eyed blinker, Arcaro, the horse's adrenaline, and all the tender, loving care that had been heaped on him for months seemed to join forces for the supreme effort. "Whirlaway came between horses on the turn, went to the front in a cyclonic burst of speed, and the colts which had been fighting for the lead ceased to be contenders." He ran faster the farther he went. The others just gave up. As the fans looked on in disbelief, Whirlaway streaked over the last ¼ in :23⅗ seconds to win by an amazing eight lengths. It was a record-breaking performance—2:01⅖—clipping ⅖ second from Twenty Grand's 1931 track mark. It was also perhaps the fastest last ¼ mile ever run in a 10-furlong race. Although the official time for the quarter was :24 seconds, Whirlaway's was less because he had to come from behind to win.

Bill Corum was ecstatic: "Oh Whirlaway, Oh Whirlaway, that you made me feel so good today," he crowed in his column. "One instant they had all been there on the bend together, the next, only the bright red blouse and the blue cap were where the race was supposed to be going on." Arcaro was hailed as a "miracle man" for having ridden a perfect race, for having held the colt thoroughly in check until the final stages of the race. It was later revealed that this was all part of a carefully mapped-out plan. Jones and his jockey had prepared an exact schedule of points on the track where the colt would be let out. "He was a 'one run' horse," claimed Arcaro, "and if he was to win his speed had to be preserved for that part of the race where they payoff." Other unusual precautions were also taken. Before he was to be saddled, Whirlaway had been walked around the track, hemmed in between the inner rail and a Calumet lead pony. Then he was marched back and forth in front of the grandstands to get him used to the noise of the crowd. The public was

"The Flying Tail" streaks across the finish line eight lengths ahead of Staretor to take the 1941 Kentucky Derby in the record time of 2:01⅖. He ran the last ¼ mile in :23⅗ seconds.

Official Chart of the Kentucky Derby

SEVENTH RACE **1 1-4 MILES. (Twenty Grand, May 16, 1931—2:01⅘—3—126.) Sixty-Seventh Running KENTUCKY DERBY. $75,000 Added. 3-year-olds. Special weights. Trainers of the winner, second and third horses to receive $3,000, $2,000 and $1,000, respectively. Breeders of the winner, second and third horses to receive $2,000, $1,000 and $500, respectively.**

06306
May-3 41-C.D

Net value to winner $61,275; second, $8,000; third, $3,000; fourth, $1,000.

Index	Horses	Eq't A Wt	PP	St	½	¾	1	Str	Fin	Jockeys	Owners	Odds $1 Str't
06106^{2}	WHIRLAWAY	wB 126	4	6	8^{1}	$6^{1\frac{1}{2}}$	4^{1}	1^{3}	1^{8}	ArcaroE	Calumet Farm	2.90
04709^{2}	STARETOR	w 126	2	1	7^{2}	$4^{1\frac{1}{2}}$	5^{3}	$2^{\frac{1}{2}}$	2^{nk}	WoolfG	H S Nesbitt	36.00
(05979)	MARKET WISE	wB 126	7	5	6^{2}	8^{4}	6^{3}	5^{3}	3^{2}	AndersonI	L Tufano	19.10
(05760)	PORTER'S CAP	wB 126	9	4	2^{h}	3^{5}	$2^{1\frac{1}{2}}$	3^{h}	4^{1}	HaasL	C S Howard	3.30
05760^{2}	LITTLE BEANS	wB 126	5	10	10^{12}	9^{5}	8^{5}	7^{2}	5^{1}	MooreG	Mrs L Palladino	12.10
05751	DISPOSE	w 126	11	2	1^{2}	1^{2}	1^{h}	4^{h}	$6^{1\frac{1}{2}}$	BiermanC	King Ranch	7.20
(06106)	BLUE PAIR	wB 126	3	3	3^{5}	2^{h}	$3^{\frac{1}{2}}$	$6^{\frac{1}{2}}$	$7^{\frac{1}{2}}$	JamesB	Mrs V S Bragg	20.60
(05922)	OUR BOOTS	w 126	10	9	4^{3}	$5^{\frac{1}{2}}$	7^{2}	8^{5}	8^{3}	McCrearyC	Woodvale Farm	3.90
(05752)	ROBERT MORRIS	w 126	8	8	$5^{1\frac{1}{2}}$	7^{1}	9^{6}	9^{8}	9^{12}	RichardsH	J F Byers	13.90
05922^{3}	VALDINA PAUL	wB 126	6	7	9^{3}	10^{15}	10^{15}	10^{15}	10^{12}	LemmonsH	Valdina Farm	†24.30
(05906)	SWAIN	wB 126	1	11	11	11	11	11	11	AdamsJ	C Putnam	†

(Complete finish confirmed by Kuprion Camera.)

†Mutuel field. Time, :23⅖, :46⅗, 1:11⅗, 1:37⅖, 2:01⅖ (new track record). Track fast.

	$2 Mutuels Paid			Odds to $1		
WHIRLAWAY	**7.80**	**5.00**	**4.40**	**2.90**	**1.50**	**1.20**
STARETOR		**35.20**	**17.00**		**16.60**	**7.50**
MARKET WISE			**10.80**			**4.40**

Winner—Ch. c, by Blenheim II.—Dustwhirl, by Sweep (trained by B. A. Jones; bred by Calumet Farm).

WENT TO POST—5:53. AT POST—1½ minutes.

Start good and slow. Won easily; second and third driving.

WHIRLAWAY, eased back when blocked in the first eighth and taken to the inside approaching the first turn, started up after reaching the final half mile, was taken between horses on the final turn, responded with much energy to take command with a rush and, continuing with much power, drew out fast in the final eighth. STARETOR, away slowly and allowed to remain well back the first five eighths, made his move gradually, drifted out slightly before straightening up in the stretch and held on well in the final drive. MARKET WISE, also well back early, was slow to respond to pressure, but rallied after reaching the last five sixteenths and, finishing with courage, was wearing down STARETOR. PORTER'S CAP, a strong factor from the start and always clear as he raced on the outside, responded to strong urging when rounding the final turn, but tired after reaching the last three sixteenths. LITTLE BEANS raced well from a very sluggish beginning, then closed courageously to pass tired horses in the stretch. DISPOSE took command easily, was allowed to run along well within himself through the back stretch, was under pressure after three quarters and held on fairly well to the closing three sixteenths, where he faltered badly. BLUE PAIR quit after showing speed for a mile. OUR BOOTS could not go with the early leaders under urging and failed to keep up after reaching the last half mile. ROBERT MORRIS began well, but dropped out of contention after a half mile and was far back thereafter.

unaware that the horse was the favorite of the race because he wore no identifying number or colors. Finally, just before he was to go out onto the track for the race, the trainer gave his jockey last-minute instructions: "Eddie, don't take the lead until you're headin' for home. This horse can pass any livin' horse. Jes' wait for the straight part of the track 'cause when he's got horses to pass he won't run wide." He did not. He hugged the rail for the entire race.

The spectacular result notwithstanding, ugly rumors and whispers suddenly cropped up, relating Whirlaway's incredible late bursts of speed to the use of drugs. On May 8, *New York Daily Mirror* columnist Dan Parker wrote of how the colt had been given a saliva test after a winter race at Hialeah and the results proved to be positive. He complained that nothing had been done about it, that the entire matter had been written off as medicine for a cold. He seemed to imply that the prestige of owner Warren Wright had prevented further inquiries. Then, he reported, Whirlaway lost the next race and the public lost its shirt. "Whirlaway's imitation of a streak of lightning at the Derby last Saturday has set tongues wagging," he continued. "One trainer came back with the story that Whirlaway had such a bad cold on Derby Day he had to have a triple dose of medicine." He even questioned whether the horse had been given a saliva test after the race.

This brought Bill Corum to the rescue, in a high state of dudgeon. He led off his column on May 9 with a verse:

> No, Dan, it wasn't the cough medicine
> that carried 'em off;
> It was the coffin, they should have
> carried the rest of those horses in,
> When he left 'em for dead at the
> head of the stretch.

"He could scarcely be expected to set a mile-and-a-quarter record in a five-and-one-half furlong dash," he concluded.

Even the normally placid Southern gentleman from Parnell, Missouri, Ben Jones, had his ire worked up: "I will, if Mr. Wright approves, match Whirlaway against any three-year-old anywhere," he cried. "I would like to bring Whirlaway out of the stable at midnight, high noon, or any time, and without any notice whatsoever throw a saddle and rider on him and let him show you what he can do to any horse of his age at any distance and under any conditions."

Parker apparently realized he had made an error, for he recanted the story, and on May 11, he reported that he had received assurances from Louis F. McNeely, sports editor of the *Louisville Times*, that Whirlaway had indeed been given the saliva test after the Derby under proper conditions and control—and that the results had been negative.

This rumor having been scotched, others cropped up in what seemed to be an effort to discredit the victory. There was the claim that Churchill Downs had been rolled until it was a "pasteboard track," that it had been packed

Trainer Ben Jones and jockey Eddie Arcaro hold the special hood with a one-eyed blinker used to keep Whirlaway from running wide on turns.

deliberately to ensure a spectacular time for the benefit of the huge crowd. Some even speculated about the long tail, claiming it was indicative of a "good doer," a good eater in track parlance. Others claimed that it served to prevent trailing steeds from closing in on the flying colt.

The net result of the controversy was to create doubts in the minds of the public. "Eastern fans just couldn't conceive another such performance in the Preakness, particularly after hearing ugly rumors about Kentucky's saliva test," observed *The Blood-Horse*. Although betting at the Pimlico track during the day was brisk, it fell off noticeably for the Preakness. Thus, on May 10, just a week after the Derby, Mr. Longtail went to the post in a field of eight at even money.

Again, he was in no hurry to get going. "Whirlaway walks out of the gate counting the house," was the way Ed Thorgersen described the start for *Movietone News*. When the field passed the grandstands for the first time, "Whirlaway was so far last that he wasn't bothered by the dust the other horses were raising," reported Joe Palmer. Coming into the backstretch, he was six or seven lengths behind the last horse. In fact, the bulk of the field was already going into the last turn when Whirlaway first passed the ½ mile mark. That was when Arcaro gave him the green light. The colt responded. He gouged huge chunks out of space in front of him with devastating strides and, quite suddenly, it appeared as though the seven other horses had slowed to a crawl.

Down the backstretch, Arcaro took Whirlaway to the outside and charged the leaders, King Cole and Our Boots. He caught them at the ¼ pole, having passed seven horses in a matter of 20 seconds. Snippets from Joe Palmer and Joe Estes' comments on the race in *The Blood-Horse* tell the story: "Somebody suggested afterward that maybe they didn't see him go past." "A small horse, as to height, he seemingly disappeared from sight as he went on the outside of the field, which was fairly well bunched." "Arcaro sent Whirlaway well out, perhaps 15 feet from the rail, and then tightened his inside rein. Whirlaway straightened out as if he were on a trolley, and the race was virtually over." The high-stepping Thoroughbred showed his heels to the field, waved his high-flying tail "bye-bye to them all," and blazed to a five-and-a-half-length victory.

The convincing win proved conclusively that the results of the Derby a week earlier had been no accident. Joe Palmer put his finger on the reason: "He carries in his armament the deadliest weapon a Thoroughbred can have—an

"Whirlaway walks out of the gate counting the house" dead last in a field of eight at the start of the 1941 Preakness.

Despite the poor start, Whirlaway achieves a six-length victory in the Preakness. King Cole finishes second, followed by Our Boots.

Official Chart of Preakness

SIXTH RACE
06600
May-10-41-Pim

1 3-16 MILES. (Seabiscuit, Nov. 1, 1938—1:56$\frac{3}{5}$—5—120.) Fifty-First Running PREAKNESS STAKES. $50,000 Added. 3-year-olds. Weight-for-age. Nominator of the winner to receive $1,500, nominator of the second horse $750, and the nominator of the third horse $250 of the added money. Net value to winner $49,365; second, $10,000; third, $5,000; third, $2,000.

Index	Horses	Eq't A Wt	PP	St	½	¾	1	Str	Fin	Jockeys	Owners	Odds $1 Str't
(06336)	WHIRLAWAY	wB 126	1	8	8	7^5	$1^{1\frac{1}{2}}$	1^5	$1^{5\frac{1}{2}}$	ArcaroE	Calumet Farm	1.15
05979^3	KING COLE	wB 126	5	2	1^1	1^1	2^2	$2^{1\frac{1}{2}}$	2^2	GilbertJ	O Phipps	25.75
06336	OUR BOOTS	w 126	8	6	$4_{\frac{1}{2}}$	$5^{1\frac{1}{2}}$	$3_{\frac{1}{2}}$	3^h	3^{nk}	McCrearyC	Woodvale Farm	3.85
06336	PORTER'S CAP	wB 126	3	3	$6_{\frac{1}{2}}$	6^h	4^h	4^5	4^9	HaasL	C S Howard	5.40
06392^3	KANSAS	wB 126	6	7	$5^{1\frac{1}{2}}$	3^h	5^3	$5^{2\frac{1}{2}}$	$5^{2\frac{1}{4}}$	HarrellJ	Millsdale Stable	45.10
06336	DISPOSE	w 126	7	4	2^h	4^h	7^6	6^2	6^3	BiermanC	King Ranch	13.60
05979^2	CURIOUS COIN	wB 126	4	5	$3_{\frac{1}{2}}$	2^h	6^h	7^{10}	7^{15}	AndersonI	Coldstream Stable	15.55
(06392)	OCEAN BLUE	wB 126	2	1	7^5	8	8	8	8	HanfordI	C Oglebay	8.65

(Complete finish confirmed by Photochart Camera.)
Time, :23$\frac{3}{5}$, :47$\frac{3}{5}$, 1:12$\frac{3}{5}$, 1:39$\frac{1}{5}$, 1:58$\frac{4}{5}$. Track good.

	$2 Mutuels Paid			Odds to $1		
WHIRLAWAY	4.30	4.40	3.30	1.15	1.20	.65
KING COLE		16.30	7.80		7.15	2.90
OUR BOOTS			3.60			.80

Winner—Ch. c, by Blenheim II.—Dustwhirl, by Sweep (trained by B. A. Jones; bred by Calumet Farm).
WENT TO POST—4:58. AT POST—1 minute.
Start good and slow. Won easily. second and third driving.

WHIRLAWAY, slow to begin, was some distance back of the field passing the stand the first time around, but improved his position after entering the back stretch while saving ground, then came to the outside of KING COLE nearing the stretch turn to dash to the front and, easily opening up on his opposition in the stretch, won with speed in reserve. KING COLE headed the field early and set a good pace to hold DISPOSE, CURIOUS COIN and OUR BOOTS down the back stretch, but was no match for WHIRLAWAY when the latter challenged, although easily best of the others. OUR BOOTS, close to the pace early while racing on the outside of DISPOSE and CURIOUS COIN, dropped back in the stretch, but was not good enough to withstand PORTER'S CAP. The latter, under restraint not far from the leaders in the first half mile, made a mild move nearing the stretch while racing rather wide and continued wide in the stretch to falter near the finish. KANSAS raced up strongly in the back stretch and was impressive for seven-eighths, then faded. DISPOSE had good early speed, but tired in the stretch. CURIOUS COIN was used up keeping up with the early leaders and tired after going seven eighths. OCEAN BLUE was off well, but was unable to keep up after going a half mile and was badly beaten at the end.

annihilating burst of speed that he can apparently turn on at any stage of a race." Ben Jones exulted, "He's like an old ham getting better with age." In the jockey room, Eddie Arcaro's fellow riders marveled: "Boy, what a horse that is you were riding. We'd sure like to get a good look at him some time." "That's all right, pals," Arcaro replied, grinning. "Just hand me a towel. I want to wipe the jam off my lips. This is too easy and you said it when you said he was a whirlwind. I was just gunning you all the way. It was just as well that my horse propped a little on the break and walked out of the box. I'd have had to run over horses because he certainly swings when he gets ready to roll."

Confidence and joy reigned supreme at Calumet. This was the first Preakness victory for Warren Wright, Ben Jones, and Eddie Arcaro. It also meant another $49,365 added to the colt's winnings. The payoff to his betting backers, however, was rather slim, a mere $1.15 to the dollar. The winning time, too, was 1:58$\frac{4}{5}$, which hardly approached Seabiscuit's 1938 track record of 1:56$\frac{3}{5}$. After the race, it was learned that Ben Jones had once more walked the colt around the track "almost within splinter distance of the inside rail."

This, plus the outcome of the Preakness, may have caused turf reporter Norris Royden to conclude: "The dumbest horse Ben Jones ever encountered finally has learned . . . how to negotiate left-handed turns."

The pressure was now off as they prepared for the final leg of the Triple Crown. However, Ben Jones refused to let up and had his mount run in a tune-up on May 20. He might have saved himself the effort. The 73rd Belmont Stakes on June 7 was hardly a contest, virtually a walkover for Whirlaway. Few doubted the end result, even among the Thoroughbreds, as only three showed up to oppose the Flying Tail, the smallest field since Twenty Grand had run in the race 10 years earlier.

At the outset, Robert Morris, Yankee Chance, and Itabo set a very slow pace, hoping to upset the timing of the favorite. But Eddie Arcaro would have nothing of this nonsense. They had gone a ½ mile when he turned to Alfred Robertson on Robert Morris and Basil James on Yankee Chance and yelled: "The hell with this, fellas, I'm leaving." He then gave Whirlaway his head, and within the next ¼ mile, moved out to a seven-length lead. To all intents and purposes, the race was won at that point. The colt had beaten the field and had nothing else to do. Therefore, he was eased to finish in an easy gallop and in the rather unimpressive time of 2:31, nearly three seconds off the track record set by Sorteado in 1939.

Owner Warren Wright missed the glory of the Triple Crown achievement. He was attending his son's graduation from the University of Denver. However, he had listened to the radio broadcast of the race and then had been interviewed by reporters. He was quick to give Ben Jones credit for "making a great consistent racer out of a temperamental, willful two-year-old." He also offered a cogent analysis of what Jones had done: "One doesn't employ a system in raising an unusual child," he said. "One studies the child, watches nervous reactions, follows awakening interests, or, in other words, carefully bends the twig." Wright, in addition to enjoying the thrill of winning the Triple Crown, could also point to the fact that his remarkable horse had just scored his 13th victory in 26 starts and had moved into 17th place, behind Bimelech, as the leading money-winner. Thus, he became only the second horse since Man o' War to lead his age division in earnings at ages two and three, and the first leading two-year-old since Big Red to have a better record at age three than at two.

For the rest of the year, the Flying Tail terrorized his competitors. His next victory was the Dwyer Stakes, which was his eighth win of the year and

Whirlaway coasts to an easy victory in the 1941 Belmont Stakes. Robert Morris finishes second, with Yankee Chance third.

fifth straight since the Derby. Other major stakes victories included the Saranac Handicap, Travers Stakes, American Derby, and Lawrence Realization. He did lose the Arlington Classic, Narragansett Special, and Jockey Club Gold Cup—the last by a nose to Market Wise in a sizzling finish down the stretch. Coming up to the Saranac Handicap, following his Arlington Classic loss while ridden by Alfred Shellhomer (because Eddie Arcaro had been grounded for rough riding), a whole raft of excuses was voiced for the defeat. It was said that Jones did not give the colt enough strenuous work, that only Arcaro raced him best, that he had been hit in the eye with a clod of dirt, that the classic was a jinx for favorites.

The fact is, he won the Saranac with Robertson in the irons, although only by a whisker in a three-horse photo finish. Some, including Samuel Riddle, owner of War Relic, refused to concede the win. Riddle displayed uncontrolled anger before fans, swinging his cane wildly and sending officials scurrying right and left.

In the Travers, they sent Whirlaway out with his tail braided to prevent him from picking up mud in the soft going.

Trainer Ben Jones holds a flower-bedecked Whirlaway, the new Triple Crown champion, in the winner's circle after the Belmont victory. Eddie Arcaro is in the saddle.

Official Chart of Belmont Stakes

SIXTH RACE **08106** June-7-41-Bel

1 1-2 MILES. (Sorteado, Sept. 23, 1939—2:28⅘—4—112.) Seventy-Third Running BELMONT STAKES. $25,000 Added. 3-year-olds. Weight-for-age.

Net value to winner **$39,770**; second, **$5,000**; third, **$2,500**; fourth, **$1,000.**

Index	Horses	Eq't	A Wt	PP	St	½	¾	1	Str	Fin	Jockeys	Owners	Odds $1 Str't
(07004)	WHIRLAWAY	wB	126	3	3	$3^{1\frac{1}{2}}$	1^{7}	1^{3}	1^{2}	$1^{2\frac{1}{2}}$	ArcaroE	Calumet Farm	.25
(07176)	ROBERT MORRIS	w	126	4	4	$2_{\frac{1}{2}}$	2^{6}	2^{7}	2^{2}	2^{5}	RobertsonA	J F Byers	4.30
07725³	YANKEE CHANCE	w	126	1	2	4	4	4	3^{3}	3^{5}	JamesB	C V Whitney	36.05
(07279)	ITABO	w	126	2	1	1^{1}	3^{2}	3^{3}	4	4	BiermanC	King Ranch	7.70

(Complete finish confirmed by James J. Jones Photo Finish Camera.)

Time, :25⅖, :49⅘, 1:13⅘, 1:39⅕, 2:05, 2:31. Track fast.

	$2 Mutuels Paid			Odds to $1	
WHIRLAWAY	2.50	2.10	No show prices.	.25	.05
ROBERT MORRIS		2.40			.20

Winner—Ch. c, by Blenheim II.—Dustwhirl, by Sweep (trained by B. A. Jones; bred by Calumet Farm).

WENT TO POST—4:56. AT POST—1 minute.

Start good and slow. Won easily; second and third the same.

WHIRLAWAY was under restraint for a quarter and, when settled rounding the first turn, moved into command with a rush, then drew away into an easy lead and was rated along steadily, came a trifle wide rounding the stretch and finished in the middle of the track with speed in reserve. ROBERT MORRIS reared at the start and broke off stride, settled quickly and was kept close up throughout, improved his position rapidly rounding the far turn and, nearing the stretch turn, was placed under pressure, but could not menace the winner, yet held the others safe. YANKEE CHANCE was fractious at the post and was taken under restraint when outrun, then began to move up when settled in the stretch and hung at the finish. ITABO was sent into command to show the pace for the early stages under sufferance, then dropped back steadily when settled after the first mile and was never a factor thereafter.

All in all, the general consensus was that there really was no telling just how good he was simply because no three-year-old appeared capable of extending him. Whatever losses he suffered were largely because of his ingrained habit of bearing out in the stretch run. The prevalent theory was that Whirlaway could go any distance that American racing called for and could carry weight. In fact, he was asked to bear as much as 130 pounds. Furthermore, by the time he had put away the Realization in September, he had pushed his earnings to $347,661, passing Challedon, Gallant Fox, and Equipoise to become the third-highest earner in history. He had been in training since August 1, 1939, had started 35 times, and had shipped a total of 12,500 miles, for which he was being touted as the new "iron horse" of racing. Never in the history of Thoroughbred racing had another horse racked up such a total of money prior to the end of his five-year-old season.

Late in October, Calumet Farm sent a string of its racers to Santa Anita, California, for the winter season. There seemed little doubt that Whirlaway, who was among them, would be able to top Seabiscuit's earnings record while participating in the stakes races there. Precautions were taken to make the Triple Crown champion comfortable during and after his cross-country journey. At the West Coast track, a special screened-in stall was built, from which the colt could extend his head but not be annoyed or petted by onlookers. He was also accompanied by his pet pony, Silver King. However, all plans were negated abruptly by the Pearl Harbor disaster on December 7 and the outbreak of World War II. Eight days later, the entire 1941–1942 Santa Anita season was canceled. Therefore, the year wound up in a state of suspended activity for Whirlaway, but not before he had been voted Horse of the Year by *Turf and Sport Digest*. He did just beat out a talented newcomer, Alsab, 96–90 votes. The rising star was voted best among the two-year-olds and was destined to confront the older star the following year. Whirlaway also won the three-year-old honors, which made it only the second time that a leading two-year-old had also captured top honors the following year. The last Thoroughbred to do this was Bimelech in 1939 and 1940.

When the war broke out, all transportation facilities were mobilized, which stranded the Calumet horses on the West Coast. It was not until March 1942 that they were able to ship east. Ben Jones claimed that Whirlaway had benefited from the rest, but that he was "crying to run."

As a four-year-old, the Flying Tail picked up where he had left off. He won 12 of 22 races, mostly handicaps, while carrying weights of up to 132 pounds.

He was second in eight events and never failed to place. His victories included the Clark, Dixie, Brooklyn, Massachusetts, Garden State, Narragansett Special, Jockey Club Gold Cup, Washington, Pimlico Special, Governor Bowie, and Louisiana handicaps. There were some notable highlights in that season. In the Suburban, at even money, $149,968 was bet on him, the most ever on a single horse, and he doubtless caused not a few heart seizures when he finished second after trailing by nearly 12 lengths at the final turn. Perhaps the biggest thrill for owner Warren Wright came at Suffolk Downs in Boston on July 15, when the colt won the Massachusetts Handicap. It was worth $43,850, and brought Whirlaway's total winnings past Seabiscuit's record of $437,730 by $16,606. Whirlaway was the world's leading money-winner and also the 1942 handicap leader, with his earnings from these races coming to $104,675 to date. Then, on October 3, he won $18,350 in the Jockey Club Gold Cup, which carried his total past the half-million-dollar mark, the first Thoroughbred ever to reach that pinnacle. In the Pimlico Special, on October 28, no other horse dared to come out against him, and he won the race in a walkover. He broke another Seabiscuit record on November 11, with his win in the Governor Bowie Handicap. The purse brought his total for the year to $198,810, which was some $30,000 higher than the previous mark for winnings by a four-year-old Thoroughbred. In fact, Whirlaway's achievements on the track also attracted glory to his dam, Dustwhirl. Largely because of him, she set a record for earnings by her produce because three of them won a total of $641,479. This beat the record of Marguerite, the dam of Gallant Fox, five of whose get won $620,080.

The year 1942 was notable for Whirlaway in another respect. It marked the third time since 1920 that the gauntlet was thrown down at a Triple Crown champion in a challenge to a match race. The challenger was the very exciting three-year-old Alsab. He was a bay with a white star, by Good Goods, out of Wind Chant. His career had had a rather unassuming start, when he was included "in a consignment largely made up of foals of untried stallions" and wound up being bought for only $700 at the Saratoga Sales. He was purchased by Albert Sabath of Chicago, Illinois, and gratefully rewarded his new owner's confidence in him by amassing winnings of $110,000 by the end of his second year.

Alsab scored 15 victories in 22 starts, finishing the season, wrote John Salvator Hervey, with a "future more eagerly looked forward to than that of almost any horse since Man o' War." Alsab had two notable races. One was a six-and-a-half-furlong match at Belmont Park with another two-year-old, Requested, which he won in 1:16, a record for a juvenile horse as of that date. The other was the Champagne Stakes, which he took in 1:35⅖ seconds, the fastest mile run by any horse in 1941, and a new world's record for a two-year-old, breaking that set by Twenty Grand in 1930. Alsab was so good that his owner entered him for the following year's Kentucky Derby on October 14, the earliest registration ever for the classic. Salvator wrote:

> In action, Alsab is not of the drum-roll stroke so common among precocious juveniles, neither had he their quickness away from the gate. He gets off, on the contrary, rather moderately, if not even slowly at times, and requires a bit of ground over which to extend himself before moving into high [speed]. . . . When at the very top of his flight, he never struggles or gives an effect of extreme exertion, rather everything he does appears easy and within his powers.

Alsab's third year was good and bad. He missed the Triple Crown by losing the Derby and Belmont to Shut Out, and won the Preakness. He ran 23 times, winning nine, placing in seven, coming in third in three, and finishing out of the money four times. His total winnings were $234,565—not a bad year's pay for any horse. The fact is, he was an exciting performer, second only to Whirlaway, which made the match race a "natural." It took place on September 19, 1942, at Narragansett, with a $25,000 purse to the winner. The distance was 1³⁄₁₆ mile at weight-for-age conditions, giving Alsab 119 pounds to Whirlaway's 126.

George Woolf, who had guided Seabiscuit to victory in the match race with War Admiral, was on Whirlaway, and Carroll Bierman rode Alsab. The crowd of thirty-five thousand anticipated excitement because both horses had reputations for coming from behind. The start saw Alsab jump out first to a half-length lead at the first quarter. Woolf, riding confidently, stayed behind, biding his time. He was never more than two lengths off. At the mile, he was only a half-length away as Whirlaway crept up on the outside and began one of his late surges. The two colts ran head-to-head in a savage, awe-inspiring stretch run, "a finish fought with exceptional bitterness and gameness on both sides." They crossed the finish line locked tightly, although Whirlaway was still moving up at the end and, in fact, was ahead by a few strides past the wire. It was a photo finish, of course, and the decision in favor

The spectacular photo finish of the match race between Whirlaway (on the outside) and Alsab at Narragansett Park on September 19, 1942.

The official photo showing Alsab winning the race by the tip of his nose.

of Alsab was made only after a magnifying-glass inspection of the film showed that he had won by the barest of possible margins, the tip of a nostril. The time was 1:56⅗. The Narragansett Championship marked the third instance when a Triple Crown champion lost out in a match race. It was notable in another respect. Never before had two such top money-winners met in a special race. The pair subsequently raced against each other in two other stakes events, with Whirlaway avenging his defeat in one and succumbing again in another.

Mr. Longtail finished up his fourth year with a win in the Louisiana Handicap at the Fair Grounds in New Orleans on December 12. He also suffered his first real injury, a hurt foreleg that subsequently was diagnosed as a bowed tendon. Four days later, his hurt was eased somewhat when he was named Horse of the Year for the second successive time. He received 76 votes to 45 for Alsab and 4 for Count Fleet. The honors would not quit, for he was also named Best Four-Year-Old and Best Handicap Horse. It was the third year in a row that he had won the top spot in his own division.

Ben Jones nursed Whirlaway carefully until the following spring and then tried him out in two races. He lost both. The last was the Equipoise Mile Handicap at Arlington Park on June 26, 1943, in which he finished fifth and pulled up somewhat lame. The losses convinced Warren Wright that his marvelous horse had reached the end of his campaigning days and had earned a life of ease in retirement. His last appearance was at Washington Park in Chicago, Illinois, on July 5, when he paraded in silks before a cheering crowd.

Not since Man o' War had a horse made such a triumphant return to Kentucky. He arrived in Lexington on July 13, and on August 8, was honored with a Whirlaway Day celebration replete with speeches from leading citizens and public officials in a manner befitting the return of a conquering hero from battle. The colt then settled down at Claiborne Farm for stud duty, where he lived a regal life as choice mares were sent to him at $1,500 per breeding effort. His first get began to race in 1947, and through 1949, he had produced 52 winners out of 71 starters, including seven stakes winners—Dart By, Duchess Peg, Going Away, Scattered, Whirl Flower, Whirl Some, and Whirling Fox. His fillies had won, or were in the money, in just about every major stakes event for the distaff Thoroughbred. These achievements of his offspring resulted in his making the list of the 20 leading sires of 1949. Finally, through 1951, his 283 starters had earned $1,631,330, or some $5,764 per starter per year. It is somewhat noteworthy, in passing, that in September

1944, a mare that had been served to Whirlaway as part of his fertility tests late in 1943 produced a foal that was registered and became a winner. It was First Whirl.

Marcel Boussac, one of Europe's celebrated Thoroughbred breeders, owners, and turf personalities, visited Lexington in 1950, took one look at Whirlaway, and exclaimed: *"C'est pour moi."* The French textile magnate and industrialist had a keen eye for Thoroughbred stock, having produced such stars as Goya II, Adaris, Hierocles, Ardan, and Djeddah, all of whom subsequently were purchased and imported by American syndicates. He was not to be dissuaded,

Proud owner Warren Wright (left) and trainer Ben Jones hold Whirlaway as he makes the final public appearance of his racing career at Washington Park, Chicago, on July 5, 1943. Devoted exercise boy Pinky Brown is astride him.

therefore, from negotiating a three-year lease for Whirlaway to stand in stud at his own farm. By then, Bull Lea had become the choice stallion at Calumet Farm, so Warren Wright was prevailed upon to send his prize champion to Boussac's Haras Fresnay-le-Bufford farm in southern Normandy. It was the first time that Calumet Farm had ever exported one of its Thoroughbreds. Before the contract had expired, though, Monsieur Boussac had become so enamored of his American stallion that he succeeded in convincing Wright to sell him outright. On the morning of April 6, 1953, at the age of 15, Whirlaway died suddenly in his stall 10 minutes after he had been bred to a mare. The cause of death was said to have been a rupture of nerve tissue.

Years after Whirlaway had retired, Eddie Arcaro perhaps best crystalized just what it was that made the colt such a unique racer. "It never was any picnic to ride Whirlaway," he said. "Once he started to climb you just couldn't slow him down. It was like stepping on the accelerator of a big Cadillac. How he could pour it on!"

Ben Jones truly loved the eccentric colt and could never reconcile himself to his eventual retirement. "If Whirlaway was my horse," he boasted early in 1943, "he would still be running when he was 10 years old. He is the soundest horse I have ever seen." The day the colt had to be retired, however, he lamented: "It's like losin' an old friend."

Count Fleet

Count Fleet
(brown colt) {
  Reigh Count {
    Sunreigh
    Contessina
}
  Quickly {
    Haste
    Stephanie
}

| Chapter 6 |

Count Fleet

~1943~

Breeding Thoroughbred horses is a treacherous business. The odds for success are so stacked against the breeder, the wonder is that so many of them keep chasing the ever-elusive prize at the end of the rainbow—another Man o' War or the next Triple Crown champion. Patience, perseverance, and unlimited, ready cash are indispensable prerequisites. It is equally true that a rich lode of luck must also accompany the fat wallet. The history of Thoroughbred racing in America is replete with stories of champion heroes emerging from the pack of thousands of foals bred each year, largely because of a twist of fate. The saga of Count Fleet is one such chapter.

John D. Hertz was a self-made millionaire. He emigrated to America from Czechoslovakia as a youngster, settled in Chicago, amassed his fortune when he founded the Yellow Cab Company, and then proceeded to put Americans in the driver's seat with his car-rental operations. His interest in Thoroughbred racing and breeding began in the early twenties. He rose rapidly to prominence in the sport, eventually heading up Arlington Park. It was he who, in 1939, tried to bring the special race between War Admiral and Seabiscuit to Chicago by offering to match the $100,000 Belmont Park was putting up as a purse.

In 1927, six years after he and his wife had joined the owner-breeder ranks, they saw a young colt catch up to the leader of a race, reach over, and bite him. The Hertzes were so taken with this remarkable display of fired determination that they made up their minds then and there to buy him. The following year, they wound up with their first Kentucky Derby trophy. The colt's name was Reigh Count, and he went on to victory in other major stakes races in the United States and England. When he eventually was retired to stud, he was among the top 20 leading sires for five consecutive years. But none of his get won a Futurity or Kentucky Derby, which convinced Hertz that he could not expect too much more success from him. However, he was not about to sell him, so he decided to breed him to no more than four mares each year for as long as he lived or remained active in stud. Considering that it is usual for a top stallion to receive between 30 and 40 mares in a breeding season, the decision was hardly a vote of confidence in Reigh Count, more likely a sentimental gesture to the stallion. On the other hand, Hertz still had it in the back of his mind that he might yet bring off the long-tried breeding theory of mating a distance-running sire, like Reigh Count, with a flashy, speedy mare, to produce a son with the best qualities of both.

Such a mare did come along, but it took better than 10 years, and it called for even more of the gambler's gambit to take a chance with her. She was Quickly, a shifty mare by Haste, out of a daughter by Stefan the Great. Hertz, in buying her for only $2,500, was bucking the wisdom of breeders, who distrust any mare that has run too much. The reasoning is that they have worn themselves out to be any good as a broodmare. On the surface, Quickly fit that theorem. She was seven years old, footsore, and in poor physical condition, having raced 85 times in six seasons, winning 32 times and earning only $21,530. Most of her victories were at six furlongs; distance obviously was not her forte. Quickly's first mating was poor. The next year she was barren. Hertz still refused to concede, and his luck, gambling instinct, and sheer stubbornness bore fruit on March 24, 1940. To the cover of Reigh Count at Hertz's Stoner Creek Farm in Kentucky, she produced an ugly duckling of a foal, "a gangling little brown chow-hound that was promptly named Count Fleet."

He was a disappointment as a yearling, showing signs of difficulty in handling. The combination of negatives nudged Hertz to offer the youngster for sale. Count Fleet, therefore, was shown to prospective yearling buyers, but the trainers shied away because of his dam. On the other hand, they snapped up two other yearlings by Reigh Count. About the only one who believed in the young Thoroughbred at the time was the stable boy, Sam Ramsen. He envisioned a great horse in the brown, gawky colt. He worked diligently with him and, when Ramsen was about to be inducted into the army, he begged the manager of Stoner Creek Farm to tell Hertz not to sell Count Fleet, because "someday he is going to be one fine racer."

Hertz had little choice. When 1942 rolled around and there was still no buyer in sight, he simply shipped the fractious problem off to the races, placing him in the hands of his trainer, the big, quiet, florid-faced Scot, G. D. "Don" Cameron. It took until June 1 before Cameron was willing to chance his educational indoctrination of the horse in an outing at Belmont Park. "The Count" swerved at the start, banged into Vacuum Cleaner, and lost. He did the same two weeks later. A few days afterward, the colt's jockey, Johnny Longdon, chanced to visit Cameron's barn at Belmont and noticed a trainer examining Count Fleet. He jumped on his bicycle, pedaled furiously to a nearby telephone booth, and called Hertz. "That was the first time I knew that Mr. Hertz had put him up for sale," recalled Longdon. "The price, they told me, was $4,500. I felt it was a bad mistake to let him go. Just his love of running, if it could ever be properly controlled, had convinced me that he would be a good one." When he explained this to the owner, he was told: "The colt's dangerous. Someday, I'm afraid he'll do you serious injury." "I'm not afraid," countered Longdon. This, coming from a 34-year-old jockey, one of the top riders of the American turf, convinced Hertz. "All right," he sighed, "if you're game enough to ride him, I'll keep him."

The tide took a dramatic turn almost immediately. Count Fleet broke his maiden in a five-and-a-half-furlong sprint in 1:06, just ⅗ second shy of the track record, and repeated on July 4 at the same distance, at ⅕ second faster, in both as if the opposition had suddenly stopped running. He lost the next time out, in the Eastview Stakes on July 15, only to rebound in the Wakefield Stakes on July 22, when three horses came out with him and he "strung them out like the proverbial 'string of suckers,'" as one reporter called it. These performances convinced the railbirds that he was probably the best two-year-old in the East. The only one who could stack up to him was Occupation, a westerner whose followers were touting him for juvenile champion honors and as unbeatable, coming off victories in the Arlington Park Futurity and other races. The showdown between the two was inevitable and was slated for the Washington Park Futurity in Chicago, Illinois, on August 15, 1942.

Eleven horses went to the post, with Occupation the favorite at 3-5. The Count trailed at the top of the stretch following a troublesome start, and then Longdon sent him after the leader. As they approached the wire, "Count Fleet seemed . . . literally to be eating him up," recalled John Salvator Hervey. He failed by a neck. It was back to the drawing board once more, and two quick wins followed as the colt was prepared for the upcoming Futurity Stakes at

111

Belmont Park on October 3. Just before the race, though, big news was made at a morning workout. Johnny Longdon was observed having his hands full trying to hold in the horse as he rocketed through six furlongs, or ¾ of a mile, in an unprecedented 1:08⅛. There were too many onlookers with stopwatches for Cameron and Longdon, who said he thought it was more like 1:12, to discount the time. Although Count Fleet had always been considered a horse of competitive temperament and a stretch runner of ability, none had seriously thought of him as a speedster. The workout changed many minds, including that of the trainer, who, for the first time, was ready to concede that the colt had tremendous potential.

It came as a rather severe shock, therefore, that "the Fleet" ran third in the Futurity, five lengths behind Occupation and a neck back of Askmenow. Many felt that he had, in track parlance, "left the race on the track in the trial"; the remarkable workout had simply drained him. There was a more

Count Fleet (far left) comes in third behind winner Occupation and filly Askmenow in the 1942 Futurity Stakes at Aqueduct. "The Fleet" played "Romeo to his Juliet" throughout the race.

practical explanation after the dust had settled. For one thing, confusion was rampant at the outset of the race, when jockey Carroll Bierman was unseated in the gate by Askmenow, the only filly in the race. Then the two ran two-three for the six and a half furlongs as the colt played "Romeo to his Juliet." Longdon later told reporters of his ordeal: "We broke all right, but Count Fleet grabbed his quarter [part of the hoof] right after the start. For the last ⅜ of a mile, he laid on Askmenow, and I couldn't drag him off. Even after the finish neither of us could pull up." It was shades of the shenanigans his sire was guilty of as a two-year-old, and it was a tribute to his taste for the fairer sex. The little lass was worth the extra look, for she subsequently was named the year's Best Two-Year-Old Filly.

A more cogent reason made the race noteworthy for turf historians. It marked the last time Count Fleet would ever suffer defeat. He went on, in 1942, to take the one-mile Champagne Stakes in a breeze, 1:34⅗, beating Alsab's record by ⅗ second and Jack High's 12-year-old track record by ⅕ second. It proved to be the fastest mile run by any horse that year, regardless of age, sex, or track. Three more victories followed, including the Pimlico Futurity, in which he equaled the track mark.

It was quite a year considering the inauspicious beginning. Count Fleet had racked up 10 wins in 15 starts, including four stakes races—the largest number of victories by a two-year-old in 1942—and had earned $76,245. He easily captured Best Two-Year-Old honors, and his prowess on the turf was further acknowledged when he was assigned 132 pounds in the Experimental Free Handicap. The race rates the best two-year-olds of the previous season, with each assigned weights as a measuring device of their potential as three-year-olds. The mark had not been equaled by any horse as of 2004.

In reviewing the year, assistant trainer Charles Hewitt tried to explain the colt's success. "They fault his conformation but he can do the job. He doesn't pound the ground like most horses. He doesn't have to dig in and push, but sort of rocks along as if it were the easiest thing in the world." The stable boys had another way of assessing Count Fleet's power. Normally, after a tough race or workout, it takes about 45 minutes of just walking about to cool out. With Count Fleet, the editors of the book *Call Me Horse* wrote, he 'just couldn't seem to amble along in leisurely fashion as most horses do. He had to make a walking-race out of it. After about 20 minutes his handler would holler for relief, and the Fleet would have the second worn out and puffing audibly by the time the 45 minutes were up."

They shipped Count Fleet to Stoner Creek Farm for the winter. Then, in late January, he went to Oaklawn Park in Hot Springs, Arkansas, where Don Cameron began to bring him back to racing form, finally taking him to Belmont in mid-March for the start of the racing season. By then, he was hardly the gaunt ghost of a horse; rather, he had grown into a handsome brown figure, having filled out at the rate of two pounds per day to improve his weight from 978 pounds in December to more than one thousand pounds within a month. He was, for sure, a good doer.

Robert Kelley claimed that 1943 was "Count Fleet's Year," that his second year of racing was like a "skyrocket flaring across the sky." Unfortunately, like the rocket, the brilliant burst of flame and color was snuffed out just as it reached the zenith of its flight. He made six starts and "demolished just about every other opponent that came along to challenge him." His first race at age three was the St. James Purse at New York's Jamaica track on April 13. He won it without urging, the victory dropping the winter book odds on him for the Kentucky Derby from 2-5 to 4-5. However, he did come out of the race with a nicked foreleg, though Don Cameron discounted the injury. On April 17, he spurted through the 1⅛-mile Wood Memorial in 1:43, within ⅗ second of the track record. What started out to be a two-horse affair wound up as a one-horse dash after six or seven furlongs. According to Arthur Daley of *The New York Times*:

> If the Count had been a man instead of a horse, he would have yawned politely in the homestretch at the total lack of opposition. But being of decidedly equine ancestry, the Count merely kept his ears pinned down in strict attention to business—and thereby pinned the ears of all who were willing to challenge him. . . . It is a lead-pipe certainty now that the parallel between Count Fleet and Man o' War is going to be more sharply drawn.

The colt was such a favorite of the fans at the track that they had backed him almost to the exclusion of the other seven horses. Of the $310,112 bet on the race, $196,192 was on Count Fleet, the largest amount ever placed on a single horse in New York since the introduction of the pari-mutuel machines. The glee of victory was muted somewhat when he trailed blood from a three-inch gash on a hind leg as he returned to the winner's circle. He apparently had sustained it when Modest Lad had pushed Vincentive into

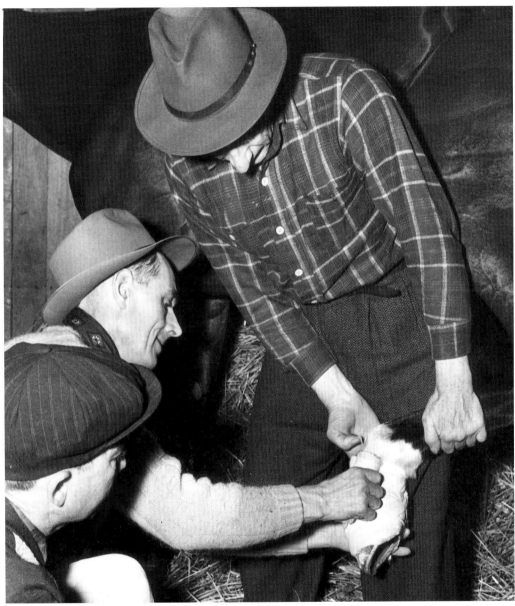

Blacksmith Stan Martin (right) and helpers bandage Count Fleet's left hind foot in his stall at Churchill Downs. The colt had cut himself with one of his hooves in the Wood Memorial.

him on the breakaway, and he cut himself with one of his own hoofs. They packed the wound with sulfa drugs and shipped him off at once to Churchill Downs. For Cameron, it meant a string of sleepless nights filled with worry over whether or not the colt would be able to run in the Derby.

The 1943 Kentucky Derby was unique in that just three months before the date there was the possibility that it might not be staged at all. It was wartime, in the midst of World War II, and there were heavy restrictions on travel, accommodations, and gasoline. Virtually everything was rationed and in short supply—even bourbon. The threat of cancelation caused Colonel Matt Winn, head of Churchill Downs, to "get his back up." He devised a plan that pledged "only neighbors and their children from greater Louisville would attend." He promised, further, to run it as a "street-car" affair, with only cars that had "A" gas-ration coupons admitted to the track grounds. Taxis were not permitted to drop off passengers less than one mile from the entrance. All of the restrictions were dutifully spelled out in a *New York Times* editorial. As a result, the 69th running of the classic did, in fact, come to be nicknamed the "Street-Car Derby," and only sixty-two thousand people made it to the track.

The word was *go* for Count Fleet on the day of the race. His handlers felt the wound was sufficiently under control and, for added protection, they covered the sulfa drugs with axle grease before he moved onto the track. As far as the fans were concerned, it made no difference. He was down to prohibitive 1-2 odds—the shortest price in the history of the race. The only colt that figured to give him trouble was Ocean Wave, a stablemate of Whirlaway and trained by Ben Jones, but he was scratched, so there was little opposition to anticipate. One reporter mused that "the Count figures to make a conga line out of this $82,750 classic like his daddy, Reigh Count, did 15 years ago." He did just that. "The Fleet sailed into port . . . without even getting up a full head of steam," reported the Associated Press, "broke out in full battle array after bouncing with some others in the field of 10 for a ½ mile, and from there on it was just a gallop." He scored by three lengths over Blue Swords. Finishing last was Burnt Cork, owned by Eddie "Rochester" Anderson, the radio sidekick of comedian Jack Benny.

Longdon, the British-born jockey, did recall a slight threat from Blue Swords. "Sure I saw him coming. I just gave the Count a little nudge and he gave out some more. That's all." He then observed that he had come to understand his horse's temperament, that the colt was bred to run and wanted to run. "Get him out on top, give him the race track, and let him run. It was what he loved to do more than anything else." He also commented that the colt had an abhorrence of defeat, "and if he didn't have racing room, he'd go to the outside or just climb over horses. If you were in close quarters with him you were in trouble." Naturally, the conversation turned to Big Red. "I don't know the great horses like Man o' War," said Longdon, "because I wasn't

Count Fleet cruises to a three-length victory over Blue Swords in the 1943 Kentucky Derby. Slide Rule was third.

Official Chart of the Kentucky Derby

SEVENTH RACE **1 1-4 MILES. (Whirlaway, May 3, 1941—2:01⅖—3—126.) Sixty-Ninth Running KENTUCKY DERBY. $75,000 Added. 3-year-olds. Weight, the scale. (Owner of winner to receive a gold trophy.)**

3 9 9 6 7

May 1-43—C.D Net value to winner $60,725; second, $8,000; third, $3,000; fourth, $1,000; trainers of the winner, second and third horses receive $3,000, $2,000 and $1,000, respectively; breeders of the winner, second and third horses receive $2,000, $1,000 and $500, respectively.

Index	Horses	Eq't	A	Wt	PP	St	½	¾	1	Str	Fin	Jockeys	Owners	Odds $1 Str't
(39413)	COUNT FLEET	wb		126	5	1	1^{h}	1^{2}	1^{2}	1^{2}	1^{3}	LongdenJ	Mrs J Hertz	.40
39413^{2}	BLUE SWORDS	wb		126	1	2	$4\frac{1}{2}$	$4^{1\frac{1}{2}}$	$2^{1\frac{1}{2}}$	2^{2}	2^{6}	AdamsJ	Allen T Simmons	9.00
39761^{2}	SLIDE RULE	wb		126	2	6	$6\frac{1}{2}$	3^{h}	$4^{1\frac{1}{2}}$	3^{3}	3^{6}	McCrearyC	W E Boeing	10.80
39546^{2}	AMBER LIGHT	wb		126	7	5	$5^{1\frac{1}{2}}$	5^{3}	$3\frac{1}{2}$	4^{2}	$4\frac{1}{2}$	RobertsonA	Dixiana Farm	17.50
39761	BANKRUPT	w		126	6	9	9^{3}	9^{1}	$7\frac{1}{2}$	$6\frac{1}{2}$	$5^{1\frac{1}{2}}$	ZufeltF	T B Martin	†21.90
39761^{3}	NO WRINKLES	w		126	10	7	8^{3}	$7\frac{1}{2}$	6^{1}	7^{h}	6^{h}	AdairR	Milky Way Farm	34.60
39546	DOVE PIE	wb		126	4	10	10	10	8^{2}	8^{1}	7^{3}	EadsW	J W Rodgers	86.50
39147	GOLD SHOWER	w		126	9	4	2^{4}	2^{1}	5^{3}	$5\frac{1}{2}$	8^{10}	AtkinsonT	Vera S Bragg	12.10
39761	MODEST LAD	wb		126	3	8	7^{h}	6^{h}	9^{4}	9^{4}	9^{8}	SwainC	Mrs H Finch	71.20
39761	BURNT CORK	wb		126	8	3	3^{1}	$8^{1\frac{1}{2}}$	10	10	10	GonzalezMN	E Anderson	†21.90

†Mutuel field.

Time, :12⅖, :23⅕, :34⅖, :46⅗, :59⅖, 1:12⅗, 1:25, 1:37⅗, 1:50⅖, 2:04. Track fast.

Mutuel Prices

	$2 Mutuels Paid			Odds to $1		
COUNT FLEET	2.80	2.40	2.20	.40	.20	.10
BLUE SWORDS		3.40	3.00		.70	.50
SLIDE RULE			3.20			.60

Winner—Br. c, by Reigh Count—Quickly, by Haste, trained by G. D. Cameron; bred by Mrs. J. Hertz.

WENT TO POST—5:30½. OFF AT 5:31½ CENTRAL WAR TIME.

Start good from stall gate. Won handily; second and third driving. COUNT FLEET began fast, was hustled along until reaching the stretch, shook off the bid of GOLD SHOWER and, responding to a shaking up, won handily. BLUE SWORDS, away well, was in hand until reaching the last half, came determinedly when subjected to punishment, but was not good enough for the winner, although easily best of the others. SLIDE RULE saved ground while outrun to the final half, was blocked when moving up approaching the final turn and, taken out for the drive, could not reach the leaders when subjected to punishment. AMBER LIGHT raced evenly under restraint until reaching the final half, made a game bid entering the stretch, but tired. BANKRUPT, outrun until the final quarter, failed to respond when called upon in the stretch. NO WRINKLES, on the outside throughout, could not better his positiion and had no excuses. DOVE PIE swerved to the inside after the start and was never a serious contender. GOLD SHOWER, much used engaging COUNT FLEET in the first three-quarters, gave way badly thereafter. MODEST LAD, bothered slightly after the start by DOVE PIE, was always far back. BURNT CORK began fast, displayed good speed in the first half and then quit.

Scratched—39761 Twoses, 126; (39761)Ocean Wave, 126.

around then. But the Count is the greatest I've ever ridden. Got everything—speed, heart—just everything."

Although the general public "felt like nothing had happened because everything had happened as expected," many were disappointed in the slow time of 2:04. The gripes started the "He Ain't So Hot Club" going, as they questioned his greatness and wondered if he was just lucky to come along when there was no competition to make him prove it. They were in agreement on one point, though, that Ocean Wave would have pushed him rather than allowed him to loaf through the last ⅛ of a mile. As one scribe put it, the "Count hardly could be put down as a P-38 [fighter plane] on the prowl." It was also reported that he had nicked his left front foot, giving fits to his handlers. He was developing a very distressing habit.

The gripes notwithstanding, the Preakness on May 8, 1943, looked like it would be merely a fight for second, with only three other horses, Blue Swords, Vincentive, and New Moon, prepared to brave the debacle. It really was no contest, virtually a replay of the Derby. "With the serenity of an old gentleman in his rocking chair on the veranda, Johnny Longdon sat down on the famous back of Count Fleet . . . and rode 1³⁄₁₆ miles to fame and glory," said Robert Kelley. "Grim-faced and unemotional, Longdon sat still. Once rounding the turn into the stretch, he looked back over his shoulder to see what the rest of the world was doing, turned around again, sat down, and came home," never using whip or heels. New Moon made an all-too-brief move to the front at the start, but Count Fleet was on top to stay by the time they reached the grandstands on the first pass-by. He led by five lengths at the ¾ pole and by eight over Blue Swords at the wire. It was a slow track, as was the time: a full second over the track record of 1:56⅖.

In analyzing the way he ran, Longdon told Emanuel Strauss of *The New York Times* that Count Fleet insisted on taking the lead early in every race and could be controlled when he was kicking dust in the faces of his rivals, after which "it's like sitting behind the steering wheel of a Cadillac." Some interesting statistics showed up following the victory. Count Fleet was the shortest-priced winner in the history of the classic at 3-20, paying $2.30 for $2.00. When he started from the paddock, the Count was 1-5. By the time he reached the starting gate, he was 1-9. The purse of $43,190 brought his total winnings to $202,260, which moved him into 26th place among the all-time money-winners. For Blue Swords, it was the sixth time he had chased the "Hertz hurricane" across the finish line, eliciting the wry comment from *The Blood-Horse*:

"If Count Fleet is the spectacular comet in the racing skies of 1943, then Blue Swords is the comet's tail."

The Withers Stakes, on May 22, was nothing more than a workout for Count Fleet before the third jewel of the Triple Crown, the Belmont Stakes. Only three horses came out against him, and he waltzed over the finish line six lengths in front of Slide Rule. To most everyone, the race was close only at the starting gate.

They sent out two horses to be "slaughtered" on the track for the running of the 75th Belmont Stakes on June 5, and the wonder is the ASPCA did not come to the rescue. The opposition to Count Fleet consisted of Fairy Manhurst, winner of only a maiden race and a Class C allowance, and Desoranto, a rather unpretentious son of Man o' War with only a maiden victory to his credit. When the farce was run, the Fleet had roared over the 1½ miles to win by an incredible 25 lengths in 2:28⅕, beating War Admiral's stakes record by ⅖ second, but shy of Bolingbroke's track mark of 2:27⅗. "There was nothing to the race, the riders of Fairy Manhurst and Desorante giving up so far as winning was

Count Fleet makes it look easy as he blasts to an eight-length win over Blue Swords in the 1943 Preakness. Vincentive is a distant third. Only three horses dared to face "the Fleet" in the race.

Count Fleet, with Johnny Longdon in the saddle, receives honors in the winner's circle after the Preakness. At left is trainer Don Cameron.

Official Chart of Preakness

SIXTH RACE **40393** May 8-43—Pim

1 3-16 MILES. (Riverland, May 1, 1943—1:56⅖—5—123.) Fifty-Third Running PREAKNESS STAKES. $50,000 Added. 3-year-olds. Weight-for-age. By subscription of $10 each, which shall accompany the nomination, with the following payments to continue eligibility: $25 additional by Aug. 15, 1942, and a further payment of $100 on or before Jan. 15, 1943. Supplementary entries may be made on or before April 15, 1943, by payment of an eligibility fee of $1,500. Starters to pay $500 additional. All eligibility, entrance and starting fees to the winner, with $50,000 added, of which $10,000 to second, $5,000 to third and $2,000 to fourth. The nominator of the winner to receive $1,500; the nominator of the second horse $750, and the nominator of the third horse $250 of the added money.

Net value to winner $43,190; second, $10,000; third, $5,000; fourth, $2,000.

Index	Horses	Eq't A Wt	PP	St	½	¾	1	Str	Fin	Jockeys	Owners	Odds $1 Str't
(39967)	COUNT FLEET	wb 126	2	1	1⁴	1⁴	1⁵	1⁵	1⁸	LongdenJ	Mrs J D Hertz	.15
39967²	BLUE SWORDS	wb 126	4	3	2²	2¹	2¹	2¹	2⁵	AdamsJ	Allen T Simmons	10.00
(40094)	VINCENTIVE	wb 126	1	4	3¹	3¹⁰	3¹⁰	3¹⁰	3²⁰	WoolfG	W L Brann	6.15
40157²	NEW MOON	wb 126	3	2	4	4	4	4	4	WrightWD	H L Straus	48.65

Time, :23⅗, :47⅖, 1:11⅘, 1:38⅕, 1:57⅖. Track good.

Mutuel Prices

	—$2 Mutuels Paid—			—Odds to $1—		
COUNT FLEET	2.30	2.10	....	.15	.05	....
BLUE SWORDS	....	2.40	....	....	.20	....
NO SHOW MUTUELS SOLD.						

Winner—Br. c, by Reigh Count—Quickly, by Haste, trained by G. D. Cameron; bred by Mrs. J. Hertz. WENT TO POST—2:41. OFF AT 2:42¼ EASTERN WAR TIME.

Start good from stall gate. Won easily; second and third the same. COUNT FLEET outran his field from the start, opened up a safe lead, came slightly wide entering the stretch and finished with speed in reserve. BLUE SWORDS was taken under restraint when outrun and steadied along to the stretch turn, where he shook off VINCENTIVE and finished well, but could not menace the winner, pulling up slightly sore. VINCENTIVE was under steady restraint, made a determined bid entering the stretch, but could not improve his position and was not unduly persevered with. NEW MOON swerved sharply after the start and was never a factor in the running and was not persevered with when hopelessly beaten.

Scratched—40316 Radio Morale, 126.

concerned after about six furlongs, even though they battled tooth and nail for the place money of $5,000. Fairy Manhurst . . . got that by a length," reported Bryan Field. Count Fleet was 8 lengths in front at the ½ mile, 20 after 10 furlongs, from where he just galloped down the stretch. It was a spectacular run in that he drove for the record despite the lack of competition. When asked why he did not shoot for the track record, Longdon replied: "It's a long summer. We're trying to beat horses. Why run against the clock and risk injury when the colt can breeze and sweep all before him?"

Practically everyone bet on the winner, $249,516 out of $261,787, thereby producing a legal minimum payoff of 1-20. America's new Triple Crown champion captured a $35,340 purse, bringing his total earnings to $250,300. The win also meant that he and Sir Barton were the only horses to add the Withers to the Triple Crown races, and he was the only Thoroughbred to win all five spring racing specials—the Wood, Derby, Preakness, Withers, and Belmont. They auctioned off his silks in the unsaddling enclosure for $50,000 in war bonds, which added a patriotic touch to the victory. Bryan Field could hardly be aware of how prophetic he was being when he also wrote, "Count Fleet achieved 21 . . . 21 races, the number run by Man o' War in his entire career." The tragic fact is, this was all for the colt, too—his last hurrah. After the race, he was reported to have struck himself in the left fore ankle during the early running. He walked soundly, and an X-ray examination showed nothing more than a slight wrench. Later, the ankle filled slightly, but soon subsided. Nobody seemed terribly alarmed. The injury, however, stubbornly refused to respond completely to treatment, finally causing cancellation of all further racing in the remaining months of the year.

The unexpected turn of events did not diminish the heroic achievements of Count Fleet during the previous six months. Certainly, they were not lost sight of when the balloting for year-end honors was conducted. There never was a doubt, and he was named Horse of the Year and Best Three-Year-Old. The tally was a testimonial of sorts in itself, for he received 135 out of a possible 143 votes from the sportswriters and broadcasters polled by *Turf and Sport Digest*. Confidence in his return to the track also remained high, especially with Hertz, who in January 1944 happily announced from Florida that the Count had recovered completely, that he would be entered "in enough handicaps to establish him further as a great horse," and that he would be retired in 1945. It was wishful thinking. July rolled around, and Don Cameron still had failed to bring the colt up to racing form. It was all too

Only Fairy Manhurst and Desoranto dare to challenge Count Fleet (center) in the 1943 Belmont Stakes.

The Belmont turns into a rout as Count Fleet charges to an incredible 25-length win. He beat War Admiral's stakes record by ⅖ of a second.

Proud owner Mrs. John D. Hertz takes "the Fleet" in hand for the parade to the winner's circle. The Belmont race was the last of his career because of the injury to his left fore ankle at the start of the race.

Official Chart of Belmont Stakes

SIXTH RACE
4 1 8 4 7
June 5-43—Bel

1 1-2 MILES (Main Course). (Bolingbroke, Sept. 26, 1942—2:27⅗ —5—115.) Seventy-Fifth Running BELMONT STAKES. $25,000 Added. 3-year-olds. Weight-for-age. (Geldings not eligible.)
Net value to winner $35,340; second, $5,000; third, $2,500.

Index	Horses	Eq't	A	Wt	PP	St	½	1	1¼	Str	Fin	Jockeys	Owners	Odds $1 Str't
(40971)	COUNT FLEET	wʙ		126	2	1	1⁸	1¹²	1²⁰	1²⁰	1²⁵	LongdenJ	Mrs John Hertz	.05
(41475)	FAIRY MANHURST	w		126	1	2	2½	2¹	2¹½	2¹	2¾	GilbertJ	Foxcatcher Farm	28.85
41475²	DESERONTO	wʙ		126	3	3	3	3	3	3	3	StoutJ	Beverley Bogert	52.70

Time, :23⅗, :48, 1:12⅗, 1:37⅘, 2:03⅗, 2:28⅕. Track fast.

Mutuel Prices {
COUNT FLEET .... 2.10 .... .05 ....
NO PLACE OR SHOW MUTUELS SOLD.

┌─$2 Mutuels Paid─┐ ┌─Odds to $1─┐

Winner—Br. c, by Reigh Count—Quickly, by Haste, trained by G. D. Cameron; bred by Mrs. John Hertz.
WENT TO POST—4:18. OFF AT 4:19 EASTERN WAR TIME.
Start good from stall gate. Won easily; second and third driving. COUNT FLEET outran his opposition from the start, drew into a long lead, was steadied along and was galloping through the stretch run. FAIRY MANHURST was under restraint and, under urging, outfinished DESERONTO. The latter was under pressure in the late stages, but had no mishaps.

apparent that the injury sustained in the Belmont race had created a splint that affected his ankle. Any further racing could aggravate the injury and perhaps cause more serious harm. Consequently, the trainer sadly recommended that Count Fleet be retired from racing for all time. The Fleet was beached.

He was retired to Stoner Creek Farm, where the skyrocket flared once more, this time to burn brightly for a long time. Count Fleet enjoyed a tremendously successful career as a stallion. Without solicitation or advertising upon his retirement, his stud book was filled with the names of 30 mares, and his stud fee was set at $1,500. The way things turned out, the price was a bargain. For example, in 1951 38 of his get were stakes winners, including Horse of the Year Counterpoint and Best Three-Year-Old Filly Kiss Me Kate. Additionally, he continued to dominate the 1951 Triple Crown races, as Count Turf, another of his standout sons, won the Kentucky Derby and Counterpoint took the Belmont Stakes.

The 1951 Derby also marked another unusual achievement. It was the first three-generation sweep of the event—Reigh Count (1928), Count Fleet (1943), and Count Turf (1951). Another measure of his importance as a sire was recorded in 1951, when John Hertz insured his prize stallion with Lloyds of London for $550,000, the largest policy ever written on any horse. The following year, One Count was named Horse of the Year, and by 1963, Count Fleet was acclaimed as the leading broodmare sire, as 88 stakes winners from his daughters included Kelso, Lamb Chop, Lucky Debonair, Quill, Tompion, Prince John, Fleet Nasrullah, and Furl Sail. Through 1972 he had 1,095 year-starters, sons or daughters who actually went to the post. His last crop was foaled in 1967.

Stoner Creek Farm, in the mid-sixties, was converted from a Thoroughbred nursery to a Standardbred breeding farm. At the time, it was stipulated that Count Fleet would live out his remaining days on the farm under the care of its manager, Charlie Kenney, and that he would be buried in the Stoner Creek graveyard. As the years went by, age seemed to embrace the great horse with grace. In the June 1971 issue of *Horsemen's Journal*, Dave Hooper was able to write a glowing report from information provided by Kenney: "He's quite sway-backed as an equine senior citizen. But he's very, very active for 31." Although he was retired from stud in 1966, he has "never lost his interest in the opposite sex. I guess he won't till he has all four feet in the grave. He still likes the girls very much. How do the French say it—he's still got that joie de vivre." Kenney further revealed that the horse had retained a dislike for the dark. "Mr. Hertz wouldn't let him stay out at night when Count Fleet was much younger. . . . We keep him out in the daytime from 7:30 until 4:00. And he still attracts a lot of sightseers."

On December 3, 1973, Count Fleet died at Stoner Creek Farm. He was 33 years old. Said *The New York Times'* Red Smith: "Under the weight of years his front legs gave out; he tried for a day or two to get up and, failing, slipped quietly away. . . ."

Assault

Assault
(chestnut colt) {
  Bold Venture {
    St. Germans
    Possible
  }
  Igual {
    Equipoise
    Incandescent
  }
}

| Chapter 7 |

Assault

~1946~

t had to happen sooner or later. It was inevitable that somewhere along the line a non-Kentucky-bred Thoroughbred would come along to challenge the three-year-old field for the Triple Crown. If he were to hail from a state other than Kentucky, it would have to be Texas, of course, where everything is proverbially bigger and better. The fact is, the state's first home-bred candidate for the Triple Crown was hardly that at the outset.

In the spring of 1943, on March 26, a chestnut colt was born to the mare Igual, a daughter of Equipoise, on the fabulous King Ranch at Kingsville, Texas. His sire was Bold Venture, winner of the Kentucky Derby and the Preakness in 1936, and his grandam was a full sister of Man o' War. The foal was named Assault. It is remarkable that he ever was born. His dam, as a foal on the ranch, was so sickly and unpromising that serious consideration was given to having her destroyed. She was saved by the intercession of the ranch's veterinarian, Dr. J. K. Northway, who discovered an abscess under her stifle, which apparently affected her whole condition. He prevailed on owner Robert J. Kleberg Jr. to allow him to treat the horse. The good doctor succeeded in curing her, but she never recovered to racing form. Instead, she was prepared for breeding.

Her first two foals were not much to brag about, hardly a recommendation for a bright future. On the third try, to the cover of Bold Venture, she produced Assault. Unlike his dam, the weanling displayed a frisky, frolicsome personality, which was almost his undoing. On one of his gambols around the ranch, he stepped on a sharp stake and ran it through the front wall of the hoof of his right foreleg, half crippling himself. Once more the doctor's

127

A close-up of Assault's forelegs, showing the malformation of his right hoof.

skill was tested, and once again he succeeded. The injury, though, was like a damaged fingernail that heals with a deformation. The foot never did grow to normal size, causing the colt to develop a peculiar walk. In fact, the wall of the hoof became so thin that it was difficult to find room enough to anchor a nail for shoeing, a ticklish problem that remained with the horse for the rest of his days. It was, in a sense, a reminder of Sir Barton, whose soft hooves made it difficult for him to keep his shoes on.

Trainer Max Hirsch was less than bullish on Assault after seeing his game leg: "When he came up from Texas, I didn't think he'd train at all. When he walked and trotted you'd think he was going to fall down. It wasn't hurting him any more but he'd gotten in the habit of favoring and protecting it with an awkward gait." Some unsympathetic observers thought the horse was clubfooted, which accounts for why he later was nicknamed "the Clubfooted Comet." However, at that early point in his career, when Hirsch had to start preparing him for his two-year-old season, it must have been a rather disheartening prospect for the trainer, especially when he could look back a few years to the glory days of Bold Venture.

The old adages might well have been applied to Assault: "looks are deceiving," and "if at first you fail, try, try again." The colt made his first start at Belmont Park, on June 4, 1945, and finished 12th in a field of maidens. It was not until his fourth start, at Aqueduct on July 12, that he won his first race. In fact, he ran nine times that year, won only once more, finished in the money just three times, and wound up with total winnings of only $17,250. Most of this total was earned in his sixth race, the Flash Stakes, on August 6, when he won a purse of $11,505. Prior to then, he had chalked up only one victory in five starts, in an allowance event. In the Flash, which was one of the races of the Saratoga meet but was held at Belmont because of the restrictions on travel imposed by World War II, he went to the post for the five-and-a-half-furlong event as a ridiculous 70-1 shot. The track was muddy, which may have had some bearing on the outcome. It was an improbable four-horse photo finish, each just noses apart, and Assault was awarded the victory to the astonishment of owner, trainer, jockey, and fans. Mist o' Gold was placed second, and Mush Mush third. Anyone who had been brave enough to bet on the Texas colt wound up with a tidy $443.20 payoff for a $2 bet. About the only other factor that could be pointed to as noteworthy is that the victory came on the very day America dropped the first atom bomb on Japan, on the city of Hiroshima.

Assault's last race of the year was at Jamaica, on October 8, after which he was shipped to Columbia, South Carolina, to winter. The general appraisal for the year was that the horse, despite a rather uninspiring record, ran well enough to try again.

The first two starts of 1946 provided some hopeful rays. He took the six-furlong Experimental Free Handicap at Jamaica on April 9, by four and a half lengths, even though he was at 9-1 odds. Next, he captured the important 1⅛-mile Wood Memorial on April 20, by two and a quarter lengths, this time going off at somewhat less than 9-1. Winning this race was particularly heartening because it is the first big event for three-year-olds before the Kentucky Derby. The elation was quickly dampened, and his chances for the classic notably dimmed, when he followed the Wood with a loss in the Derby Trial at Churchill Downs by a four-length margin. Bandages and a muddy track were given as excuses for the poor showing. "Assault had a tendency to strike himself, and usually ran with small adhesive bandages inside his hocks, and

Assault leads 16 straining opponents across the finish line at the end of the 1946 Kentucky Derby. An 8-1 underdog, he won by eight lengths over Spy Song in a classic come-from-behind run.

a long one down his left cannon in front," wrote Joe Palmer in *American Race Horses*. "For the Derby Trial Hirsch also added 'Oregon Boots' on Assault's hind legs, and once these got properly water-soaked and filled with mud, Assault had little chance."

The explanation failed to allay the apprehension of turf fans, and he went to the post on Derby Day at long odds, 8-to-1, behind the favorites, Lord Boswell, Knockdown, and Perfect Bahram. There was an extra measure of excitement in the air as the field came out on the track. This was the first Derby with a $100,000-added purse, making it the richest race of the series to date. With Warren Mehrtens in the saddle, Assault settled into fifth position among the 17 straining horses at the first turn. In the backstretch, he moved up to third place, but only because some of the other horses had dropped back.

It was at the ¼ pole that Mehrtens made his Run for the Roses. He pushed his colt hard along the rail. Assault responded by moving to the lead at the ⅛ pole and continuing his drive until he crossed the finish line an astonishing eight lengths ahead of Spy Song. Lord Boswell ran well out of the picture. The classic come-from-behind run confounded everyone, including his backers, who were paid off handsomely; his owner, who picked up first-prize money of $96,400; and Warren Mehrtens, who chalked up his first Derby win. The

Trainer Max Hirsch with Assault and jockey Warren Mehrtens in the winner's circle at Churchill Downs.

Official Chart of the Kentucky Derby

SEVENTH RACE
9 7 5 9 5
May 4-46—C.D

1 1-4 MILES. (Whirlaway, May 3, 1941—2:01⅖—3—126.) Seventy-Second Running KENTUCKY DERBY. $100,000 Added. 3-year-olds. Weight, the scale. (Owner of winner to receive a Gold Trophy. Trainers of the winner, second and third horses to receive $3,000, $2,000 and $1,000, respectively, of the added money, and the breeders of the winner, second and third horses to receive $2,000, $1,000 and $500, respectively, of the added money, whether or not they are the owners of the horses when the race is run.
Net value to winner $96,400; second, $10,000; third, $5,000; fourth, $2,500. Mutuel Pool, $1,202,474.

Index	Horses	Eq't	A	Wt	PP	St	½	¾	1	Str	Fin	Jockeys	Owners	Odds to $1
97370	ASSAULT	wb		126	2	3	5½	4^{h}	3½	$1^{2\frac{1}{2}}$	1^{8}	W Mehrtens	King Ranch	8.20
97370^{2}	SPY SONG	w		126	6	2	1^{2}	1½	1½	2^{2}	2^{h}	J Longden	Dixiana	7.80
(97226)	HAMPDEN	wb		126	17	14	6^{1}	5^{h}	$4^{2\frac{1}{2}}$	5^{2}	3^{1}	J Jessop	Foxcatcher Farm	5.80
(97136)	LORD BOSWELL	w		126	3	1	9½	7½	$9^{1\frac{1}{2}}$	3½	$4^{1\frac{1}{2}}$	E Arcaro	Maine Chance Farm	a-1.10
95332	KNOCKDOWN	w		126	11	4	2½	2½	$2^{1\frac{1}{2}}$	4½	5^{4}	R Permane	Maine Chance Farm	a-1.10
97370	ALAMOND	wb		126	7	8	11½	8½	11^{2}	6^{1}	6^{1}	A Kirkland	A C Ernst	65.30
97136	BOB MURPHY	wb		126	13	16	13½	11½	6^{2}	7½	7½	A Bodiou	D Ferguson	f-31.80
97136^{2}	PELLICLE	wb		126	8	11	12^{2}	9½	8^{h}	8^{h}	$8^{1\frac{1}{2}}$	G Hettinger	H P Headley	16.10
(97324)	PERFECT BAHRAM	w		126	5	12	15^{3}	13^{2}	10½	11½	9½	T Atkinson	Maine Chance Farm	a-1.10
(97370)	RIPPEY	w		126	14	7	4^{h}	6^{1}	5^{h}	9^{1}	10^{1}	F Zufelt	W Helis	10.20
97226	JOBAR	w		126	16	17	17	17	16^{4}	16^{4}	$11^{1\frac{1}{2}}$	J R Layton	H W Fielding	f-31.80
(97135)	DARK JUNGLE	wb		126	12	6	$3^{1\frac{1}{2}}$	3^{h}	7½	10½	12^{2}	A LoTurco	Lucas B Combs	60.70
97324^{3}	ALWORTH	wb		126	4	10	10^{1}	12^{1}	13^{h}	13^{3}	13½	O Scurlock	Mrs R D Patterson	f-31.80
97370^{3}	WITH PLEASURE	wb		126	10	9	7½	10^{1}	14^{2}	14^{2}	$14^{1\frac{1}{2}}$	C Wahler	Brolite Farm	48.30
97370	MARINE VICTORY	wb		126	15	15	14^{1}	14^{3}	15^{3}	15½	15^{1}	D Padgett	Bobanet Stable	45.00
97370	WEE ADMIRAL	wb		126	9	5	$8^{1\frac{1}{2}}$	16^{1}	12½	12^{2}	16^{3}	R Watson	R S McLaughlin	59.40
97136	KENDOR	wb		126	1	13	16^{6}	15^{1}	17	17	17	W L J'nson	Mrs D M Hollingsworth	f-31.80

a-Coupled, Lord Boswell, Knockdown and Perfect Bahram. f-Mutuel field.

Time, :12, :23⅖, :35⅖, :48, 1:01⅕, 1:14⅕, 1:27⅖, 1:40⅘, 1:53⅗, 2:06⅗. Track slow.

Mutuel Prices	$2 Mutuels Paid			Odds to $1		
ASSAULT	18.40	9.60	6.80	8.20	3.80	2.40
SPY SONG		9.00	6.60		3.50	2.30
HAMPDEN			5.20			1.60

Winner—Ch. c, by Bold Venture—Igual, by Equipoise, trained by M. Hirsch; bred by King Ranch.

WENT TO POST—5:17. OFF AT 5:20 CENTRAL DAYLIGHT TIME.

Start good from stall gate. Won driving; second and third the same. ASSAULT, forwardly placed and saving ground from the beginning, came through on the inside entering the stretch, quickly disposed of SPY SONG and drew out to win with little left. SPY SONG assumed command early, made the pace until reaching the stretch, then gave way to the winner, but continued resolutely to hold HAMPDEN. The latter, on the extreme outside at the beginning, raced in the middle of the track the entire trip, was pulled up sharply when his rider misjudged the finish, then came again when roused, but could not better his position. LORD BOSWELL, in hand for six furlongs, was blocked near the upper turn, came again when clear, but could not overhaul the leaders when hard ridden through the stretch. KNOCKDOWN forced the pace to the mile, then gave way. ALAMOND, on the outside for the drive, failed to rally under punishment. BOB MURPHY, also on the outside entering the stretch, could not threaten. PELLICLE raced evenly and had no excuse. PERFECT BAHRAM lacked his usual early speed and was never dangerous. RIPPEY could not keep up after displaying brief speed. JOBAR began slowly. DARK JUNGLE was through after six furlongs. ALWORTH was always far back. WITH PLEASURE could not threaten and tired badly. MARINE VICTORY was never a serious factor. WEE ADMIRAL had speed for a half mile, then gave way. KENDOR was overmatched.

slow track resulted in the unimpressive time of 2:06⅘, but the victory reversed a year-and-a-half-long trend in Assault's career. He had won not only one of the most prestigious classic races in turfdom, but also his biggest purse. Suddenly he was respectable.

The proof of that respect was all too clear at Pimlico, where he suddenly found himslef the favorite, at 7-5—the first time in his life that he had been so honored. It was a particularly startling development because through most of the spring he had been going off at long odds. Lord Boswell, conversely, was cast as the runner-up at a little less than 2-1. The 1946, 71ˢᵗ running of the Preakness, like the Derby, also had a new look as it, too, moved into the $100,000-added-purse bracket. Consequently, both new price and purse appeared to be sufficient motivation for greater efforts by the Texas Thoroughbred.

They were, but the colt's performance was enough to give his backers fits. First, he was hampered through the first ⅟₁₆ of a mile, when Natchez veered in toward the rail. Then his jockey made him move too soon to recoup his position. "Mehrtens may have been a bit scared, and he made up the lost ground quickly. When he asked Assault for his run, a little earlier than in the Derby, the colt came with a burst which carried him four lengths out from the field at the furlong pole, but then he had nothing left," wrote Joe Palmer. Lord Boswell put on a "frightening display of finishing power" in the stretch. "When Mehrtens hit him, as the challenge materialized, Assault ducked in badly, so the jockey, afraid to hit him again, hand-rode and hoped for the finish line." He just barely won by a neck. The race was exciting; the time was not very good—2:01⅖; the purse was substantial—$96,620.

As for Assault's admirers, a noticeable chill developed between him and them. According to many, the Preakness showed a chink in Assault's armor. They discounted his spectacular showing in the Derby and suggested that the slow times in both races established the colt's inability to finish well at distance. Therefore, mindful of the grueling 1½-mile grind that faced him in the Belmont Stakes on June 1, they dropped him out of the favorite's spot, although not by much, and rated him at 7-to-5 behind Lord Boswell, who was at a little less than that.

Six other starters went to the post at Belmont, and Assault promptly made them all look good as he stumbled at the bell. But he righted himself quickly, and Mehrtens, feeling him running with his old power, held him back, biding his time, refusing to fall into the same trap as in the Preakness. Down the

Assault barely wins the 1946 Preakness by a neck over Lord Boswell. Hampden is third. The race was the first of Assault's career in which he was favored.

Official Chart of Preakness

SIXTH RACE
9 8 0 2 4
May 11-46—Pim

1 3-16 MILES. (Riverland, May 1, 1943—1:56⅖—5—123.) Fifty-Sixth Running PREAKNESS STAKES. $100,000 Added. 3-year-olds. Weight-for-age. (All eligibility, entrance and starting fees to the winner, with $100,000 added, of which $20,000 to second, $10,000 to third and $5,000 to fourth. The nominator of the winner to receive $2,500; the nominator of the second horse, $1,000; and the nominator of the third horse $500 of the added money.)

Net value to winner $96,620; second, $20,000; third, $10,000; fourth, $5,000. Mutuel Pool, $446,140.

Index	Horses	Eq't A Wt	PP	St	½	¾	1	Str	Fin	Jockeys	Owners	Odds to $1
(97595)	ASSAULT	wb 126	5	6	6¹½	3h	1¹½	1⁴	1ⁿᵏ	W Mehrtens	King Ranch	1.40
97595	LORD BOSWELL	w 126	2	7	9⁶	6½	4¹	2½	2³½	D Dodson	Maine Chance Farm	a-2.25
97595³	HAMPDEN	wb 126	4	5	5¹	4¹½	3²	3¹½	3⁴	E Arcaro	Foxcatcher Farm	3.00
97595	KNOCKDOWN	w 126	3	4	4¹	5²	5h	5h	4¹½	R Permane	Maine Chance Farm	a-2.25
97595	ALAMOND	wb 126	8	9	7½	8⁴	6⁶	6⁵	5³	K Scawth'n	A C Ernst	67.35
97226²	NATCHEZ	wb 126	9	2	2¹	1h	2¹½	4²	6⁴	J Gilbert	Mrs W M Jeffords	22.60
97784²	LOVEMENOW	wb 126	6	8	8²	9⁵	8²	7²	7³	A Snider	Cedar Farm	10.75
97595	WEE ADMIRAL	wb 126	1	1	3h	7½	9⁶	8⁴	8³	N Wall	R S McLaughlin	42.55
97595	MARINE VICT'RY	wb 126	7	10	10	10	10	10	9⁵	D Padgett	Bobanet Stable	30.15
97226	TIDY BID	wb 126	10	3	1²	2½	7½	9¹	10	S Clark	W Helis	34.75

a-Coupled, Lord Boswell and Knockdown.

Time, :12⅕, :23⅖, :35⅖, :48, 1:00⅖, 1:13, 1:27⅖, 1:40, 1:54⅖, 2:01¼. Track fast.

Mutuel Prices

	—$2 Mutuels Paid—			—Odds to $1—		
ASSAULT	4.80	3.10	2.20	1.40	.55	.10
LORD BOSWELL (a-Entry)	3.10	2.20		.55	.10	
HAMPDEN			2.30			.15

Winner—Ch. c, by Bold Venture—Igual, by Equipoise, trained by M. Hirsch; bred by King Ranch.

WENT TO POST—4:57. OFF AT 4:57½ EASTERN STANDARD TIME.

Start good from stall gate. Won ridden out; second and third driving. ASSAULT, well handled while escaping trouble soon after the start, rallied well when called upon, circled the leader while forging to the front leaving the backstretch, drew clear rapidly on the turn and was ridden out through the final sixteenth. LORD BOSWELL, sluggish early, worked way into contention gradually, drove between horses entering the stretch and closed with a late rush to be getting to the winner. HAMPDEN, always forwardly placed, was in close quarters briefly when ASSAULT moved on the outside of him, followed ASSAULT while moving into contention, then hung in the drive. KNOCKDOWN raced prominently placed throughout, but was not good enough. ALAMOND, shuffled back when NATCHEZ moved over at the break, took the overland route throughout and could not seriously threaten. NATCHEZ cut across sharply at the start, disposed of TIDY BID for the lead, then weakened. LOVEMENOW showed nothing. WEE ADMIRAL was pinched back at the first turn and failed to recover. MARINE VICTORY was outdistanced. TIDY BID had early speed, but quit.

Scratched—96393² Billy Bumps, 126.

backstretch, they held fourth position some five lengths behind the front-running Natchez. Once again, at the ⅛ pole, Mehrtens called on the colt to show his mettle and, once more, the Thoroughbred responded in stirring fashion. Between the furlong pole and the finish line, he closed the gap and tacked on a three-length lead. Lord Boswell never challenged, coming in a poor fifth. It was another exciting race but, again, the time was unspectacular—2:30⅘.

For trainer and owner, the win was all that mattered. Assault was the new Triple Crown champion, the first from Texas. He had picked up another hefty purse, $75,400, and had run his total winnings from the "three jewels" to $268,420, an astronomical figure when compared to the $57,275 earned by Sir Barton in the same three races 27 years earlier.

Two weeks later, on June 15, Assault ran his winning streak to four straight by taking the Dwyer Handicap at Aqueduct, four and a half lengths to the

Assault, on the rail, stumbles at the start of the Belmont Stakes.

Assault beats Natchez by three lengths after catching him at the furlong pole to win the 1946 Belmont Stakes.

good. He had been the odds-on favorite at 2-to-5 and had run his by now typical race, sitting back at the early stages and then making his charge. His time was still slow, 2:06⅗, which prompted the experts to conclude that Assault was merely the best of another poor crop of three-year-olds. The appraisal gained substance on July 27, in Chicago, when he finished sixth and last in the Arlington Classic. He started fast and then went dull. Every time Mehrtens used his whip, the horse seemed to fall back. It was a puzzling performance that mystified everyone until he was back in the barn. There, in obvious pain, he was forced to lie down in his stall. Medical tests soon pinpointed the cause. It was a kidney infection, which necessitated his withdrawal from action for a month.

The interruption of his training started an unfortunate chain reaction. For a while, he just could not win a race. Assault returned to the campaign trail on September 7, in the Discovery Handicap at Aqueduct. The Triple Crown champion was promptly ruled the favorite, at 7-to-10, and asked to give away weight. He carried 126 pounds, to 115 by Mighty Story and 112 by Mahout. Although he came in third, he ran with something of his old determination, so the loss was accepted as the result of his long layoff and the extra weight. The following week, though, he lost in the Jersey Handicap by a half-length as he gave Mahout 12 pounds.

Left to right: owner Robert J. Kleberg Jr., jockey Warren Mehrtens, trainer Max Hirsch, and Mrs. Kleberg enjoy the victory around the Belmont Stakes trophy. Assault was the first Texas-bred horse to win the Triple Crown.

Official Chart of Belmont Stakes

SIXTH RACE
9 9 5 3 0
June 1-46—Bel

1 1-2 MILES. (Bolingbroke, Sept 26, 1942—2:27$\frac{3}{5}$—5—115.) Seventy-Eighth Running BELMONT STAKES. $100,000 Added. 3-year olds. Scale weight. Colts, 126 lbs.; fillies, 121 lbs. (Nominators of the winner, of the second and third horses to receive $2,000, $1,000 and $500, respectively. Geldings not eligible.)

Net value to winner $75,400; second, $20,000; thmird, $10,000; fourth, $5,000; owners of starters other than first four horses, $20 each. Mutuel Pool, $640,495.

Index	Horses	Eq't A Wt	PP	St	½	1	1¼	Str	Fin	Jockeys	Owners	Odds to $1
(98024)	ASSAULT	wb 126	1	7	4^2	4^h	3^2	$3^{1\frac{1}{2}}$	1^3	W Mehrtens	King Ranch	1.40
98390^2	NATCHEZ	wb 126	6	3	2^3	2^2	$2^{1\frac{1}{2}}$	1^2	2^2	C McCreary	Mrs W M Jeffords	a-8.60
98850	CABLE	w 126	2	1	7	7	4^h	$4^{\frac{1}{2}}$	3^h	T Atkinson	Mrs A Wichfeld	45.50
(98390)	HAMPDEN	wb 126	7	5	1^{nk}	1^2	1^2	2^h	$4^{\frac{1}{2}}$	E Arcaro	Foxcatcher Farm	3.75
98850^2	LORD BOSWELL	w 126	5	4	5^1	5^2	5^2	5^8	5^5	E Guerin	Maine Chance Farm	1.35
(98850)	MAHOUT	w 126	4	2	6^h	$6^{\frac{1}{2}}$	6^4	6^2	6^h	J Longden	Mrs W M Jeffords	a-8.60
98850	WAR WATCH	wb 126	3	6	3^2	3^4	7	7	7	A Scotti	Mrs A Roberts	92.80

a-Coupled, Natchez and Mahout.

Time, :24$\frac{4}{5}$, :49$\frac{3}{5}$, 1:14$\frac{1}{5}$, 1:39$\frac{2}{5}$, 2:04, 2:30$\frac{4}{5}$. Track fast.

Mutuel Prices	$2 Mutuels Paid			Odds to $1		
ASSAULT	4.80	3.10	2.70	1.40	.55	.35
NATCHEZ (a-Entry)		5.70	4.10		1.85	1.05
CABLE			6.50			2.25

Winner—Ch. c, by Bold Venture—Igual, by Equipoise, trained by M. Hirsch; bred by King Ranch.

WENT TO POST—4:40. OFF AT 4:40 EASTERN DAYLIGHT TIME.

Start good from stall gate. Won driving; second and third the same. ASSAULT stumbled at the start but recovered quickly, was sent up on the inside, was steadied along to the far turn, where he began to improve his position, came to the outside for the stretch run, swerved slightly, disposed of the leaders and drew away. NATCHEZ bore out slightly rounding the far turn, was straightened out, moved up entering the stretch turn, assumed command, but could not stave off the winner. CABLE was steadied along, was well up under pressure in the stretch run and closed with good courage. HAMPDEN was sent into command after the first quarter, was steadied along and had no mishap. LORD BOSWELL was taken under steady restraint in the early running, improved his position going to the far turn, but flattened out when placed under pressure in the final furlong. MAHOUT was unable to improve his position in the stretch run. WAR WATCH raced evenly and was never a formidable factor.

Scratched—98850 Cedar Creek, 126; 98850^3 Manor Lad, 126; (99177) Windfields, 126.

In his next race, he moved out of his three-year-old division for the first time to run against older horses in the 1½-mile Manhattan Handicap at Belmont Park on September 25, 1946. His reputation preceded him, for here too he was asked to give up weight to the field as he was burdened with 116 pounds, the equivalent of 124 pounds on older horses. The event marked the first of Assault's series of bitterly waged battles with the vaunted Stymie. The race was won by Stymie, who carried 126 pounds, as Assault wound up in a dead heat for third. The losing streak continued into the Roamer Handicap on October 19, when the filly Bridal Flower, with an 8-pound advantage, beat him by half a length. On October 26, it was back to the older horses in the Gallant Fox Handicap. Assault carried 114 pounds, the equivalent of 121 pounds for those out of his division. Stymie, with 126 pounds, was his nemesis one more time, catching him in the stretch as he fell to third place.

This defeat, though, was blamed on the jockey. The verdict was that Mehrtens had lost faith in the horse and was unwilling to ride him to his fullest capabilities. Trainer Max Hirsch was convinced that a change of jockeys was imperative, and he called in Eddie Arcaro to ride in the important winner-take-all Pimlico Special November 1. Hirsch made no bones about his determination and his confidence in the horse's ability to win: "This horse can beat Stymie at any distance . . . two miles . . . four miles." Then he spelled out just what Arcaro was to do: "You watch Stymie," he ordered. He then told Arcaro to hold up making any move with Assault, regardless of what the other horses in the field were doing, until he saw Stymie come up on him. Arcaro obeyed and, as soon as Stymie crept alongside, he drove his mount and won the race. The result was a regeneration of some of the lost faith in the horse. He ran once more in 1946, in the Westchester Handicap on November 9, won it by two lengths, and wound up the year with eight firsts out of 15 starts.

As Assault retired for the winter, the racing experts scratched their heads in trying to evaluate him. There was no gainsaying that he had had a spectacular year. The colt had captured the Triple Crown against all odds and had surpassed Gallant Fox's record of $308,275 by winning $424,195—the most ever by a Thoroughbred in one year. Yet, more than three-fourths of the total had been won in only three races with very large purses. His times were rather slow, and he was considered a poor risk in distance races. Then again, he had given away considerable weight advantages to older horses and had even mastered Stymie. Furthermore, as the year progressed, his times improved. As Joe Palmer put it, he "was flying in the fall." Thus, in summing up, the writers found that the positives outweighed the negatives and voted him Horse of the Year. Still, he lacked charisma and failed to generate excitement. The consensus, again according to Palmer, was that against three-year-olds he was "good, maybe, but not great." He would have to show a lot more the next year.

Assault, himself, seemed to be aware of this and was giving signs that he was doing something about the matter. Early in 1946, he was a sort of matter-of-fact horse, but he appeared to gain more confidence as the year wore on and he won important races. Suddenly, he was all business when he went to the track. In the barn, however, it was another thing. He became a character, pulling off high jinks that dismayed his handlers and that would never have been tolerated with an ordinary horse. His enormous appetite was a case in point. "He's perpetually hungry," trainer Hirsch would lament. No groom would dare to enter his stall without first giving him a mouthful of grain out of a feed tub. When he was particularly hungry, he would create such a commotion in the barn that he would force an earlier feeding to avoid the possibility of his injuring himself as he stomped about in his stall, let alone upsetting all of the other horses.

Then, too, he began to develop physically. Although not a big horse, standing just above 15 hands, he looked to have grown over the winter from a rather plain but substantial three-year-old into a very handsome four-year-old. When the spring of 1947 rolled around, he gave the illusion of being taller than he really was. Most important of all, there was no mistaking that he was a more assured Thoroughbred.

Two factors dominated the thinking of racing fans as the 1947 turf campaign prepared to swing into action. It was apparent that, as a result of handicap purses becoming increasingly inflated, year-end honors would very likely be determined by the amount of money earned. It was equally obvious that the year would see this goal challenged by three Thoroughbreds: Robert J. Kleberg's four-year-old Assault, Warren Wright's five-year-old gelding Armed, and Hirsch Jacobs' six-year-old Stymie—each of whose earnings gave any of the horses a clear shot at surpassing Whirlaway's world record.

Assault began his junior year like a demon possessed, reeling off five straight victories, seven in all if his last two wins in 1946 are included. The first was in the 1⅛-mile Grey Lag Handicap at Jamaica on May 3, just one year after he had won the Kentucky Derby. Carrying 128 pounds and jockey Warren Mehrtens, he beat Let's Dance, who carried only 110 pounds, by a neck in 1:49⅘. Stymie, with 126 pounds, did not even place. On May 9, it was the Dixie Handicap at Pimlico, with Eddie Arcaro up. His margin of victory was a half-length, as he bested Rico Monte, to whom he had given 9 pounds. The time for the 1³⁄₁₆ miles was 1:57⅖, an improvement over his winning time in the Preakness on the same track the year before. Two weeks later, he came out for the Suburban Handicap at Belmont saddled with 130 pounds to Stymie's 126. It was a fantastic victory. With Arcaro riding, he reached the stretch in second place, some six lengths behind Natchez, yet he flashed over the last ¹⁄₁₆ of a mile to beat him by two lengths, and Stymie by eight. The fourth victory in the skein, the Brooklyn Handicap, on June

Assault slashes across the finish line at Aqueduct two lengths in front of archrival Stymie to take the Brooklyn Handicap. The victory was the fourth in a row at the start of Assault's fourth year of racing. It also boosted his earnings past Whirlaway's world record.

21, was a milestone for the colt. Forced to carry 133 pounds to Stymie's 124, he again waited for his archrival to make his move before he streaked to a three-length win. The victor's purse was worth $38,100, which boosted Assault's total earnings to $576,670, thereby surpassing Whirlaway's existing world record of $561,161.

Later on, the picture of Assault and Stymie charging one-two down the homestretch was to take on special significance. It was the first time in the history of Thoroughbred racing that a horse had ever crossed the finish line as "the world's leading money-winner hotly pursued by one who would displace him twice."

"By now, Assault looked like the best horse in training. He had given weight and beating to everything in the East, and if ever there was a horse to run with him it would have to be Calumet Farm's Armed," wrote Joe Palmer when reviewing the 1947 racing scene. Armed, since the beginning of the year, had been creating his own excitement. He had picked up purses totaling $100,000 in two races early in the year. These continued his brilliant record from 1946, when he had won 11 out of 18 races, been unplaced in only one, and had earned $288,725. Overall, in his three years of racing through 1946, his winnings amounted to $385,175, making him the richest gelding in history. He was so good that in 1946, his fourth year, he had never failed to get part of the purse in 36 consecutive races. By the end of June 1947, he had run his total winnings to $487,775.

Stymie, on the other hand, had not been standing by idly. Through 1946, in four years of campaigning, he had amassed winnings of $546,285. After his loss to Assault in the Brooklyn Handicap, he went on to win two races, the second of which was the Sussex Handicap, on July 5, and which pushed him ahead of Assault as the new money-leader, with $595,500. The reign was short, only one week, as he lost to Assault in the $50,000-added Butler Handicap. The victory and loss were both tough, but for the winner it brought new respect. Coming into the homestretch, Assault was wedged between Stymie and Gallorette. It seemed for sure that he was trapped and slated to lose. However, jockey Arcaro touched his whip to him, and the colt bolted through a virtually impossible opening to win by a head over Stymie. This fifth consecutive triumph was all the more remarkable because the Texas colt carried the heaviest impost of his career, 135 pounds, as compared to Stymie's 126. First prize amounted to $36,700, and Assault moved back into first place as his earnings total soared to $613,370.

It was the pinnacle of Assault's career. A week later, the winning streak came to an end in the International Gold Cup at Belmont Park. This time, his usual strategy against Stymie and Natchez failed. He waited for Stymie's move while Natchez set the pace, but he ran out of steam in the stretch. Nevertheless, the third-place finish was good for $10,000, which narrowly preserved Assault's money-winning position.

While all of the leap-frogging went on between Assault and Stymie, the call could be heard from the fans for a match race between Assault and Armed, obviously the two most exciting horses of the year. Negotiations began in the middle of July between Warren Wright and Robert J. Kleberg Jr. The plan was to stage the match at Washington Park in Chicago, Illinois, on August 30, for a purse of $100,000, which would enable either one of the horses to achieve top money-winning honors. The race was then called off when Assault injured his right foreleg. It was rescheduled for September 27 at Belmont Park, under the auspices of Joseph E. Widener, who had figured so prominently in trying to set up the $100,000 match race between War Admiral and Seabiscuit in 1937.

However, the race seemed destined for trouble. On September 22, after a workout, Assault suddenly walked lame. Trainer Hirsch suspected an old splint on the left foreleg was acting up, but the ailment seemingly healed soon. They watched it carefully for three days. Because of the uncertainty, things reached a pass where all of the principals were unhappy about continuing with the race. However, they felt obligated to the public. Kleberg finally issued a candid statement: "Because of the great public interest and long preparation for the race, we have decided to run Assault and hope he will be at his best." He then told of the colt's miseries: "In an ordinary stakes or other race," he continued, "I doubt that I should start him." Then, Wright and Kleberg agreed that neither would hold the purse if their horse won. Rather, they would split it up between the Red Cross and the Damon Runyon Cancer Research Foundation. Finally, it was decided that no betting would be allowed on the race, that it would be only an exhibition. There was so much confusion that even the ASPCA got into the act, showing up at the track on the morning of the race to demand proof that Assault was in condition to run and was not being abused.

Armed was favored at 1-to-3, with Assault at 7-5. It was a hollow victory for the gelding, who won by eight lengths as Eddie Arcaro eased Assault when he found that his horse could not keep up with the winner. It was an equally

The gelding Armed beats Assault by eight lengths in their match race at Belmont Park on September 27, 1947. The loss was attributed to a leg injury. Before the race, the ASPCA had demanded proof that the colt was in condition to run.

sad ending to an otherwise glorious year for the Triple Crown champion. He did not race again in 1947, and lost out to Armed for Horse of the Year honors, to the bitter recriminations of his handlers.

The gelding took the Sysonby Handicap on October 9, won $18,000, and became the leading money-winner of the year with $376,325. His grand total was $761,500. Stymie, on the other hand, cracked the world's mark with total earnings of $846,060. Assault's record for the year was equally respectable, including five victories in seven starts, one second, one third, and winnings of $181,925. His total at the end of the year was $623,370, and twice during the year he had been the world's leading money-winner. Max Hirsch was thoroughly disgusted by the voting. He was particularly angry because he felt that Assault had been penalized unjustly for having run two bad races at the end of the season. "You'd think my horse wasn't worth 15 cents," he groused.

Assault was shipped to Columbia, South Carolina, for rest and treatment of his leg splints. He made his first start in 1948 in the Widener Handicap, only to finish fifth. The result convinced his owner that the time for retirement had arrived, and the colt was sent to the King Ranch's Kentucky stud farm. A routine chemical analysis of his semen disclosed the sad fact that the horse was sterile. Two weeks later, a second check was made, which substantiated the first report, and the colt thereupon was returned to Texas.

By August, Assault showed sufficient improvement in his physical condition to prompt a return to racing. His preparation continued into the following spring, and his first start in 1949 was at Aqueduct on June 24. He lost by a nose. On July 2, though, he raised some hopes by taking the Brooklyn Handicap and the $40,600 purse. Then, on August 13, he finished fourth in the Massachusetts Handicap and was bleeding from a nostril. A brief rest healed the problem, enabling him to race in the Edgemere Handicap at Aqueduct on September 10. He came in third. It was after he ran seventh in the Manhattan Handicap on September 24 and eighth in the Grey Lag Handicap on October 15, bleeding again following the latter race, that the announcement went out that Assault would be retired for the second time.

However, the story of America's seventh Triple Crown champion still had a few more interesting wrinkles. In 1950, he was allowed to run out with a band of young quarter horse mares and got four of them in foal, which raised not a few eyebrows, especially among the breeders at the King Ranch. They felt so good about the news that they even brought out Assault for races in his seventh year. He ran in three, winning one, placing in another, and losing the third, earning $2,950. These were his very final flings on the turf. He was retired for keeps thereafter.

Dr. Northway, in a letter dated August 2, 1971, explained what had happened:

> As you know (and which is rather known throughout the Thoroughbred horse breeders) Assault did prove sterile, and has continued sterile to Thoroughbred mares and also to each examination of semen sent to many of the best veterinarians in the field. He was retired here and has remained sterile, with the exception (nobody knows from a genetic standpoint) when mated to young open Quarter mares, he did succeed in settling four out of eight from natural service in the pasture. We were very much elated over

Venerable Triple Crown champion Assault at age 22 in retirement on the King Ranch in Texas. He was put to sleep six years later after fracturing his leg in a fall.

the outcome as he produced two fillies and two colts from these eight mares. We sent him to California to give him a chance to increase his winnings. . . . He is now definitely retired here on the ranch and is living happily and in good condition for his age. His appetite is good (he is fed twice a day) and he has a good pasture in which to exercise. He is quite a pet to all of the owners and to all who know him . . . this grand old champion horse.

Alas, the end came on September 2, 1971. The 28-year-old stallion stumbled and fractured his left front leg near the shoulder. Time had run out on him. The good Dr. Northway had no panacea for him this time, so he put him to sleep. The story of Assault thus ended almost the way it began.

Citation

and trainer Jimmy Jones

Citation (bay colt)	Bull Lea	Bull Dog
		Rose Leaves
	Hydroplane II	Hyperion
		Toboggan

| Chapter 8 |

Citation
~1948~

I t could be said that the squire of Calumet Farm, Warren Wright Sr., had a sixth sense for making the right buy at the right time. In 1936, while in the process of converting his breeding farm from trotters to Thoroughbreds, he was instrumental in organizing a syndicate that went to England for a top stallion and came home with Blenheim II. The result was Whirlaway. That same year, at the Saratoga Sales, he picked up a real buy when he paid $14,000 for the colt Bull Lea. By the time the horse entered stud, after a fairly successful racing career, Whirlaway was the number one stallion on the farm, enjoying the pick of the best mares. This created a need for a choice mare to accommodate Bull Lea.

To fill the void, Wright went to England once more and purchased Hydroplane II from Lord Derby's stable. It was the spring of 1941, and the British and Nazi Germany were at war. Wright wanted the mare badly but did not want to see his investment lost because of a U-boat's torpedo. Therefore he arranged for the mare to be shipped to America via the safer Pacific route. She arrived in July. Her first two foals proved to be rather ordinary. On April 11, 1945, out of a mating with Bull Lea, she dropped her third foal, a blood-like dark bay colt, who also was given somewhat short shrift at the outset. He was Citation, but unlike the previous offspring of the British mare, he was destined for top honors at Calumet Farm and in the racing world. Within three years, he would make Wright the proud owner of his second Triple Crown winner, a distinction enjoyed by only one other owner, William Woodward.

A sentimentalist could be pardoned if he were to claim that the colt was destined for great things in his lifetime if only because of the way he came by his name. Normally, Mrs. Wright, wife of the Chicago baking-powder magnate, enjoyed the honor of naming the Calumet foals. On this occasion, however, the pleasure was given to Mrs. Otto W. Lehmann, a close friend of the Wrights. "It was during the war, when you were hearing a lot about citations," said Mrs. Lehmann in retrospect. "It seemed like a good name for a good horse: an honorable mention for distinguished performance." She could not have been more clairvoyant.

On the way to the pinnacle in racing, Citation earned a distinction, joining a select group of Thoroughbreds who have been compared favorably with the 20th century's turf touchstone, Man o' War. Racing experts reached the conclusion that Citation was equal to, if not better than, Big Red. For example, noted trainer James "Sunny Jim" Fitzsimmons stated unequivocally early in 1948, before the colt had even won the Kentucky Derby: "Up to this point Citation's done more than any horse I ever saw. And I saw Man o' War." By October, the rangy bay's trainer, Ben Jones, unabashedly boasted to the *New York Journal-American*'s Pat Lynch:

> Citation is a better horse. . . . I think Citation shades him. Man o' War was an erratic sort and Citation has a perfect disposition. I've talked to a lot of men that saddled horses against Man o' War and they feel the same. . . . Two things make Citation a great horse. First, he is far above average in intelligence. Secondly, he can run any kind of race. Come from behind or make his own pace . . . I've tried to fault him, but I just can't find any holes. He's the best. Maybe we'll never see his likes again in our time.

From a jockey's viewpoint, Eddie Arcaro said: "Riding him is like driving a Cadillac. You get that chunk of speed whenever you ask for it."

In the twilight of Citation's career, other owners would sigh with envy at his earnings. Citation was the first millionaire in turf history, the first Thoroughbred to reach the exalted seven-figure mark. He was remarkable in other respects. He was a horse who loved to run and hardly cared where, when, or how. During his third year, he raced in Florida, Maryland, Kentucky, New Jersey, New York, Illinois, and California, on all kinds of tracks and handled by five different jockeys. As early as February, he gave up to 22 pounds to older horses on two occasions and beat the daylights out of them. So great was his stamina that in a period of seven weeks he won four races, at distances of six furlongs, 1¼ miles, and two miles. He began the year with a $3,250 win in Florida and closed it out in California with a total of $709,470, a record for earnings in one year. He was all horse.

His achievements at age three were hardly a surprise, considering his sensational season at age two, when he won eight of nine starts and $155,680. Ironically, for a while at the outset, it appeared as though he might never get the chance to prove his ability. That he succeeded at all is a credit to his tremendous racing power, which could not be denied, rather than to immediate recognition of this by his handlers. It was all because he had arrived at Calumet in the midst of a plethora of exceptional horses. Truly, the stable could crow that its cup runneth over. Its string had grown to such an extent that it had to be divided into two training camps, one handled by the boss, Ben Jones, in Florida, and the other by his son, H. A. "Jimmy" Jones, in Maryland. The luminaries of the pack included Armed, Coaltown, Bewitch, and Faultless, each of whom enjoyed distinguished careers. As far as young Citation was concerned at this stage of his life, he was in a spot you would hardly give to a dog, let alone a Thoroughbred. Actually, Calumet had so little need for a new top colt that there was no rush to get him going. This state of affairs prevented him from making his first stakes start until the end of July. Prior to then, he was "merely getting a race now and then to keep him sharp."

"Big Cy" made his debut on April 22, 1947, at Havre de Grace in a four-and-a-half-furlong race for maiden colts and geldings, which he won by a length. He followed this with four consecutive wins, including a record-breaking :58 performance in a five-furlong sprint at Arlington Park on July 24, and his first stakes victory in the Elementary Stakes at Washington Park on July 30, in which he gave 12 pounds to the runner-up, Salmagundi. His next outing was in the rich Washington Park Futurity, on August 16, in a confrontation with two stablemates, the filly Bewitch and the colt Free America. The filly, also an offspring of Bull Lea, was the darling of Calumet. She boasted seven consecutive victories, was probably the fastest two-year-old in the country, and was well on her way to the title of the year's Best Two-Year-Old Filly. Citation, on the other hand, had won "only" five in a row. Free America was the poor relation of the group, having lost once and won only his last three. Calumet wanted the race badly enough to go full blast by starting all three in it. However, in order to avoid a family donnybrook, in which his own horses might be punished by his own riders in their zeal to win, trainer Jimmy Jones ordered the jockeys to let whichever horse was leading win. He then sweetened the command by arranging for the winning purse to be split three ways. Everyone would be a winner.

Calumet scored a one-two-three finish—Bewitch, Citation, Free America—in a race that saw Big Cy make up a five-length deficit in the last furlong to lose by just a length. There were many, though, who felt that Citation could have caught Bewitch in the stretch had he been pushed hard enough, and that his second-place finish was a deliberate sacrifice to maintain Bewitch's unblemished record.

Thereafter, the colt went on to win Belmont's Futurity Trial and Futurity, and Pimlico's Futurity. His three-length victory in the Belmont Futurity, America's outstanding race for two-year-olds, on October 4, was notable for several reasons. He won a purse of $78,450, and the win automatically assured his position as the Best Two-Year-Old of the year. It was also sweet revenge, for he beat Bewitch. In the Pimlico race, only four horses faced him. It was an easy win worth $36,675 to close out a fantastic first year of campaigning. "Practically all of his victories found him going easily at the end, and once he gave evidence he could stay as well as sprint, he went into retirement as the winter favorite for the 1948 Kentucky Derby," said turf historian H. P. Robertson in reviewing the 1947 racing season. Citation's record also helped appreciably to make it a banner year for Calumet Farm in its phenomenal 1947 sweep. Besides its two two-year-old stars, the stable could point to Armed, who had prevailed over Assault and Stymie for Horse of the Year honors.

Citation started his third year in high style with two impressive races at Hialeah. The first, a six-furlong allowance for three-year-olds and over, found him the only sophomore unafraid to show up. In fact, he even was asked to give away weight to his elders, so strong was his reputation from the previous year. He carried 113 pounds, equal to 129 on a four-year-old in February and 131 on older horses. Thus Armed, with 130 pounds, had a 1-pound advantage, and four other entries had upward of 22 pounds. With it all, he won the race by a length. The second start was in the Seminole Handicap on February 11, and once more he beat Armed. Both victories represented an unusual coup because it is rare for a Thoroughbred to be matched against horses out of his division so early in his third year. The theory is that such a horse has not yet reached his full development and so is at a decided disadvantage with the older Thoroughbreds. As a result, Citation's esteem rose sharply in the eyes of the racing community, causing trainer Fitzsimmons to compare him glowingly with Man o' War and Ben Jones to exult: "This is the best horse I've ever had." Then there was the California turfman E. O. Stice, who made the first of a series of fruitless offers by breeders to purchase Citation. His $250,000 bid fell on deaf ears.

The next triumphs were in the Everglades and Flamingo stakes, the latter resulting in the colt's first big purse of the year: $43,500. Jockey Ted Atkinson remembered the Flamingo race all too well. He was aboard Pennant Day, when he suddenly heard a horse pounding up behind him on the final turn. "I knew it was Citation," he said, "and I got the hell out of the way. I didn't want to get run over." It was an indication of the increasing measure of respect Citation was beginning to command from those who were in a position to

Citation, with Al Snider up, wins over Big Day and Saggy in the Flamingo Stakes at Hialeah on March 1, 1948. Jockey Ted Atkinson, on Pennant Day, heard "Big Cy" pounding up on the final turn and "got the hell out of the way."

know and care. The victory skein was broken on April 12, with a loss to Saggy in the mud in the Chesapeake Trial at Havre de Grace. The defeat, however, could be attributed to some extenuating circumstances and could not be construed as a reflection on the horse's performance.

First, a tragic event struck Calumet when their regular rider, Al Snider, was lost on a fishing trip in the wilds of the Florida Everglades. An emergency call went out to Eddie Arcaro to ride Citation in the six-furlong race. One writer likened it to "inviting a guy to rob a bank." Then the track turned up muddy, and Jimmy Jones cautioned Arcaro not to take any chances with the horse in this, his first race aboard him. The jockey, being the pro that he was, candidly took the blame for the loss, admitting to an error in pacing judgment. He even claimed that he could have recovered from the mistake and won, but felt it would have meant punishing the horse too much and risking possible injury. It was just not worth it with the Triple Crown races coming along soon. "I knew Jimmy . . . didn't want me to beat up his horse," he said after the race. "You can't tell how much you're taking out of a horse in the mud." The decision was apparently a wise one, for the colt went on to capture the Chesapeake Stakes on April 17, by four and a half lengths over Bovard, after running his rivals into the ground, and the Derby Trial, 10 days later, before moving up to the 1948 Kentucky Derby.

Derby day was clear, but the track was sloppy from an early rain. Calumet had two of its stars entered—Citation and Coaltown. The tandem was a powerful threat because Coaltown had come back in 1948 from a throat ailment, which had curtailed his racing the year before, and had reeled off four straight sizzling wins. Therefore, Coaltown went off as the odds-on favorite at 2-5, but not before an earlier surprise. Presumably reasoning that because the entry would pay such prohibitively short odds that it was senseless to back it, the early bettors had poured money on My Request. There was some merit to this, for the three-year-old B. F. Whittaker colt was also on a four-win streak, which included a clean sweep at Jamaica of the Experimental Handicap and Wood Memorial. Furthermore, the general public had had little opportunity to see what was happening before post time. It seems that betting on the Derby, the seventh race on the program, that day was being handled in the morning at special windows in a remote area of Churchill Downs. With the exception of quotations written on a nearby blackboard, no information was readily available until the tote board had been cleared of all data on the other races after they had been completed. Therefore, when the board blinked on for the Derby, it showed My Request as the favorite. The early odds also may have reflected the reservations of those who reasoned that Citation was riding two jinxes: never before had a winner of the Belmont Futurity or the Derby gone on to take the big race as well. However, by post time, the fans had apparently thought better of it and sent My Request off at almost 4-1.

Turf lore is filled with colorful tales, not the least of which is the one of Eddie Arcaro's doubts about Citation in the race, as reported by Robert Kelley. Arcaro was more favorably disposed to Coaltown but was slated to ride Citation. He had made a wrong decision in the 1942 Derby, under similar circumstances, having elected to ride Devil Diver instead of Shut Out, who won the race. Both horses had been Greentree Stable entries. Therefore, his anxiety over the Calumet horses in 1948 was understandable. Ben Jones tried to reassure Arcaro, telling him not to worry about Coaltown. "Citation can catch any horse he can see," he said. Then, in the paddock just before the parade to the post, Arcaro is alleged to have muttered: "Gee, Ben. Are you sure I'm on the right one?" "You're on the right one," snapped Jones as he helped the jockey up.

Citation had the rail position, but his stablemate moved out fast to a commanding six-length lead in the backstretch, which gave Arcaro a few anxious moments and seemed to support his earlier premonitions. However, he was not about to give up easily as he gunned for another Derby victory, one more than any other jockey had ever ridden. "I knew I had the rest of the field beat at the ½-mile pole," he recalled. "I looked back and I knew the other horses were too drunk to cause us any trouble. We moved when I clucked to him, and I could see we'd move on out at Coaltown."

In a relatively short period the jockey had come to know his horse well, and what he could expect from him at the appropriate moment. He was aware that Citation was lazy and inclined to loaf, but at the same time was ready always to respond at the first cluck. Therefore, he was able to push him and bring him even with Coaltown going into the stretch. The two ran head-to-head in a momentary struggle, after which Citation darted with a closing kick to finish handily four lengths in front, his "ears pricked—looking for more horses to run down," according to writer George Russell. Coaltown was second and My Request third.

The only real problem Arcaro had with Citation was the crowd. The colt appeared to be scared by the howling din sent up by the throng as they

Citation wins handily by four lengths with "ears pricked" in the 1948 Kentucky Derby. Stablemate Coaltown is second. Jockey Eddie Arcaro, who had wanted to ride Coaltown, wound up with his fourth Kentucky Derby win.

Official Chart of the Kentucky Derby

SEVENTH RACE
4 7 7 3 0
May 1-48—C.D

1 1-4 MILES. (Whirlaway, May 3, 1941—2:01⅖—3—126.) Seventy-fourth running KENTUCKY DERBY. $100,000 added. 3-year-olds. Scale weights. (Owner of winner to receive gold trophy.)
Gross value, $111,450. Net value to winner $83,400; second, $10,000; third, $5,000; fourth, $2,500. Mutuel Pool, $670,833.

Index	Horses	Eq't	A	Wt	PP	St	½	¾	1	Str	Fin	Jockeys	Owners	Odds to $1
(47451)	CITATION	w		126	1	2	2^{h}	2^{3}	2^{5}	1^{2}	$1^{3\frac{1}{2}}$	E Arcaro	Calumet Farm	a-.40
(47189)	COALTOWN	wb		126	2	1	1^{6}	$1^{3\frac{1}{2}}$	$1^{\frac{1}{2}}$	2^{4}	2^{3}	N L Pierson	Calumet Farm	a-.40
(47326)	MY REQUEST	w		126	6	3	4^{h}	4^{3}	$3^{1\frac{1}{2}}$	3^{1}	$3^{1\frac{1}{2}}$	D Dodson	B F Whitaker	3.80
47189^{2}	BILLINGS	w		126	5	6	$5^{\frac{1}{2}}$	$3^{\frac{1}{2}}$	4^{8}	4^{15}	4^{20}	M Peterson	Walmac Stable	14.70
47282^{3}	GRANDPERE	w		126	4	4	3^{2}	6	6	$5^{\frac{1}{2}}$	5^{nk}	J Gilbert	Mrs J P Adams	17.80
47451^{2}	ESCADRU	wb		126	3	5	6	5^{6}	$5^{1\frac{1}{2}}$	6	6	A Kirkland	W L Brann	7.10

a-Coupled, Citation and Coaltown.
Time, :12⅕, :23⅖, :34⅗, :46⅗, :59⅕, 1:11⅖, 1:24⅗, 1:38, 1:51⅖, 2:05⅖. Track sloppy.

Mutuel Prices

	$2 Mutuels Paid			Odds to $1		
CITATION (a-Entry)	2.80	....	....	.40	....	...
COALTOWN (a-Entry)	2.80	....	....	.40	....	...

NO PLACE OR SHOW MUTUELS SOLD.

Winner—B. c, by Bull Lea—Hydroplane II., by Hyperion, trained by B. A. Jones; bred by Calumet Farm
WENT TO POST—4:32. OFF AT 4:32½ CENTRAL STANDARD TIME.

Start good from stall gate. Won handily; second and third driving. CITATION, away forwardly and losing ground while racing back of COALTOWN to the stretch, responded readily to a steady hand ride after disposing of the latter and drew clear. COALTOWN began fast, established a clear lead before going a quarter and, making the pace on the inside in the stretch, continued willingly, but was not good enough for CITATION, although easily best of the others. MY REQUEST, bothered slightly after the start, was in hand while improving his position to the stretch, then failed to rally when set down for the drive. BILLINGS suffered interference after the break when GRANDPERE bore to the outside, was in close quarters on the first turn when caught between ESCADRU and CITATION, then could not better his position when clear. GRANDPERE broke into BILLINGS at the start, displayed speed for a half mile, then gave way. ESCADRU, forced to take up when in close quarters entering the backstretch, could not reach serious contention thereafter and tired badly after going three-quarters of a mile.

Scratched—47451^{4} Galedo, 126.

moved into the homestretch, and Arcaro whacked him for the first time with the whip to keep his mind strictly on the race. "Maybe I didn't have to hit him, but I wasn't in any mood to take any chances," he said somewhat apologetically. The time was 2:05⅘ on the off footing, and the price was $2.80 for $2.00, with no place or show bets permitted. The payoff equaled that of Count Fleet, the smallest price since pari-mutuel betting was introduced at the Derby. The victory produced an extra measure of satisfaction for the principals. Calumet Farm enjoyed its third Derby win—Citation, Pensive, and Whirlaway. It was the fourth for trainer Ben Jones—Citation, Pensive, Whirlaway, Lawrin. To Eddie Arcaro, it meant the fourth crossing of the finish line in front in a Derby—Citation, Hoop Jr., Pensive, Whirlaway. Aboard Big Cy, he collected $83,400 and thumbed his nose at the jinxes.

The Preakness at Pimlico was a breeze for the son of Bull Lea. He was the odds-on favorite at 1-10, with only win bets permitted, as only three horses challenged him: Vulcan's Forge, Better Self, and Bovard. It had rained for two days before the race, and again Citation went off on a sloppy track. The result was a lazy time of 2:02⅖, the slowest since the distance for the Preakness had been changed from 1 mile to 1³⁄₁₆ miles in 1925. Eddie Arcaro shrugged this off, remarking instead that it had been an easier run than in the Derby. He had tapped Citation once at the head of the stretch and again in the middle of it. He claimed the colt was under stout restraint throughout and that at no time had there been any serious opposition. Big Cy merely galloped along in front until the stretch, at which point he was allowed to increase his advantage. "If that's all the competition we're going to have," said the jockey, "he and I are going to have a picnic."

The only real difficulty Citation faced that day in the Preakness was the ceremony in the winner's circle. He balked at having the blanket of black-eyed Susans draped over him for the traditional picture taking. Trainer Jimmy Jones solved the problem by covering the colt's eyes as the flowers were put in place. The day also proved to be a cash windfall for Calumet Farm. In fact, it was the biggest haul for a stable in racing history. While Citation was picking up $91,870 at Pimlico, Calumet's Faultless was taking down $60,300 by winning the Gallant Fox Handicap at Jamaica in New York, and another stablemate, Fervent, was earning $15,000 by coming in second. All told, the afternoon's purses totaled $167,170.

With two down and one to go for the "really big win," most trainers might have rested their horse to prepare for it without pressure. It was not so as far

Citation breezes to an easy victory in the 1948 Preakness. Only three horses opposed him.

Official Chart of Preakness

SIXTH RACE
4 8 7 5 5
May 15-48—Pim

1 3-16 MILES. (Riverland, May 1, 1943—1:56$\frac{2}{5}$—5—123.) Seventy-Second Running PREAKNESS STAKES. $100,000 added. 3-year-olds. Scale weights. (All eligibility, entrance and starting fees to the winner, with $100,000 added, of which $20,000 to second, $10,000 to third and $5,000 to fourth. The nominator of the winner to receive $2,500; the nominator of the second horse, $1,000, and the nominator of the third horse, $500 of the added money.)

Gross value, $134,870. Net value to winner $91,870; second, $20,000; third, $10,000; fourth, $5,000. Mutuel Pool, $191,004.

Index	Horses	Eq't	A	Wt	PP	St	½	¾	1	Str	Fin	Jockeys	Owners	Odds to $1
(47730)	CITATION	w		126	4	1	$1^{1\frac{1}{2}}$	1^{2}	$1^{2\frac{1}{2}}$	$1^{2\frac{1}{2}}$	$1^{5\frac{1}{2}}$	E Arcaro	Calumet Farm	.10
48359^{3}	VULCAN'S FORGE	wb		126	2	4	2^{2}	$2^{2\frac{1}{2}}$	3^{3}	2^{1}	$2^{3\frac{1}{2}}$	D Dodson	C V Whitney	30.00
(48259)	BOVARD	w		126	1	2	$3^{1\frac{1}{2}}$	3^{2}	2^{h}	3^{2}	3^{nk}	W Saunders	S W Labrot Jr	9.30
47326^{3}	BETTER SELF	w		126	3	3	4	4	4	4	4	W Mehrtens	King Ranch	12.60

Time, :13, :24$\frac{4}{5}$, :37$\frac{2}{5}$, :50$\frac{2}{5}$, 1:03, 1:16, 1:29, 1:43, 1:55$\frac{3}{5}$, 2:02$\frac{2}{5}$. Track heavy.

Mutuel Prices		$2 Mutuels Paid			Odds to $1		
	CITATION	2.20	....	....	.10	....	....
	NO PLACE OR SHOW MUTUELS SOLD.						

Winner—B. c, by Bull Lea—Hydroplane II., by Hyperion, trained by H. A. Jones; bred by Calumet Farm.

WENT TO POST—5:15. OFF AT 5:15½ EASTERN DAYLIGHT TIME.

Start good from stall gate. Won easily; second and third driving. CITATION sprinted to the front while under stout restraint, was without serious opposition, merely galloped along in front to the stretch, felt the sting of the whip twice and easily increased his advantage. VULCAN'S FORGE, raced kindly after breaking slowest of all, raced in the runner-up position to the stretch, gave way briefly to BOVARD and was easily better than the latter in the drive. BOVARD was not rushed early, exhibited a mild rally along the inside rounding the final turn, then flattened out under pressure. BETTER SELF failed to rally at any stage and apparently disliked the going.

as Citation was concerned. Jones figured to keep him sharp by entering him in the Jersey Stakes on May 29, which he proceeded to polish off by a "mere" 11 lengths.

There may have been some misgivings about Citation's winning streak at the start of the Belmont Stakes on June 12. For one thing, seven opponents went to the post, apparently hopeful that a hole in his stamina might show up. For another, he stumbled at the bell, to give one and all conniptions. However, he steadied himself quickly and was in front to stay at the far turn. "I just let him run a little, up that turn," said Arcaro. "Then I took him up again because he went so fast it scared me." Citation waltzed over the finish line eight lengths ahead of Better Self, $77,700 richer and the eighth Triple Crown champion. The colt's road to the crown had been by far the easiest of them all. In reaching the goal, he also made Arcaro the only jockey ever to pilot two Triple Crown winners.

It was fellow jockey Ted Atkinson who subsequently revealed the cause of the stumble at the top of the race. He was sitting on Faraway in the starting gate stall next to the one occupied by Citation. "I looked over and this big dude [a gate crew member] had his left forefoot on a ledge alongside the gate. I yelled to Eddie to look, and he [Arcaro] reached down with his whip and smacked Citation's leg." Just then, the gates opened and the startled colt lost his composure for the moment, but not enough to spoil his march to the "most glorious crown."

There was no stopping Citation. He remained unbeaten for the rest of the year, with victories in the Stars and Stripes Handicap, Buckingham Purse, American Derby, Sysonby Mile, Jockey Club Gold Cup, Empire City Gold Cup, Pimlico Special, Challenge Purse, and Tanforan Handicap. In the Sysonby Mile, no three-year-old other than his stablemate Coaltown wanted any part of him. However, the field did have some of the fastest sprinters of all ages in the land. Once again, Citation lay back, biding his time.

Rounding the far turn of the Sysonby, with $\frac{1}{2}$ mile to go, the front-runners were Spy Song, Natchez, and Coaltown. Citation was fourth, trailing by some six lengths. Then he suddenly took off. Arcaro said it was like a jet plane gunning. At the head of the stretch, they had caught up to and passed the field, moving into a two-length lead. They extended this to three en route to the wire, with the jockey standing in the saddle for the last $\frac{1}{16}$ of a mile. Jimmy Jones was somewhat puzzled. "Why did you move so soon?" he asked. "The sonofagun just took off on me," exclaimed Arcaro. But it was a rather simple remark by a groom who worked for Alfred G. Vanderbilt and who had witnessed the race that really said it all: "Boss," he said, shaking his head, "that there horse just ain't human."

Respect for Citation continued to grow apace. Not one horse at all showed up to challenge him in the Pimlico Special on October 29, because the race called for level weights and a winner-take-all purse. It was a walkover, but Citation had to do it in grand style. According to H. P. Robertson, "He almost pulled Arcaro out of the irons to 'walk' over in 1:59⅗," a time that was faster than some of the previous competitive runnings of the event. The gallop was worth $10,000, and Arcaro had his arms massaged afterward to ease the muscles that had been strained from trying to hold in the horse.

The last race, and win, of the year for him was in the Tanforan Handicap at Bay Meadows near San Francisco on December 11. It gave him a record of 19 victories in 20 starts, 15 of them in succession, as he nailed down the best of everything in 1948: Best Three-Year-Old, Handicap Horse, and Horse of the Year. His earnings of $709,470 topped Assault's mark of $424,195, and only Stymie and Armed had won as much as his total in their entire careers.

The winning team—Citation, jockey Eddie Arcaro, and trainer Jimmy Jones—in the traditional parade to the winner's circle after the Belmont victory.

It is no contest in the 1948 Belmont as Citation is all by himself at the finish line, eight lengths in front of Better Self. Citation won in spite of a stumble at the start.

Official Chart of Belmont Stakes

SIXTH RACE

5 0 9 6 9

June 12-48—Bel

Gross value, $117,300.

Pool, $433,818.

1 1-2 MILES. (Bolingbroke, Sept. 26, 1942—2:27⅗—5—115.) Eightieth running BELMONT STAKES. $100,000 added. 3-year-olds. Scale weights. Nominators of winner, second and third horses to receive $2,000, $1,000 and $500, respectively. Colts, 126 lbs.; fillies, 121 lbs. (Geldings not eligible.)

Net value to winner $77,700; second, $20,000; third, $10,000; fourth, $5,000. Mutuel

Index	Horses	Eq't A Wt	PP	St	½	1	1¼	Str	Fin	Jockeys	Owners	Odds to $1
(49854)	CITATION	w 126	1	1	1h	1¹	1⁴	1⁵	1⁸	E Arcaro	Calumet Farm	.20
(50522)	BETTER SELF	wb 126	8	2	6²	5ⁿᵏ	5⁵	3⁶	2½	W Mehrt'ns	King Ranch	a-12.50
(50437)	ESCADRU	w 126	3	3	4½	4¹	2³	2³	3⁵	A Kirkland	W L Brann	6.85
50437	VULCAN'S FORGE	wb 126	5	6	7⁵	7⁴	7⁴	5⁴	4³	D Dodson	C V Whitney	15.10
49854	GASPARILLA	wb 126	7	7	5¹	3½	3¹	4ʰ	5⁴	R Donoso	A J Sackett	a-12.50
50522²	SALMAGUNDI	wb 126	6	5	3²	6¹⁵	6³	6³	6²	E Guerin	W Helis	22.45
50645³	GOLDEN LIGHT	wb 126	4	8	8	8	8	8	7⁵	N Combest	Belair Stud	82.50
49854³	FARAWAY	wb 126	2	4	2³	2³	4½	7½	8	T Atkinson	Glen Riddle Farm	28.10

a-Coupled, Better Self and Gasparilla.

Time, :24, :48⅖, 1:12⅗, 1:37, 2:02⅗, 2:28⅕. **Track fast.**

	—$2 Mutuels Paid—			—Odds to $1—		
Mutuel Prices CITATION	2.40	2.30	2.10	.20	.15	.05
BETTER SELF (a-Entry)		3.70	2.10		.85	.05
ESCADRU			2.10			.05

Winner—B. c, by Bull Lea—Hydroplane II., by Hyperion, trained by H. A. Jones; bred by Calumet Farm.

WENT TO POST—4:45. OFF AT 4:46 EASTERN DAYLIGHT TIME.

Start good from stall gate. Won easily; second and third driving. CITATION stumbled at the break, but recovered quickly and was sent along under steady restraint and shook off FARAWAY when ready and, rounding the far turn, drew away and in the stretch run was shaken up slightly, then again drew away to finish with speed in reserve. BETTER SELF was taken under restraint in the early stages and was sent through on the inside rounding the stretch turn and disposed of ESCADRU in the final seventy yards. ESCADRU, on the outside and well up all the way, made a determined bid rounding to the stretch turn, but could not menace the winner and tired. VULCAN'S FORGE was outrun early, improved his position in the final half mile, but could not gain on the leaders. GASPARILLA was kept in a forward position from the beginning, but flattened out badly when roused rounding the far turn. SALMAGUNDI was steadied along in the running, but failed to respond when roused. GOLDEN LIGHT was outrun and was never a factor. FARAWAY was in near pursuit of the early pace, but tired badly and began to drift out and was not persevered with when beaten.

Scratched—49814² Coaltown, 126.

Finally, his overall figure of $865,150 was only $53,335 short of Stymie's all-time record.

Unfortunately, the sweet was laced with bitters. After the Tanforan, he developed a "hot spot" on an ankle, which proved to be an osselet on the left fore ankle. Later, he was bothered by tendon trouble. The ailments became so persistent that he was finally forced to sit out the entire fourth-year season. Things were never the same again.

Citation returned to action on January 11, 1950, winning a six-furlong race at Santa Anita, California, and regenerating all of the old excitement among his followers. It was his 16th consecutive win, the longest streak in modern racing history. This was followed by a series of tough losses, an overnight by a neck at Santa Anita, January 26; the San Antonio Handicap by a length, February 11; the Santa Anita Handicap by a nose, February 25; the San Juan Capistrano Handicap by a nose, March 4; and the Surprise Purse at Golden Gate Fields in Albany, California, May 17. He returned to his winning ways on June 3, when he took the Golden Gate Mile to boost his earnings to a record high of $924,631, thus topping Stymie's mark by about

Citation takes the Pimlico Special in a walkover on October 29, 1948. "Big Cy" almost pulled Eddie Arcaro out of the irons even though there were no other horses in the race.

$6,000. He then lost the Forty-Niners Handicap on June 17, and the Golden Gate Handicap on June 24, after which he was shipped to Chicago. There it was discovered that he had sore ankles, so back he went to Calumet Farm for a rest.

On the surface, his 1950 record might appear to be disappointing. It was far from that. He won two of nine starts, finishing no worse than second in the others. His losses were mostly to the talented, Irish-bred Noor, who had been imported by Charles S. Howard, the owner of Seabiscuit, and who captured honors as the 1950 Handicap Horse. Actually, Citation ran exceptionally well. He set a world's record of 1:33⅗ in the Golden Gate Mile and came in second in four world-record runs and one track-record run. Some of the losses were attributed to the weight he was forced to give away, in addition to coming up against a hot Noor. Those losses were: the Santa Anita Handicap, 1¼ miles, track record of 2:00, won by Noor carrying 110 pounds to Citation's 132; the San Juan Capistrano Handicap, 1¾ miles, world record of 2:52⅘, won by Noor carrying 117 pounds to Citation's 130; the Surprise Purse, six furlongs, world record of 1:08⅖, won by Roman Inn at level weights; the Forty-Niners Handicap, a mile and a furlong, world record of 1:46⅘, won by Noor carrying 123 pounds to Citation's 128; and the Golden Gate Handicap, 1¼ miles, world record of 1:58⅕, won by Noor carrying 127 to Citation's 126, the first race in which he had ever been given weight and his only bad defeat—by three lengths.

Normally, at this stage of his life, Citation should have been retired. He was not. Warren Wright, before he died during the year, expressed his desire that the horse should be allowed to race until he topped not only Stymie's earnings record but had also become the first millionaire of the racing world. Consequently, the colt was brought out again in 1951. The first start was at Bay Meadows on April 18, in a six-furlong race. It was his first event in about 10 months, and he finished third. He came in third once more on April 26, winning only $400. On May 11, he wound up fifth in the Hollywood Premiere Handicap, the first time in 41 races he had ever finished out of the money. He lost again on May 30, in the Argonaut Handicap, a race that was noteworthy to the Triple Crown champion because it marked the last time he would be a loser. Apparently reaching back into memory, he racked up three consecutive wins, in the Century Handicap, American Handicap, and Hollywood Gold Cup. He ran the latter on July 14, completing the 1¼ miles in 2:01 to win by four lengths. The purse, a guaranteed $100,000, pushed Citation's earnings well past the million-dollar level.

Irish-bred Noor crosses the finish line ahead of Citation in the 1950 Santa Anita Handicap.

Noor (No. 3) beats Citation by a nose in the San Juan Capistrano on March 4, 1950.

Citation becomes the first horse to win $1 million as he defeats the filly Bewitch in the Hollywood Gold Cup on July 14, 1951. It was his last race, and he avenged the first defeat of his career, which was by Bewitch.

"Millionaire" Citation prances proudly before wildly cheering fans in his last public appearance, at Arlington Park in Chicago on July 28, 1951. A handler rides him.

There was an interesting sidelight to the race. The horse Citation beat to the wire in this, his last race, was Bewitch, the filly who had hung on him his first defeat in 1947. She picked up $20,000 for her second-place finish, which made her the leading money-winner of her sex, with a total of $462,605.

Two weeks later, on July 28, Big Cy was formally retired. He made his last public appearance that day at Arlington Park, Chicago, in a parade before a wildly cheering throng. Well-deserved rest had come to the superb colt after 45 starts and 32 victories. On his way back to Calumet Farm, his train car was shared by Coaltown and Bewitch, also headed for retirement, a rather valuable cargo indeed. His stud record was favorable; by 1962 he had sired four $100,000 winners, including Guadalcanal and Fabius. However, by his own standard, he never produced any offspring that compared remotely to him, which caused the experts to consider his career as a stallion somewhat less than successful.

Citation, Big Cy, died on the night of August 8, 1970, at Calumet Farm at the age of 25. He was buried near the side of his sire, Bull Lea, and his dam, Hydroplane II.

Secretariat

and jockey Ron Turcotte

Secretariat
(chestnut colt)
{
  Bold Ruler { Nasrullah
             Miss Disco

  Somethingroyal { Princequillo
                     Imperatrice
}

| Chapter 9 |

Secretariat

~1973~

Exactly a quarter of a century elapsed, from 1948 to 1973, before American Thoroughbred racing fans were able to salute a new Triple Crown champion. He had the improbable name of Secretariat, a blazing-red coat, and such awe-inspiring performances that some were inclined to believe he was a veritable Pegasus incarnate.

This enthusiasm was stimulated, no doubt, by the 25 years of frustration that saw only six horses make it to the Belmont Stakes with victories in the Kentucky Derby and Preakness, only to fail in the tortuous 1½-mile classic. Of these, half wound up with an assortment of ailments, provoking the cynics to call it the "Cripple Crown." For example, Canonero II (1971) developed a bad hock, Carry Back (1961) came back gimpy, and Tim Tam (1958) fractured a bone in a foot. Consequently, there were more than a few skeptics who were ready to write off all possibility for a new champion. Considering the fluke circumstances surrounding Secretariat, his owners, and his trainers, it is truly a miracle that he even came into being, let alone made it to the "most glorious crown" as America's ninth Triple Crown champion.

The colt was born on March 30, 1970, at the Meadow Farm, in Doswell, Virginia. His owner was Christopher T. Chenery, a utilities magnate who collected board chairmanships of companies such as Southern Natural Gas. He had gone into the breeding business as an avocation in 1936, when he purchased twenty-six hundred acres of rolling countryside some 15 miles north of Richmond. The farm, originally known as the Meadow, had belonged to his ancestors from 1810 until they lost it during the Civil War.

Chenery had a philosophy about horses: "The purchase price does not always represent what a horse is worth. It's only what some fool thinks he's worth." Therefore, in 1939, he shopped cautiously and purchased a yearling mare, Hildene, for only $750. "She showed speed," he liked to recall later on, "but stopped eight times in eight races. Then I stopped racing her." In the parlance of the track, she turned into a "blue hen," producing a string of top stakes winners and fillies, even though she went blind with her first foal. One of her distinguished sons was First Landing, who became the sire of Riva Ridge.

Seven years after this remarkable purchase, Chenery boldly shelled out $35,000 for another mare, Imperatrice, who proceeded to justify the price tag with an equally impressive lineup of offspring, including an unraced daughter, Somethingroyal, who became the dam of Secretariat. Thus, from the blood of these two mares, the fortunes of Meadow Farm, Stable and Stud flourished. From 1939 to 1972, 40 stakes winners were produced, and earnings totaled $8,500,000 in purses and more than $12,000,000 in overall breeding sales and purses.

All did not progress that smoothly straight through. Financial troubles began to crop up in the sixties, coincident with Chenery's failing health and increasing senility. By 1967, the industrialist's three children, Dr. Hollis B. Chenery, Mrs. Margaret Carmichael, and the youngest, Mrs. Helen "Penny" Tweedy, were forced to make a tough decision. Dr. Chenery, a distinguished economist with the World Bank, was for selling all of the horses and investing the money in a rising stock market. Mrs. Tweedy demurred. "We probably have the legal right to do that," she conceded, "but we know Dad wouldn't want us to give up the horses. So I don't think we have the moral right to do it." Furthermore, she continued, "The land has supported the horses, and the horses have supported the land." Finally, she pointed out, "I at least know how to read a balance sheet," from having attended Columbia University's Graduate School of Business. Her arguments prevailed, and she was given the green light to take a stab at managing the whole operation.

Her first move was to reduce the overhead by cutting the stable from 130 to 68 horses. The next decision, however, was momentous in its future ramifications: whether or not to continue with an odd agreement her father had had for years with Mrs. Henry Carnegie Phipps and her son, Ogden. They were the owners of the stallion Bold Ruler, who had dominated racing for a decade in the breeding shed of Claiborne Farm as the leading American sire. So priceless did they regard his services that money could not buy "romance" with him. Rather, payment had to be made with a unique form of currency.

"It was all part of a very complicated arrangement," recalled Tweedy. "They agreed that each season Mr. Phipps' great sire, Bold Ruler, would be bred to two of my father's broodmares. Every two years they flipped a coin. The winner had first choice of the two foals that year and the loser had first choice the year after." As far as she was concerned, it was a bad arrangement: "It was a great deal for the Phippses, because they would end up with the off-spring of the best mares in the country. It hadn't been good for Dad, though. He hadn't been lucky with his Bold Ruler foals. But, I decided since he had made the deal, I'd give it two more years."

Penny Tweedy had learned fast that crossing bloodlines can help over-come flaws in horses. So, on the advice of A. B. "Bull" Hancock, owner of Claiborne Farm, she sent two Meadow mares to Bold Ruler, Somethingroyal and Hasty Matelda. It was the former that suggested the greatest promise. The consensus was that Bold Ruler's offspring were precocious and brilliant racers at the age of two and at short distances. At three, they were disappointments, particularly when asked to run farther, as in the classic races of 1¼ miles and

Mr. and Mrs. Ogden Phipps. Phipps flipped a coin with Mrs. Tweedy to determine the ultimate owner of Secretariat.

more. On the other hand, Somethingroyal's sire was Princequillo, whose foals were tough, durable, long-running, but "seldom blessed with speed." As one breeder told her: "The Princequillos will run all day—and if the races get long enough and the other horses get tired, sooner or later they'll win for you."

The mating was accomplished and, in the spring of 1969, the mistress of Meadow Stable, Penny Tweedy, and the master of Wheatley Stable, Ogden Phipps, met in the office of Alfred G. Vanderbilt at Belmont Park for the coin flip. "We were joking," said Penny Tweedy, "because we both wanted to lose." It seems that both parties knew then that Somethingroyal had already foaled a filly and was impregnated a second time. On the other hand, Hasty Matelda had had a colt, but was to be barren the next year. Therefore, whoever won the toss would have the first choice of the new foals, but would lose out the second year because there would be only one foal. Thus, only one of the owners would wind up with two horses.

Phipps won the toss and, because he always preferred Meadow fillies, took the Somethingroyal foal. They named her The Bride and eventually raced her four times, but she never finished better than sixth. As one wag put it, she "couldn't outrun a fat lady with gout." By the same token, Mrs. Tweedy's new colt, Rising River, also had problems and was finally sold for $50,000. The following year, at the Meadow Farm on March 30, 1970, Somethingroyal dropped a bright red colt foal with three white stockings and a star. He was christened Secretariat, a name suggested by Elizabeth Ham, executive secretary for 35 years for the elder Chenery and formerly an employee of the old League of Nations in Geneva. Three years later, while reflecting on the subsequent turn of events stemming from this odd deal, the astute turf scribe William Rudy wrote: "On such vagaries are racing fortunes founded."

It became obvious soon that Tweedy's father's longtime trainer, Casey Hayes, was finding it difficult adjusting to her measures, so she replaced him. The new man was Roger Laurin, 34, son of the well-known French-Canadian trainer Lucien Laurin, who was employed by Claiborne Farm and who had taught his son everything he knew about the business. Young Laurin was operating his own public stable and came well endorsed by Bull Hancock for the job. "We lost about $85,000 the first year," Tweedy frankly admits, "but I would go into my father's trophy room and look around, and I would think that with all that breeding as a foundation Meadow Stud would have better times." There was a small profit of $65,000 the second year, but until Riva Ridge showed up, it was strictly a "holding operation."

There were some bright spots, nevertheless, not the least of which was the new youngster on the farm, Secretariat. The first time she saw him gamboling in the fields, Tweedy made a succinct entry in the book she kept on her horses: "Wow!" He was big, bright-eyed, and barrel-chested, with legs that "promised to be straight and flawless." Farm manager Howard Gentry enjoyed watching him, too, because "he always liked to lead the field, even when he was running with other yearlings across the pasture."

By June 1971, when everything seemed to be settling down to a smooth routine, another far-reaching decision was made. Roger Laurin suddenly quit as trainer, lured away by the Phippses to replace their own trainer, who had died of a heart attack. The Wheatley Stable was a great opportunity for him and he grabbed it, but in so doing, he added a bit of chutzpah and nepotism to the situation by suggesting his father, Lucien, as his replacement. Penny Tweedy was hardly enthused. Lucien Laurin, who by now was no longer with Claiborne Farm and was operating a public stable, was pushing 60 and on the verge of retiring. He had, in fact, booked a European vacation for his wife and himself.

"Mrs. Tweedy was reluctant at first to take on a trainer who might stay only a couple of months," admits Laurin, "but Mr. Hancock told her: 'He'll stick around. He's a good trainer and he'll stay.'" Bull Hancock must have been a good judge of character because the trainer did choose to stay, bringing a wealth of experience to the Meadow horses. Laurin, a native of St. Paul De Joliette, Quebec, was a jockey from 1920 until 1942, and thereafter a trainer with a reputation for converting slow or lame mounts into winners. By 1971, he had amassed the impressive record of winners in 1,137 races with earnings of $6,434,303.

In taking over the training assignment, he took 10 Meadow Stable horses to his barn, including Riva Ridge, Upper Case, and Quill Gordon, all promising Thoroughbreds, who joined stakes winner Spanish Riddle, whom he was training for another owner. An assessment of the checkerboard moves by the trainers caused *The Blood-Horse* to comment wryly: "A man can repay to his father all that he owes him, but Roger Laurin that day came as close to evening the score as a man can expect to come."

Eight days later, Lucien Laurin sent out his first Meadow horse, Riva Ridge, for his first race as a two-year-old. "The colt was bumped, raced greenly and was not impressive," finishing seventh, hardly an auspicious start for both trainer and horse. It was a wholly different story by year's end, when the colt was named Best Two-Year-Old and Penny Tweedy and Lucien Laurin could indulge themselves in the luxury of dreaming of the Triple Crown.

They did not know it at the time, but they had the wrong horse in mind. Riva Ridge did, in fact, go on to win the 1972 Kentucky Derby and Belmont Stakes, but faltered in the Preakness because of a distaste for mud. However, down on the Virginia farm, a young colt was getting set to make his move into the racing wars and to historic fame and fortune.

"It was when he was a yearling, playing in the fields, that I first suspected. And by the time he left the farm as a two-year-old, I was sure he was one of the best we'd ever raised," is the way Howard Gentry recalled the fateful moment when Secretariat "left home." Lucien Laurin was somewhat more philosophical when he studied the big frame of the colt. Along with Secretariat's size came an insatiable appetite. He ate anything that resembled food and grew quite chubby. That simply meant that the horse would have to be brought along more slowly. "You have to have more forbearance with a fat horse," the elder Laurin said.

The training progression more than substantiated the early suspicions. In his early workouts, Secretariat trailed his stablemates. Gradually, he caught up to them. Finally, by late spring, he moved ahead, prompting the trainer to seek out the impatient Mrs. Tweedy and happily break the good news: "He's ready to run." In fact, Laurin was so impressed with the horse he began to wonder if his own ardor deluded him. "He was so damned good-looking that I said to myself he probably wouldn't be worth 10 cents as a racer." The response he got from the owner was a typical sample of human foible. After all the impatience and anxiety at preparing for the moment, she said she would not be able to stay for the race, that she had to be away on business. "I'll wait," Laurin said quietly. "I think you ought to be here when he runs." The comment made Tweedy sit up and reflect. Laurin normally was a rather taciturn individual who wasted few words. Therefore, she reasoned, he must have something special for her to see, so she arranged to be in New York on July 4, 1972, for the colt's debut at Aqueduct.

It was a five-and-a-half-furlong sprint for two-year-old maidens, colts, and geldings, and, like Riva Ridge's first race a year before, it was a nightmare— only more so. Coming out of the gate another horse bumped into Secretariat and knocked him sideways, at the same time pinching him back with no place to run. "He came this close to being knocked down," said jockey Paul Feliciano. "If he wasn't such a strong horse, he would have fallen." Despite the rough handling, Secretariat managed to finish a credible fourth, making up seven of eight lengths in the last ¼ mile. He also learned a lesson about competing at the track, which he never forgot. "It's no kidding," commented Laurin sometime later. "He sure remembered because, in his second start, he took himself back out of the gate . . . took himself back out of trouble." Indeed he did, but then he ran for daylight and won handily by six lengths.

On July 31, two and a half weeks later, at Saratoga, Secretariat showed he meant business by winning a six-furlong allowance by a length and a half. That race also marked his first ride by Ron Turcotte, who from then on became his regular jockey. Turcotte was the second French Canadian on the Tweedy-Laurin team. A native of Grand Falls, New Brunswick, he became an apprentice in 1961, began riding in the United States in 1964, and proceeded to rack up more than $1,000,000 in purses. He did well for the team in 1971 and 1972 aboard Riva Ridge, giving the Chenery family their first Kentucky Derby victory.

With two quick wins under his belt, the time arrived for Secretariat to prove that now he was to be taken seriously. The test would be his first stakes event, the six-furlong Sanford on August 26, against his first real competition. The favorite was Linda's Chief, at 3-5, who had reeled off five consecutive victories. Only five horses were entered, and Secretariat proved he was fearless as well as swift. Seemingly trapped going into the final turn, reported Joe Nichols in *The New York Times*, the "Meadow colt gave a spectacular exhibition as he knifed his way between horses in the stretch to flash into the lead and score by three lengths." An ecstatic Ron Turcotte later said, "That was the day he convinced me. When a horse is going a quarter in 26 seconds, you're forcing him, pushing him. At 24 or 25, you're working together with him. But when it's faster than that, you're picking his head up and he's pulling harder, putting everything into it, and it's a really good feeling. That's the way it is with Secretariat." The win provided the Meadow Stable with an added heady taste of success because Secretariat followed Upper Case and classic winner Riva Ridge as the third stakes winner racing for them in 1972.

The impressive wins by Secretariat sent a faint quiver through the racing community. There was no question that the horse was a major factor to be reckoned with, particularly in the six-and-a-half-furlong Hopeful Stakes coming up on August 26. The race is one of the more important of the year. As the name implies, people hope it can give a clue to potential champions: 12 former Hopeful winners captured the Belmont Stakes, and since 1936, 14 were voted Best Two-Year-Old.

Just about everyone pegged Secretariat the heavy favorite. The only one seemingly in the dark about him was the copy editor of the *New York Daily*

News, who, on the day of the race, published an improbable headline: FILLY SECRETARIAT 1-2 PICK IN $86,550 HOPEFUL

The colt won in typical fashion for him, shooting from last place to a five-length victory. His time of 1:16⅕ was ⅗ second slower than the stakes and track records.

The faint quiver now became a distinct quake. For the first time, some began to talk of him as a "super horse." Kent Hollingsworth, editor of *The Blood-Horse*, in marveling at the end-of-the-race surge, said: "Secretariat . . . has demonstrated a lick not seen since Damascus approached the last turn trailing by about thirteen lengths and came out of it six lengths on top to win the 1967 Travers by twenty-two lengths in track-record time." Even Lucien Laurin began to believe: "Secretariat, the two-year-old, is better geared for immortality than Riva, the three-year-old." And so it was, coming up to the prestigious Belmont Futurity on September 16.

Only six horses dared to face Secretariat, the odds-on favorite, which provoked Michael Strauss of *The New York Times* to report: "Even members of the Baker Street Irregulars, a group devoted to the perpetuation of the memory of Sherlock Holmes, who made their annual appearance at the Big B . . . could find nothing mystifying about the installation of Secretariat as an overnight 2-to-5 choice." If anything, it was "an easy-does-it performance," even though he was next to last on the far turn. "My horse broke all right," remarked Turcotte, "but took himself back like he has been doing, but not so much this time. Maybe he's beginning to forget that bumping he got in his first race." Stop the Music made a brief move at him at the end of the six and a half furlongs, but to no avail. The victory was worth $83,320, bringing Secretariat's total to a respectable $162,580 for the year, and it marked the first back-to-back wins in the Belmont Futurity by the same stable in 30 years. Riva Ridge, with Turcotte riding, had won the race the previous year.

There are five stakes races that are regarded as barometers for determining the best of the two-year-olds: the Hopeful, Futurity, Champagne, Laurel Futurity, and Garden State. Any horse that can take these, or most of them, will win the title hands down and, in all probability, wind up as "the wealthiest horse in the country." Secretariat had a good leg up on the title by dint of wins in the first two of the five. Consequently, he came up to the $125,000-added Champagne Stakes at Belmont Park, New York's richest race for juveniles, on October 14, 1972, as the 7-10 favorite. However, there were some doubters or wishful dreamers. "Secretariat is just about everyone's choice for leading two-year-old colt," wrote William Rudy in the *New York Post*, "but he has not scared anyone out of today's race at one mile. In fact, the fields opposing him keep getting bigger." Only four challenged him in the Sanford, six in the Futurity, but eleven made up the field in the Champagne. There were some, too, who felt the big colt had been tiring at the end of the Futurity when Stop the Music charged him in the stretch, an opinion no doubt fired by the widely held theory that Bold Ruler's offspring could not handle longer distances.

"For the first time in three years, a disqualification turned champagne into vinegar for a great two-year-old in the . . . Champagne Stakes," is the way one writer summed up the race. "Belmont ended Saturday not with a bang but with a whimper, as the best horse was disqualified," another disheartened scribe began his report. To put it more bluntly, 31,494 fans were in a state of shock. Secretariat did, in fact, race home two lengths in front while drawing out, but the "steward inquiry" sign flashed immediately and then indicated that the colt had been dropped to second and Stop the Music had won.

The race had started in typical fashion. Secretariat ran last down the backstretch, biding his time until the far turn. Then, as William Rudy in *The Blood-Horse* described it:

> Three-sixteenths of a mile from the finish . . . Secretariat was moving strongest between horses in a move that had brought him from last place. Stop the Music, racing inside of him, had made his move, too, and for 50 yards or so the two colts had raced stride for stride with Secretariat having just a bit of an advantage over his stubborn rival. At that point, Ron Turcotte . . . went to the whip and hit the Meadow Stable colt right-handed. The colt ducked in sharply. . . .

173

Secretariat seemed to bump Stop the Music. When Turcotte switched his whip to his left hand, the horse straightened out and went on to finish in front. The jockey was dumbfounded because he could not recall Secretariat ever ducking in before in a race.

Laurin, somewhat bitter, commented that the colt "never had to be hit before," so why now—especially since he appeared to be on his way to a win anyhow. For Mrs. Tweedy, the outcome was a terrible disappointment: "This was to be Secretariat's coronation race. He had the two-year-old championship in the bag," she lamented. Laurin's bitterness was further evidenced by his recalling how the colt had been "knocked against the gate and met with all kinds of traffic" in his first start. The decision of the stewards stood, nevertheless.

The sour taste of the race was washed away, however, when Secretariat emerged on the track two weeks later. "Saturday, October 28, at Laurel was designed for young lovers—and the bettors loved it," waxed *The Blood-Horse*. "The nation's two outstanding two-year-olds, La Prevoyante and Secretariat, ran on the same program, and each was backed down to 1-10." La Prevoyante was a Canadian-bred filly owned by electronics magnate Jean-Louis Levesque. She had won all of her eleven races to date (nine of them stakes), was the only two-year-old filly ever to win more than eight straight, was certain of being named Champion Two-Year-Old Filly, and was in the running for Horse of the Year honors. She was competing that day in the $121,990 Selima Stakes.

Secretariat also had quite a bit on the line. He was a shoo-in for Best Two-Year-Old honors, but, he was also competing for Horse of the Year—not only against the fetching filly, but also against the three-year-olds Riva Ridge and Key to the Mint, who were to duel it out in the Jockey Club Gold Cup at Aqueduct that same day. In essence, the day was a track fan's dream, for the best of America's Thoroughbreds would be in action in New York and Maryland. It augured a weekend of decision by the pollsters whose minds, no doubt, would be influenced by the results of the day.

Lucien Laurin had a moment of decision of his own. He was torn between two loves—should he stay in New York with Riva Ridge, or should he go to Laurel to be with Secretariat? Not only did he choose the chestnut colt, but he also assigned Ron Turcotte as his jockey. He was not disappointed. Secretariat again made an unhurried start. In his first experience with a sloppy track, he kept to the outside and handled the track as though he were out for a morning breeze. He loped home by eight lengths to the good in 1:42⅖ for the 1¹⁄₁₆ miles, just ⅕ second slower than the track record. Turcotte looked back over his shoulder in mid-stretch and saw nothing. As they say, he was "lookin' and cookin'"; it was no contest. It was also sweet revenge over Stop the Music, who finished second, and to whom Secretariat had given up first place in the Champagne Stakes on the foul claim. After the race, Lucien Laurin once more tried to explain his colt's hang-up stemming from the knocking-about he had experienced in his first race. "It happened near the ⅜ pole; apparently it made him gun-shy because when he gets to the ⅜ pole now he turns on the gas regardless of what distance he is running."

La Prevoyante apparently had no such problems in the Selima race. She merely took off, spread-eagled the field by 14 lengths, and coasted home for her 12ᵗʰ win in a race of that distance, in 1:46⅗. It brought her earnings to $417,109 and made her the only two-year-old to win so many times in an undefeated season since Colin did it in 1907. Her owner, after the race, either wittingly or not, voiced a prediction on Secretariat's future that was to make headlines throughout the following year: "I know Mrs. [Helen] Tweedy very well. The deal has already been made. La Prevoyante will be bred to Secretariat the first year they are at stud."

Meadow Stable was considerably less fortunate in New York, where Riva Ridge was soundly thrashed in the Jockey Club Gold Cup. He came in 3 lengths behind Key to the Mint, who, in turn, lagged behind Autobiography by 15 lengths. The loss suggested unhappy tidings in the year-end balloting.

The last race of the year for Secretariat, the Garden State Stakes in New Jersey, went as expected. Going off at 1-10, he "left the players laughing," after first "giving them a mass attack of jitters as he dawdled along in last place during the early stages of the race," was Gene Ward's colorful account of the race in the *New York Daily News*. It was only when the track announcer voiced what had become a familiar refrain during his races—"Here comes Secretariat with a big rush on the outside"—that they headed for the win windows. Rudy Turcotte, Ron's brother, who raced Angle Light to a second-place finish three and a half lengths behind, for one fleeting moment had an illusion of an upset in the making. "Then I looked over my shoulder," he recalled, "and saw those blue and white checkers on the outside. I knew if Secretariat was close to me with a quarter of a mile to go it was all over for me."

Voting for champion horses is conducted by a poll of the handicappers of the Thoroughbred Racing Associations (TRA), the staff of the *Daily Racing Form* (DRF), and members of the National Turf Writers Association (NTWA). Until 1971, each group held its own voting, and prior to that, the distinguished chronicler of the turf, Walter S. Vosburgh, made the selections. The 1972 nominees produced a rare ballot-box battle. It was no contest as far as champion two-year-old colt and filly were concerned. It was for the top honors that the voting became somewhat sticky. *Sports Illustrated* reported:

> Much has been made of the contest between the two-year-old colt Secretariat and the two-year-old filly La Prevoyante for Horse of the Year Honors, but less excitable members of the racing fraternity felt

that either choice was unrealistic. No two-year-old, they argued, could properly be named horse of any year. It was as illogical as naming a particularly brilliant college junior as Man of the Year. Promise and precocity are not the same as mature achievement, and a two-year-old colt or filly is essentially promise.

The final tally, as a result, was something of a mishmash in which Secretariat received 77 votes to La Prevoyante's 56, with the TRA and DRF favoring the colt. On the other hand, NTWA members submitted 58 ballots for Horse of the Year with 26 going to the filly, 21 to the colt, and 11 to the Chilean-bred Cougar II. There seemed to be a consensus that while the filly indeed had won all 12 of her races, Secretariat, in chalking up seven victories in nine starts and winning $456,404, had had tougher opposition. Thus, in taking turfdom's top award, the Eclipse, Secretariat became only the third two-year-old to achieve the feat. The others were Native Dancer in 1952 and Moccasin in 1965. In addition, he was the fifth home-bred champion for Christopher T. Chenery's Meadow Stable, following in the footsteps of Hill Prince, First Landing, Cicada, and Riva Ridge.

The one disappointment for Meadow Stable was Riva Ridge, who failed in his bid for the three-year-old title, losing out to Rokeby Stable's Key to the Mint. After having won the Belmont Stakes, Riva Ridge was victorious only once more during the rest of the year, in the Hollywood Derby, which obviously must have affected the balloting. *Sports Illustrated* seemed to object: "Now a new controversy rages over why Key to the Mint was picked instead of Riva Ridge, who won the Kentucky Derby and the Belmont Stakes, the two most prestigious races for three-year-olds. What it all comes down to, obviously, is that races and reputations are won on the track, not in the polling places."

With the start of 1973, a year that was to see Secretariat produce some of the most spectacular turf histrionics and headlines ever recorded by a three-year-old Thoroughbred in America, Lucien Laurin was no longer hesitant about the future. "I want another shot at the Triple Crown," he stated boldly, "and I think this colt . . . is going to give me a real look at our classics again. He doesn't have to carry his track around with him, either. He has handled all kinds," he concluded, in an obvious allusion to Riva Ridge's problems with racing in mud.

Three days into the new year, Christopher T. Chenery, the founder of Meadow Stable, was dead at the age of 86. His demise created a mountainous tax problem for the heirs. Although he had arranged for the orderly transfer of most of his assets, the taxes on the horses owned by him would have been so prohibitive that they would have necessitated a dispersal sale. As things stood, it was apparent that the "Secretariat bloodline was the most salable asset" of the Meadow operation. A little over a month later, therefore, it was announced that Secretariat had been syndicated for the unheard-of sum of $6,080,000. It was a world-record price, and it made the colt the most valuable breeding prospect in the history of Thoroughbred racing anywhere. The previous high was $5,440,000, the price attached to the European champion Nijinsky II in 1970.

Dr. Hollis Chenery prevailed this time. "My brother's an economist," said Penny Tweedy, "and it made him nervous to think of owning an asset worth $6,000,000 that depended on a single heart beat." The syndication was put together by Seth Hancock, 24-year-old son of Bull Hancock, who had also died. It called for 32 shares in the horse, each worth $190,000. Two would be retained by Mrs. Tweedy; two would go to the Chenery Corporation, a family-owned enterprise; and the other 28 would be offered to breeders.

Several of the biggest breeding farms balked at the price, but the shares were quickly subscribed to by Thoroughbred owners in the United States and throughout the world. Each shareowner received the privilege of sending a mare to Secretariat once a year for the rest of his life, commencing with the start of the breeding season in February 1974. It was further stipulated that the colt would be allowed to continue racing until November 15, 1973, with the Meadow Stable retaining all purses won.

Mrs. Tweedy was somewhat philosophical about the price: "I guess the price was based on the Macy's basement theory; $190,000 sounded more reasonable than two hundred." Seth Hancock was more practical: "I'd say it wasn't really a gamble. Even if he doesn't win the Triple Crown, he's worth the money. He's got all three things you want in a sire: pedigree, looks, and performance." The records tended to belie this, however, because many past two-year-old champions failed to duplicate their form at three.

Despite the controversy surrounding the price, Penny Tweedy nevertheless maintained an admirable candor about the syndication deal. "Secretariat was really a sort of deus ex machina for us. He came along at exactly the right time. And what I thought was particularly nice was that Mr. Phipps was the first subscriber to the syndicate." Phipps was somewhat less sanguine. "It's unlikely that any of his offspring will be as good as Secretariat, but then again a horse doesn't have to be that good to be successful." He may have been thinking of the foal he wound up with following the coin toss with Mrs. Tweedy in 1969. He may also have been thinking of what an expert breeder once said: "What you really need to get a good foal is a male horse, a female—and a lot of luck."

Commercial breeders in the syndicate, perhaps more than the others, could expect a quick return on their investment. It was possible for them to receive six-figure sums for Secretariat foals at Saratoga or Keeneland yearling sales. If the colt raced well in 1973, they could easily recoup with just three or four foals.

It was also revealed at the time that there would be heavy insurance coverage against anything happening to the horse. He was covered for his entire syndication value, which called for a premium of $500,000 for 1973 alone. When Penny Tweedy indicated that Secretariat was insured against everything from illness to infertility, one sportswriter wanted to know: "Where do you go to apply for that infertility policy?" Another found it hard to cope with the price. "In the bullish world of horse breeding," wrote Steve Cady in *The New York Times*, "buying Secretariat at $190,000 a share makes as much sense as buying I.B.M. at $431."

The big red horse made other headline news early in 1973, even though he was still residing at his winter training quarters at Hialeah. On January 11, Kenneth Noe Jr., handicapper for the New York Racing Association and the Jockey Club, released his figures for the Free Experimental Handicap. Some 137 Thoroughbreds, including 67 fillies, were evaluated, and Secretariat was assigned 129 pounds. Only five other horses had topped him since the handicapping was begun in 1933 by Vosburgh. They were: Bimelech, 130 (1939); Alsab, 130 (1941); Count Fleet, 132 (1942); Native Dancer, 130 (1952); and Bold Lad, 130 (1964).

The time was finally at hand for Secretariat to start moving to the track. He arrived in New York early in February and was immediately prepared for his three-year-old debut in the Bay Shore at Aqueduct. He was fit; he had grown amazingly over the winter, adding an inch and a quarter to his height in six months. Laurin was worried. "I knew he had filled out well over the winter, he was training well and he was sound. But, still, until they race again, you wonder." He could have saved himself the concern. The colt drove through a sloppy track and a traffic jam of horses to win by four and a half lengths on St. Patrick's Day, March 17, 1973. "It told us all we wanted to know," said Penny Tweedy with relief. "It told us that he still has the heart, the will, the courage to win, that he still knows how to win. This is the greatest test, when they come out as three-year-olds." After the race, Ron Turcotte for the first time admitted the growing pressure when he told Pete Axthelm of *Newsweek*: "I never thought that six million would feel so heavy."

His second outing was on April 7, in the one-mile Gotham Stakes. There, he proved he was warming up to the task by equaling the track mark of 1:33⅗, while carrying 126 pounds, which prompted one reporter to look upon the results as "just another preliminary exercise of the kind made by circus acrobats as they limber up for their more spectacular maneuvers." In winning both the Gotham and the Bay Shore, Secretariat became only the third horse ever to be victorious in both races. This brought him to the important Wood Memorial on April 20. At 1⅛ miles, it would be the longest race for him thus far, and it would match him against the other best-rated three-year-old in the country, Sham. The flashy bay had a peculiar record. He was a flop early in his juvenile year and was auctioned off for $200,000 to Sigmund Sommer, a real estate and construction businessman. He finally broke his maiden on December 9 at Aqueduct, and then polished off three more wins in five tries to earn $115,250. His last victory was on March 31, when he beat Linda's Chief in the Santa Anita Handicap in 1:47—⅕ of a second faster than the mark at Aqueduct for the same distance and the distance of the Wood Memorial.

The Wood, traditionally, is regarded as the most important in the East before the Kentucky Derby and is supposed to indicate the probable favorite of the Run for the Roses. Three of the eight previous Triple Crown winners— Gallant Fox, Count Fleet, and Assault—used the Wood as the springboard to their final climb to glory. Therefore, in 1973, it had an extra measure of excitement when Sham and Secretariat were entered. "Seldom do two three-year-olds rated as the best in the land meet before the Derby," wrote William Rudy in the *New York Post*.

As the day of the race approached, a first-class rhubarb erupted. Secretariat was to be paired with his stablemate, Angle Light, who was also trained by Laurin but owned by Edwin Whittaker. There was talk that Sham would have two running stablemates, Knightly Dawn, who had acted as his pacemaker in the Santa Anita, and Beautiful Music. All three were owned by Sommer. In all, it appeared that 11 horses would be running, which caused the venerable Charles Hatton to voice some disgust in his column in the *Daily Racing Form* on April 19: "We hope it will narrow down to a horse race, not another donnybrook." Because the race is started on the first turn of the track, and because it is only for nine furlongs, he feared a "bloody awful scrimmage for position."

It was his hope, rather, that the race would be "virtually horse-against-horse, in the old tradition exciting to contemplate" between Sham and Secretariat. He went on to say that there "is nothing in the Rules of Racing to prevent a horse from bringing his gang with him, so long as they are paid-up eligibles. But the Wood is supposed to decide who had the best horse, not the most horses." He concluded by writing that "neither Sham nor Secretariat strikes us as the sort who need blockers," and that he did not think Frank "Pancho" Martin, Sham's trainer, really wanted to run two horses, let alone three.

The following day, Martin was quoted as saying that he would likewise prefer it if only the two colts ran. "I am running Knightly Dawn only because Lucien is running Angle Light. I will not run an entry if he will take out the other horse." He also boasted that he felt Sham was the best in the race. "I am going to give Secretariat a good try," he cried. "We have to try him and this is the time to do it." He even offered to bet Laurin $5,000 that Sham would win, so confident was he.

Hatton, in the meantime, kept up his drumbeat of complaint. "There still were indications the stage would be cluttered by a lot of spear carriers when the protagonists, Sham and Secretariat, make their entrance," he warned. Then, he went on to lambast the caliber of the horses, proclaiming that some "could not get a job pulling the track harrow." Finally, he predicted, "We shall not be surprised if the tote board lights up with foul claims like Times Square on Saturday night." It was on the morning of the big race, however, that he threw out his most telling barbs. He quoted Lucien Laurin as saying earlier in the week about his horse's chances: "The only way they can beat him is to steal it," while, at the same time, reporting that the track stewards were determined that nobody was going to "purloin the race."

The volatile Martin roared with anger, and that morning scratched both Knightly Dawn and Beautiful Music. He later explained his reason: "But after the remark in the paper, I don't want to be a friend of his. I never made a remark about him. He called me a thief. I didn't call him a thief." He also claimed Laurin was in effect saying that Sham could not beat Secretariat without help. Lucien Laurin, on the other hand, explained that he could not withdraw Angle Light because he had a different owner and, therefore, each of his two horses had "to run his own race." As for his "steal" remark, this was merely track parlance, which meant that by opening a long early lead with a false pace, or by setting a very slow pace to preserve his strength for the stretch run, a horse could just manage to throw a favorite off his race plan and sneak home in front. Throughout the protracted argument, all Tweedy could say was: "From here on out it's Tums and Rolaids." It was a most prophetic comment.

Only eight horses went to the post, with the entry of Secretariat and Angle Light the 3-10 favorite. When the race was over, 43,416 people, the largest crowd of the season, could not believe what they had just seen. They were dumbstruck. Angle Light scored a smashing upset, finishing ahead in front of Sham and four lengths over Secretariat. He had come out fast and had stayed in front all the way. Jockey Jacinto Vasquez did in fact slow the pace and "steal the race from Sham and Secretariat." Bob Ussery, on sixth-place Flush, gave the clue in noting the time for six furlongs. "When they went 1:12 and change, it was good night. Any good horse can finish after that, and Angle Light is a good horse." A disappointed, puzzled Ron Turcotte could only say that his mount "just didn't have his punch today. I had him clear on the backside and I tried to move him up, but he didn't respond when I hit him at about the ½ mile pole." Turcotte tried again after a wide turn into the stretch, but the colt only lugged in a bit and lacked his usual kick. Sham also seemed to be wanting in a finishing drive, although his jockey, Jorge Velasquez, felt he would have won in a longer race. Obviously caught in the middle, the rider had to worry about letting Angle Light get away while making sure he had enough left to cope with Secretariat's expected late charge. As for Lucien Laurin, he looked like the world had come to an end, not like the trainer of a horse who had just won $68,940. He was so dazed by Secretariat's futile stretch run that he did not realize which horse had won. It was Tweedy who told him: "You won it; your horse was first." Pancho Martin, too, felt that his jockey had been conned by the slow pace, and Tweedy said it "looked to me as though we were racing one horse, Sham, and forgetting the rest of the field." Furthermore, she had the uncomfortable experience of having had in her box 10 bankers from the Chase Manhattan Bank, which had become co-executor of the Chenery will. The outcome of the race could have made her wonder if she still had a "friend at the Chase."

Needless to say, the press had a field day with the speculations on Secretariat's future even though he had come in first in his previous 10 races. "So Secretariat is only human after all, though the squeamish might insist he's only equine. Racing people and the racing public had begun to regard this newest folk hero as invincible," wrote Red Smith in *The New York Times*. Gene Ward, in the *New York Daily News*, was more cutting: "This was the horse that was going to win the Triple Crown for the first time since Citation turned the trick in 1948. This was the syndicated marvel whose backers had invested $6,000,000, and Ron Turcotte, his rider, just didn't want to admit that it was the horse's own fault—he got beat." Whitney Tower, in *Sports Illustrated*, looked ahead to the Kentucky Derby. "It may not be necessary to start the race in rows, Indianapolis 500 style, but following Secretariat's defeat a lot of guys are going to be cranking up three-year-old maidens from New England to Nevada and shipping them to Louisville." Pete Axthelm in *Newsweek* was of the opinion that ". . . the brilliant colt seemed a very shaky proposition as an even-money Derby favorite," while *Time* intoned that the Derby shaped up "as more of a horse race than the smart money had previously predicted. . . . In fact, a modicum of suspense was needed to save the Derby from tedium," and that element apparently was now present.

The doubts, concerns, bewilderment, and second-guessing engendered by the Wood Memorial followed all of the principals to Churchill Downs. Opinions and predictions were available by the yard. Most prominent among these, of course, was the old shibboleth of Bold Ruler sons, that none had ever won a Derby. Laurin and Turcotte tried simply to write off the Wood as just "a bad race thrown in by a good horse," who would fire up in the Derby. The diminutive trainer, however, was highly incensed over reports that Secretariat had some heat in his legs and was below form. "Last week," he lamented, "Jimmy the Greek claimed my horse was standing in ice with knee trouble and there was talk of laying odds that the colt wouldn't get to the Derby. . . . Secretariat has not been put in ice," he said, "and there's nothing in the world wrong with him." Still, with 28 syndicate members looking over his shoulder at his every move with their $6 million investment, the pressure was intense. He took to taking sleeping pills for the first time, but still had sleepless nights.

Some other distinguished trainers offered little solace. Jimmy Jones, for example, who helped saddle eight Derby winners including Citation, was unimpressed with all of the horses in the Derby: "It doesn't measure up as a good field. There are some good horses, no great ones. No superstars." Referring to the Wood, he added: "A great horse will win under any conditions—slow track, fast track, mud, slow pace, fast pace. Citation was that kind of horse. He was an arrogant rascal. He could lick them all any time, and he knew it." Then there was Horatio Luro, who had trained Northern Dancer when he won the 1964 classic and set the still-standing 2:00 mark. He said, "A horse of Secretariat's 'blocky' build would not be [my] first choice in selecting a 1¼-mile horse." There was also the theory that Laurin had not raced the

Angle Light (front right) scores a stunning upset over Sham (center) and Secretariat (left) in the Wood Memorial.

big colt enough before the Derby. "Pancho" Martin also got in his jabs by renewing his $5,000 bet offer to the little white-haired ex-jockey and trainer. He also said he would run just Sham.

The bay colt was, in fact, shaping up as a growing favorite. The day before the race, fans at Churchill Downs gave Sham a slight edge against the Secretariat–Angle Light entry. They bet $44,915 on Sham as against $41,711 on the entry. The other horses came in for short shrift. Sportswriter Gene Ward had a rather dim appraisal of the field and he selected Sham, My Gallant, and Secretariat—in that order. He said Angle Light had had a nosebleed, Royal and Regal had a blister, and Shecky Greene was said by his critics to be able to "travel a mile and a quarter only in a van."

In New York, interest in the horse race heated up. The Off-Track Betting Corporation reported $1,131,724 in bets on Friday and, by 11:00 A.M. on the day of the race, $1,648,940. A secretary refused to support the big, red colt because "you can't make money with him." However, a United Nations Soviet executive ignored the warning. It was also reported that the OTB office on "flaky" 42nd Street was outdrawing its neighbors, the Roxy Burlesk and a double-feature sex bill of *Hetro Sexuals* and *Street of a Thousand Pleasures*.

Derby Day, May 5, 1973, for the 99th running of the renowned classic, opened with a record and never quit. At the outset, 134,476 people poured through the turnstiles of Churchill Downs, the biggest crowd ever. They then charged the betting windows to plunk down a total of $7,627,965 on all of the day's races, which topped all previous American marks, and $3,200,000 on the Derby alone, also a record. In New York, a record $3,050,194 in bets were received by the OTB. The gross value of the race was $198,880, with $155,050 going to the winner, making it the richest of all Kentucky Derbys. Thirteen Thoroughbreds marched to the post, the first time in 13 years that that exact number of horses was entered. Angle Light was in the number two position, Sham in number four, and Secretariat in number ten. He and Angle Light went off at 3-2, with Sham the second favorite at 5-2.

Secretariat came out of the gate slowly as usual, cut sharply to the rail, and settled back to last place as the field came past the stands. Near the first turn, Bill Hartack, on Warbucks, shouted at Turcotte: "Stay out, stay out, stay away," apparently remembering the big colt's veering during the Wood Memorial. Secretariat began to pick up horses on the backstretch and went to the middle of the pack. Sham, in the meantime, had moved into second and remained there. On the far turn, Sham went into the lead while Secretariat continued to loop the field on the outside, finally moving up to the leader, "his handsome head held low, heavy muscles grouping and stretching beneath the glistening coat." At that moment, according to Gene Ward, the "real Secretariat stood up and ran over Sham . . . careening past horses as though they were standing still." In the final furlong, it was a two-horse race. They met eye-to-eye at about the 3/16 pole and, although Sham "held on with courage," the big colt inexorably drew away. "Secretariat had his blood up, the Wood Memorial was behind him," reported *The Blood-Horse*, and he swept down the stretch to a record-breaking victory by two and a half lengths. The time was 1:59⅖, which stripped ⅗ second from the old mark. An incredible performance, awe-inspiring, monumental as any ever in the history of the race, was the consensus of the press, particularly because Secretariat and Sham "ran a classic in a non-American way—the last part faster than the first part." Secretariat was clocked in 0:23⅕ for the final quarter, breaking the mark of

0:24 for that distance set by Whirlaway in the 1941 Derby. He ran the first quarter in 0:23⅗.

Sham, for his part, also ran a remarkable race. He was timed at 2:00, thereby tying the old record, and finished eight lengths in front of Our Native. He completed the first mile in 1:36⅕, which meant he, too, ran the last quarter in less than 0:24. In fact, he became the fastest losing horse in the history of the Derby. To put it another way, he had run the Derby faster than 97 winners. His achievement was even more startling considering his mishap at the start. Another colt, Twice a Prince, had acted up in the starting gate, disturbing Sham and causing him to bang his head against the side of his stall. On his return to the barn, his mouth was bloodied, with two teeth dangling by a thin strip of his gum, causing trainer Frank "Pancho" Martin to remark that he looked "like a four-legged hockey player."

Ron Turcotte, in the jockey room after the hectic festivities, let go of some pent-up sarcasms, apparently reflecting some of the feelings of the Meadow Stable team: "He ran pretty good for a crippled horse. You know something, he might have run that in 1:56 if he was all right."

The result of the race produced a number of new and significant statistics and equaled others. It was the first time that the same owner-breeder-trainer-jockey combination had saddled two consecutive Derby winners. It also meant consecutive winning mounts for groom Eddie Sweat and exercise rider Charlie Davis. Mrs. Tweedy became the fourth breeder and third owner with consecutive winners. Lucien Laurin was the fourth trainer with consecutive winners. Ron Turcotte became the first jockey in 71 years to have back-to-back victories. Secretariat was only the second two-year-old champion since Needles in 1956, and the second Free Experimental Handicap topweight since Middleground in 1950, to fulfill his juvenile promise by taking the Derby. He was the second Virginia-bred horse since Reigh Count in 1928 to win the Derby. Of particular interest to breeders—he destroyed the myth about Bold Ruler's sons.

There was a wholly different attitude toward Secretariat as the Preakness approached two weeks later. By then, the opposition dwindled down to just five, with the owners and trainers of some horses exhibiting considerably more respect. Bill Resseguet, owner of Our Native, stated: "I'm going to tell my jockey to hold onto Secretariat's tail and see if we can get second money." Fred Menke, owner of Deadly Dream, candidly admitted: "Our best chance is if the others collapse." Buddy Delp, trainer of Ecole Etage, had a unique race

Secretariat completes a remarkable, record-breaking race ahead of Sham in the 1973 Kentucky Derby. He stripped ⅗ of a second from the old mark and ran the last ¼ mile in 0:23⅕.

Official Chart of the Kentucky Derby

NINTH RACE CD May 5, 1973 — **1¼ MILES. (2:00). Ninety-ninth running KENTUCKY DERBY. SCALE WEIGHTS. $125,000 added. 3-year-olds. By subscription of $100 each in cash, which covers nomination for both the Kentucky Derby and Derby Trial. All nomination fees to Derby winner, $2,500 to pass the entry box, Thursday, May 3, $1,500 additional to start, $125,000 added, of which $25,000 to second, $12,500 to third, $6,250 to fourth. $100,000 guaranteed to winner (to be divided equally in event of a dead-heat). Weight, 126 lbs. The owner of the winner to receive a gold trophy. Closed with 218 nominations.**
Value of race, $198,800. Value to winner $155,050; second, $25,000; third, $12,500; fourth, $6,250.
Mutuel Pool, $3,284,962.

Last Raced	Horse	EqtA	Wt	PP	¼	½	¾	1	Str	Fin	Jockeys	Owners	Odds to $1
4-21-73^7 Aqu^3	Secretariat	b3	126	10	11^h	6½	5^1	$2^{1½}$	1½	$1^{2½}$	RTurcotte	Meadow Stable	a-1.50
4-21-73^7 Aqu^2	Sham	b3	126	4	5^1	3^2	2^1	1½	2^6	2^8	LPincayJr	S Sommer	2.50
4-26-73^6 Kee^2	Our Native	b3	126	7	6½	$8^{1½}$	8^1	5^h	3^h	3½	DBrumfield	Pr'ch'd-Thom's-R'q't	10.60
4-26-73^6 Kee^5	Forego	3	126	9	$9^{1½}$	9½	6½	6^2	4½	$4^{2½}$	PAnderson	Lazy F Ranch	28.60
4-28-73^7 CD^2	Restless Jet	3	126	1	$7^{1½}$	7^h	$10^{1½}$	$7^{1½}$	$6^{1½}$	$5^{2¼}$	MHole	Elkwood Farm	28.50
4-28-73^7 CD^1	Shecky Greene	b3	126	11	$1^{1½}$	1^3	$1^{1½}$	3^3	5^1	$6^{1½}$	LAdams	J Kellman	b-5.70
4-26-73^6 Kee^6	Navajo	b3	126	5	$10^{1½}$	10^1	11^4	$8^{1½}$	8^2	7no	WSoirez	J Stevenson-R Stump	52.30
4-26-73^6 Kee^7	Royal and Regal	3	126	8	3^1	4^3	4^3	4^1	$7^{1½}$	$8^{3½}$	WBlum	Aisco Stable	28.30
4-26-73^6 Kee^1	My Gallant	b3	126	12	8^h	$11^{1½}$	12^3	11^2	10½	9^h	BBaeza	A I Appleton	b-5.70
4-21-73^7 Aqu^1	Angle Light	3	126	2	4^h	$5^{1½}$	7^1	$10^{1½}$	$9^{1½}$	$10^{1¾}$	JLeBlanc	E Whittaker	a-1.50
5- 1-73^8 CD^5	Gold Bag	b3	126	13	2^h	2^h	3½	9^1	11^1	11no	EFires	R Sechrest-Gottdank	68.30
4-28-73^7 CD^6	Twice a Prince	b3	126	6	13	13	13	13	12^2	$12^{1½}$	ASantiago	Elmendorf	62.50
4-26-73^6 Kee^3	Warbucks	3	126	3	12^1	12^3	9^h	$12^{1½}$	13	13	WHartack	E E Elzemeyer	7.20

a-Coupled, Secretariat and Angle Light; b-Shecky Greene and My Gallant.

Time, :23⅖, :47⅖, 1:11⅘, 1:36⅕, 1:59⅖ (new track record). Track fast.

$2 Mutuel Prices:			
1A-SECRETARIAT (a-Entry)	5.00	3.20	3.00
5-SHAM		3.20	3.00
8-OUR NATIVE			4.20

Ch. c, by Bold Ruler—Somethingroyal, by Princequillo. Trainer, L. Laurin. Bred by Meadow Stud, Inc. (Va.).
IN GATE—5:37. OFF AT 5:37 EASTERN DAYLIGHT TIME. Start good. Won handily.

SECRETARIAT relaxed nicely and dropped back last leaving the gate as the field broke in good order, moved between horses to begin improving position entering the first turn, but passed rivals from the outside thereafter. Turcotte roused him smartly with the whip in his right hand leaving the far turn and SECRETARIAT strongly raced to the leaders, lost a little momentum racing into the stretch where Turcotte used the whip again, but then switched it to his left hand and merely flashed it as the winner willingly drew away in record breaking time. SHAM, snugly reserved within striking distance after brushing with NAVAJO at the start, raced around rivals to the front without any need of rousing and drew clear between calls entering the stretch, was under a strong hand ride after being displaced in the last furlong and continued resolutely to dominate the remainder of the field. OUR NATIVE, reserved in the first run through the stretch, dropped back slightly on the turn, came wide in the drive and finished well for his placing. FOREGO, taken to the inside early, veered slightly from a rival and hit the rail entering the far turn, swung wide entering the stretch and vied with OUR NATIVE in the drive. RESTLESS JET saved ground in an even effort. SHECKY GREENE easily set the pace under light rating for nearly seven furlongs and faltered. NAVAJO was outrun. ROYAL AND REGAL raced well for a mile and had nothing left in the drive. MY GALLANT, outrun at all stages, was crowded on the stretch turn. ANGLE LIGHT gave way steadily in a dull effort and was forced to check when crowded by GOLD BAG on the stretch turn. GOLD BAG had good speed and stopped. TWICE A PRINCE reared and was hung in the gate briefly before the start and then showed nothing in the running. WARBUCKS was dull.

plan: "We'll try to go to the head. That's where [Ecole Etage] likes to be. And we're going to put high-speed roller skates on him so he'll be able to stay in front." Sham's trainer Frank Martin simply said: "Anybody that beats him will have to do some running." There would be no excuses.

The day of the Preakness was clear and bright, and a record crowd of 61,657—15,000 in the infield alone—invaded the track and invested it with a carnival atmosphere, replete with rock bands, dance contests, and a special promotion by the Baltimore Colts football club to honor their ace quarterback Johnny Unitas. The Harry M. Stevens Company even came out with a special black-eyed Susan drink of vodka, rum, and fruit juice to match the mint julep of Kentucky. Even Bob Marisch, of the *Baltimore Sun*, was motivated to uphold civic pride and espouse the importance of the Maryland classic. He wrote of a Louisville newsman quoting Irvin S. Cobb's famous description of the Kentucky Derby: "But, what's the use? Until you go to Kentucky and with your own eyes behold the Derby, you ain't never been nowhere and you ain't never seen nothin'." Marisch countered with an Ogden Nash rhyme:

> The Derby is a race of autocrat sleekness
>> For horses of birth to prove their worth to run in the Preakness
> The Preakness is my weakness.

The tight turns of the Pimlico track are always items of concern for trainers. On the day before the race, Lucien Laurin discounted this hazard for his horse and vowed not to fall into the same trap he had with Riva Ridge in 1972. "I may not win tomorrow, but I'll guarantee you I won't lose 10 lengths in the first turn. And I'll make every one of them run every step of the way." He did.

Secretariat went off as the 5-10 favorite and "looked like a mine of pure gold . . . instead of a mere $6,000,000," to sportswriter Joe Nichols. The colt broke well and sat back in fourth place, five and a half lengths behind the leader, Ecole Etage. After the first quarter, going into the first turn, the pace seemed slow to Turcotte. He chirped, and his mount accelerated, going three-wide around horses to the dismay of the fans and near heart failure for Lucien Laurin. Later, Turcotte revealed that Secretariat seemed to feel the pace, too, and drew out on his own.

Laffit Pincay Jr. had Sham running well and was waiting for Turcotte to apply the whip. "He went by us flying in the backstretch," Pincay recalled, hardly expecting the move so early in the race. With ¾ of a mile to go, the chestnut colt took the lead and headed for home, never touched by the whip. Pincay figured he might have a chance at the top of the stretch because of Secretariat's early move. He never did. For Turcotte, the biggest threat he faced was the crowd in the infield, some of whom began to climb the rail. To prevent his horse from being spooked, he cocked his head to the right, so that the move and the blinkers would block out the turmoil on the left.

It was a delightfully easy victory by two and a half lengths over Sham and ten and a half over Our Native, marking the first time in the history of the Preakness that the one-two-three horses duplicated exactly the windup of the Derby. The official time was announced as 1:55, which set off an unusual controversy. In the stands, two staffers of the *Daily Racing Form* timed the race with their own stopwatches and came up with 1:53⅗, better than the record of 1:54 set by Canonero II in 1971. The track's time was recorded electronically. The embarrassed track officials stood by their guns until two days later, when they changed the time to 1:54⅖. It was explained that the official track clocker had also timed the race manually, and that was his result. The decision seemed to be a compromise, although many felt that Secretariat was being finessed out of a record-breaking credit.

After the race, Laurin and Turcotte explained their strategy. Both felt that they had lost the Wood Memorial when Turcotte restrained Secretariat at the start of the race, which seemed to confuse the colt. Now, they "let the horse run his own race." For "Pancho" Martin, it was another cruel blow. Although he refused to offer any excuses, it was a fact that Sham ran into some more bad luck at the start of the race. He brushed with Deadly Dream coming out of the gate and then hit the rail on the clubhouse turn. "I just have to see him go in the big one at Belmont, where there's plenty of room on the track," he moaned. Clem Florio, in the *New York Post*, found it easier to explain Martin's dilemma in baseball terms. He "understandably finds it difficult to accept his .300 hitter had been overshadowed by one that can bat .400 with only one eye open."

Winning the race broke a jinx for Laurin. It was his first Preakness. In the happy glow of victory, he commented: "I thought Mrs. Tweedy did not charge enough for membership in the syndicate. I suggested $250,000 and I guess I'm right now, eh?" Apropos of this, one such member told Seth Hancock that he had, indeed, been offered a quarter of a million dollars for his share. As for the Tweedys, the day was a succession of rather odd experiences. Their car was

Jockey Ron Turcotte hand rides Secretariat to a two-and-a-half-length victory over Sham in the 1973 Preakness Stakes. Our Native was third, thus duplicating the 1-2-3 finish of the Kentucky Derby.

smacked into in the parking lot; there were no Meadow Stable credentials at the track, so they had to pay their way in; Mrs. Tweedy's arm was burned by a cigarette; and Mr. Tweedy's pocket was picked. Later, Jack Tweedy remarked: "Boy, we needed to win this one today, just to get even."

Early in June, as the date for the running of the 105th Belmont Stakes neared, it appeared as though newsmen were searching lexicons and thesauri for appropriate adjectives with which to describe the wondrous attributes of Secretariat. His tremendous wins in the Kentucky Derby and Preakness, once and for all, dispelled any notions of his ability to go on and take the Triple Crown. One could be accused of blasphemy if he were even to suggest that remotest of possibilities. His popularity was at such a seething boil that three national magazines, *Time*, *Newsweek*, and *Sports Illustrated*, featured him in cover stories within the same week. The remarkable coincidence impelled *Newsweek*'s editor, Osborn Elliott, to remark: "We're going from Watergate to Starting Gate."

Trainer Lucien Laurin and owner Helen Tweedy lead Secretariat and Ron Turcotte to the winner's circle following the Preakness victory. The race produced hot controversy over whether or not the colt had broken the record.

Official Chart of Preakness

EIGHTH RACE
Pim
May 19, 1973

1$\frac{3}{16}$ MILES. (1:54). Ninety-eighth running PREAKNESS STAKES. SCALE WEIGHTS. $150,000 added. 3-year-olds. By subscription of $100 each, this fee to accompany the nomination. $1,000 to pass the entry box, starters to pay $1,000 additional. All eligibility, entrance and starting fees to the winner, with $150,000 added, of which $30,000 to second, $15,000 to third and $7,500 to fourth. Weight, 126 lbs. A replica of the Woodlawn Vase will be presented to the winning owner to remain his or her personal property. Closed Thursday, Feb. 15, 1973 with 194 nominations.

Value of race $182,400. Value to winner $129,900; second, $30,000; third, $15,000; fourth, $7,500.
Mutuel Pool, $922,989.

Last Raced	Horse	EqtAWt	PP	St	¼	½	¾	Str	Fin	Jockeys	Owners	Odds to $1
5- 5-73^9 CD^1	Secretariat	b3 126	3	6	$4^{\frac{1}{2}}$	$1^{\frac{1}{2}}$	$1^{2\frac{1}{2}}$	$1^{2\frac{1}{2}}$	$1^{2\frac{1}{2}}$	RTurcotte	Meadow Stable	.30
5- 5-73^9 CD^2	Sham	b3 126	1	4	$3^{3\frac{1}{2}}$	4^3	$2^{1\frac{1}{2}}$	2^5	2^8	LPincayJr	S Sommer	3.10
5- 5-73^9 CD^3	Our Native	b3 126	4	5	5^h	5^8	4^3	3^3	3^1	DBrumfield	Mrs M J Pritchard	11.90
5-12-73^5 Pim^1	Ecole Etage	b3 126	6	1	$1^{1\frac{1}{2}}$	2^2	$3^{\frac{1}{2}}$	4^{10}	4^{10}	GCusimano	Bon Etage Farm	11.30
5- 5-73^7 Pen^1	Deadly Dream	b3 126	2	3	6	6	6	6	5^3	ASBlack	Wide Track Farms	35.50
5-12-73^6 Pim^5	Torsion	3 126	5	2	$2^{\frac{1}{2}}$	3^h	5^{14}	5^3	6	BMFeliciano	Buckland Farm	39.00

Time, :24⅖, :48⅕, 1:11⅖, 1:35⅗, 1:54⅖. Track fast.
(Daily Racing Form Time 1:53⅖ New Track Record).

$2 Mutuel Prices:			
3-SECRETARIAT	2.60	2.20	2.10
1-SHAM		2.20	2.20
4-OUR NATIVE			2.20

Ch. c, by Bold Ruler—Somethingroyal, by Princequillo. Trainer, L. Laurin. Bred by Meadow Stud Inc. (Va.).
IN GATE—5:40. OFF AT 5:40 EASTERN DAYLIGHT TIME. Start good. Won handily.

SECRETARIAT broke well and was eased back and relaxed nicely as the field passed the stands the first time. He was guided outside two rivals entering the clubhouse turn and responding when Turcotte moved his hands on the reins, made a spectacular run to take command entering the backstretch. SECRETARIAT was not threatened thereafter and was confidently hand ridden to the finish. SHAM broke to the right and brushed with DEADLY DREAM leaving the gate, then drifted in and hit the rail entering the clubhouse turn. Pincay swung SHAM out entering the backstretch and roused him in pursuit of the winner but he could not threaten that rival in a game effort. OUR NATIVE, reserved between rivals early, rallied to gain the show. ECOLE ETAGE, hustled to the lead, gradually weakened after losing the advantage. DEADLY DREAM stumbled then was brushed by SHAM just after the break and was outrun thereafter. TORSION, stoutly rated early, could not menace when called upon.

(The :25, :48⅘, 1:12, 1:36⅕ and 1:55 as posted by the electric timer during the running was invalidated after a 48-hour interval by a stewards' ruling, and the above time reported by official timer E. T. McLean Jr. was accepted as official. **Scratched—The Lark Twist.**

"He has a neck like a buffalo, a back as broad as a sofa. . . . At full speed, this huge and powerful combination of bone and muscle and glistening red chestnut coat covers just an inch short of 25 feet in a single stride," marveled *Time*. The editors sagely concluded that his success was a "compound of good genes, good training, and good luck." Pete Axthelm, in *Newsweek*, waxed somewhat more poetic:

> Secretariat generates a crackling tension and excitement wherever he goes. Even in the kind of gray weather that shrouds lesser animals in anonymity, Secretariat's muscular build identifies him immediately; his glowing reddish coat is a banner of health and rippling power. Magnificent enough at rest . . . when he accelerates . . . he produces a breathtaking explosion that leaves novices and hardened horsemen alike convinced that, for one of those moments that seldom occur in any sport, they have witnessed genuine greatness.

To *New York Post* columnist Larry Merchant:

> Secretariat is the kind of Big Horse that makes grown men weep, even when they are flint-hearted bettors, even when he goes off at 1-10. He is the apparently unflawed hunk of beauty and beast that they search for doggedly in the racing charts every day, and never seem to find. His supporters rhapsodize over him as though he is a four-legged Nureyev, extolling virtues of his musculature, his grace, his urine specimens.

If he were to lose the Belmont, Merchant warned, the "country may turn sullen and mutinous."

All of these platitudes notwithstanding, it was a simple occurrence on the Belmont track early one morning that really mattered. In a one-mile workout, Secretariat was clocked in 1:34⅘, just 1⅕ slower than the track record. When he returned to the barn Willie Wright, his "walker," announced that the colt was jumping, happy, playful, and not at all tired. It was a signal of things to come on June 9.

Secretariat roared out of his rail post position like a demon possessed. He faced only four challengers, of which Sham was the one to give him any concern. This time there was no settling back; this time he was the leader and moving. They had gone past the grandstand for two furlongs, when an hysterical fan screamed at him: "You can't win a Belmont with a ¼ in :23⅗." Into the clubhouse turn they slammed with all indications suggesting that it was shaping up as a match race, as Sham ran head and head with him, even moving into the lead momentarily. They straightened out into the backstretch at the ½-mile pole, and a shiver of fear gripped Lucien Laurin. The second quarter's time was a searing :22⅗ seconds. The worrisome trainer knew that "Belmonts, by modern customs, are not for front-runners," and that since 1950, no horse who had led after a ½ mile in this classic had managed to finish first. In fact, his greatest fear was that his horse might stop in the last ¼, as so many potential wonders of the past had. It was at this moment in the race that Secretariat seemed to ignite a second-stage rocket within him, and off he streaked. Turcotte took a quick look behind and saw Sham and the others drop back swiftly and fade in size. One mile into the race, the two were quite alone, some seven lengths in front.

When they moved into the homestretch, Turcotte spotted the fraction times on the tote board and suddenly realized there was a record to be had. He ducked his head down, tightened his grip on the reins, and for the only time in the race really rode Secretariat through the last ⅛ of a mile to the wire. The 69,138 fans, watching with incredulity a Thoroughbred racing within himself, ignored the 90-degree heat and humidity and went wild with excitement as he barreled home a fantastic 31 lengths ahead of his next pursuer, Twice a Prince, in the startling time of 2:24. It was an unbelievable record, shattering Gallant Man's 1957 mark by 2⅗ seconds. His time for the mile was 1:34⅕, which topped his Derby time of 1:36⅕, while his 1¼ mile was ⅖ second faster than his Louisville run.

The superlatives for America's new Triple Crown champion were endless. One called it the greatest performance by a racehorse in this century. Another ranked it with such great sporting events as Joe Louis' one-round knockout of Max Schmeling and the Olympics feats of Jesse Owens, and likened the smashing of the old record equivalent to Joe Namath tossing 10 touchdowns in one game or Jack Nicklaus coming in with a 55 in the U.S. Open. Kent Hollingsworth, editor of *The Blood-Horse*, wrote: "He ran so far beyond known reference points, he left us with no measurable comparison." As for the other participants in the race, sportswriter Ed Bowen saw them as

Official Chart of Belmont Stakes

EIGHTH RACE
Bel
June 9, 1973

1½ MILES. (2:26⅗). One Hundred-fifth running BELMONT. SCALE WEIGHTS. $125,000 added. 3-year-olds. By subscription of $100 each to accompany the nomination; $250 to pass the entry box; $1,000 to start. A supplementary nomination may be made of $2,500 at the closing time of entries plus an additional $10,000 to start, with $125,000 added, of which 60% to the winner, 22% to second, 12% to third and 6% to fourth. Colts and geldings. Weight, 126 lbs.; fillies, 121 lbs. The winning owner will be presented with the August Belmont Memorial Cup to be retained for one year, as well as a trophy for permanent possession and trophies will be presented to the winning trainer and jockey. Closed Thursday, Feb. 15, 1973, with 187 nominations.

Value of race $150,200. Value to winner $90,120; second, $33,044; third, $18,024; fourth, $9,012.
Mutuel Pool, $519,689. Off-track betting, $688,460.

Last Raced	Horse	EqtAWt	PP	¼	½	1	1¼	Str	Fin	Jockeys	Owners	Odds to $1
5-19-73^8 Pim^1	Secretariat	b3 126	1	1^h	1^h	1^7	1^{20}	1^{28}	1^{31}	RTurcotte	Meadow Stable	.10
6- 2-73^6 Bel^4	Twice a Prince	3 126	4	4^5	4^{10}	3^h	2^h	3^{12}	$2^{\frac{1}{2}}$	BBaeza	Elmendorf	17.30
5-31-73^6 Bel^1	My Gallant	b3 126	3	3^3	3^h	4^7	3^2	2^h	3^{13}	ACorderoJr	A I Appleton	12.40
5-28-73^8 GS^2	Pvt. Smiles	b3 126	2	5	5	5	5	5	$4^{\frac{3}{4}}$	DGargan	C V Whitney	14.30
5-19-73^8 Pim^2	Sham	b3 126	5	2^5	2^{10}	2^7	4^8	$4^{1\frac{1}{2}}$	5	LPincayJr	S Sommer	5.10

Time, :23⅗, :46⅕, 1:09⅘, 1:34⅕, 1:59, 2:24 (new track record) (against wind in backstretch). Track fast.

$2 Mutuel Prices:

2-SECRETARIAT	2.20	2.40	...
5-TWICE A PRINCE		4.60	...

(NO SHOW MUTUELS SOLD)

Ch. c, by Bold Ruler—Somethingroyal, by Princequillo. Trainer, L. Laurin. Bred by Meadow Stud, Inc. (Va.).
IN GATE—5:38. OFF AT 5:38 EASTERN DAYLIGHT TIME. Start good. Won ridden out.

SECRETARIAT sent up along the inside to vie for the early lead with SHAM to the backstretch, disposed of that one after going three-quarters, drew off at will rounding the far turn and was under a hand ride from Turcotte to establish a record in a tremendous perfomance. TWICE A PRINCE, unable to stay with the leaders early, moved through along the rail approaching the stretch and outfinished MY GALLANT for the place. The latter, void of early foot, moved with TWICE A PRINCE rounding the far turn and fought it out gamely with that one through the drive. PVT. SMILES showed nothing. SHAM alternated for the lead with SECRETARIAT to the backstretch, wasn't able to match stride with that rival after going three-quarters and stopped badly.

Scratched—Knightly Dawn.

Exacta (2-5) Paid $35.20; Exacta Pool, $274,110; Off-Track Betting, $334,273.

"merely moving yardsticks whose only function was to provide a measure of Secretariat's mastery."

There were sidelights galore, before and after the Belmont Stakes. Mrs. Helen Tweedy drew spontaneous applause from the crowd when she entered her box, as if they were paying tribute to a queen. In the last 16 runnings of the Belmont, eight favorites had been defeated, which gave some pause to wonder at Secretariat's odds of 1-10, the only horse since Citation to be so heavily favored to win the Triple Crown. Twice a Prince, who had created such a rumpus in the stall at Churchill Downs and upset Sham, was led into the starting gate blindfolded. After the race, Ron Turcotte said he had noticed during the warm-up that Sham was not striding impressively, so he "decided to deliver Secretariat's knockout punch early." And the Belmont Stakes had a theme song of its own for the first time, when the band played "Sidewalks of New York" as the horses came onto the track.

Following the presentation ceremonies, Secretariat was taken to the New York State Racing Commission Test Area, where saliva was swabbed from his mouth into a basin, causing an onlooking woman to exclaim: "To think they're treating him like any other horse." Ron Turcotte, ever the loyal Canadian and hockey enthusiast, crowed: "This horse is like Boom-Boom

Secretariat slams into the clubhouse turn, leading Sham and the rest of the field at the start of the 1973 Belmont Stakes.

Secretariat flies into the final turn and homestretch, all four feet off the ground, far out in front of the field.

Jockey Ron Turcotte turns to see what happened to the opposition as he guides Secretariat to an incredible 31-length victory and the Triple Crown.

Geoffrion, big and bold." Mrs. Tweedy commented: "It seems a little greedy to win by 31 lengths." Sigmund Sommer, owner of Sham, candidly admitted to being so terribly saddened by the defeat that he went home after the race, had a few drinks, and then cried. Laffit Pincay Jr., his jockey, said he refused to punish his horse in a vain attempt to try to take second and fell back. The crowd was so thick at the paddock that Lucien Laurin could not get through to help Turcotte into the saddle, so his assistant trainer, Benny Hoefner, handled this chore.

In the course of the Triple Crown races, *The New York Times'* Tom Rogers ran across and traced a continuing story that graphically illustrated the sagacious ingenuity of horse players. At 7:30 A.M. on the day of the Kentucky Derby, a man carrying an attaché case stepped from a taxi in front of the Times Square OTB parlor. He bet $5,000 in cash on Secretariat, then took his cab to the airport and flew to Churchill Downs to witness the race. He did the same thing on the day of the Preakness, only this time he bet $10,000 on Secretariat. He was playing a hunch that OTB would pay off more than the tracks. It did. Churchill Downs paid $5 to OTB's $5.80, so he wound up with a profit of $2,000. Pimlico paid $2.60 against $2.80, which gave him $1,000 profit. On Belmont Stakes day, the same bettor, who by now had been dubbed "the Masked Marvel," again arrived, at 7:30 A.M. He now pulled out $26,000 in $100 bills. He said he wanted to bet $35,000 on Secretariat to win and $5,000 on an Exacta ticket with Secretariat to win and Sham to place. He also produced $10,000 in win tickets on Secretariat in the Preakness, with a payoff value of $14,000, to make up for the additional money he needed. It took the clerk 10 minutes to punch out 400 tickets for the bets, at which time he revealed he was hoping for a win price of $2.40. As so often happens with ingenious schemes, he could not anticipate the unexpected. He could not foretell that OTB would funnel all bets into the Belmont tote system a half-hour before post time, making its payoffs the same as the track's. The result was a loss of $1,500 for the man, when his win bet on Secretariat paid off at 1-10 odds, or $3,500, but his Exacta was a $5,000 loser. Had OTB kept its betting pool separate, Secretariat would have paid $2.40 to win, which would have doubled his take to $7,000, thereby assuring him a final profit for the day of $2,000.

In becoming America's ninth Triple Crown winner, the big colt suddenly became the object of intense scrutiny. His every move and the decisions of Mrs. Tweedy and Lucien Laurin were discussed, analyzed, and second-guessed, resulting in stories, headlines, and controversy. Leading off was the decision to race him at Arlington Park in Chicago in what was called the $125,000 Arlington Invitational. The race was dreamed up by John F. Loome, president of the track, with the approval of Mrs. Tweedy and Laurin, who thought it would be nice to let the people in the Midwest see Secretariat run. Also, Mrs. Tweedy insisted on televising the race, and it was scheduled for June 30, with the owner and trainer set to provide the commentary for ABC-TV's *Wide World of Sports*. His opposition would be Our Native, My Gallant, and Blue Chip Dan, two of whom he had already beaten soundly, and the third had won only two minor races in his career. The prizes would be $75,000, $30,000, and $20,000, respectively, for the first three across the line. Laurin justified the race, too, by claiming it was getting difficult to keep Secretariat inactive. "If I don't run this horse he's going to hurt himself in his stall."

News of the race brought no cheers. It was considered little more than an exhibition, a "manufactured race." The complaint was that the colt had not beaten older horses yet and had not carried high weight. Therefore, it hardly could be classified as his "finest hour." "To be Horse of the Century," wrote Kent Hollingsworth, "Secretariat must meet every genuine challenge. The only such challenge left for Secretariat, in all the world, is the 1½ miles, uphill and down around irregular turns, clockwise, at weight for age against Europe's best classic and older horses, the Prix de l'Arc de Triomphe, the greatest prize of all, run the first Sunday in October, in Paris."

Chicago's Mayor Daley disagreed and issued a 200-word proclamation declaring it Secretariat Day. The colt's first visit to Middle America produced a sellout crowd of 41,223. One reporter wrote: "Chicago hasn't had an animal as celebrated as Secretariat since Mrs. O'Leary's cow." Another, describing the security precautions, claimed he was "surrounded by the most formidable band of bodyguards since Al Capone's day in Chicago."

To nobody's surprise, Secretariat "casually circled the small field and galloped away by nine lengths, without urging from Ron Turcotte," in the 1⅛-mile event. With only win bets allowed, and with Secretariat paying off at the legal minimum of $2.10 for $2, the track had a minus pool of $17,941.35. Not enough had been lost on the other horses, who had been running as one entry. He was timed in 1:47 flat—⅕ second off the track record by Damascus in 1967—while carrying 126 pounds to 120 for the others. The victory brought his total earnings to $970,242.

Ten months later, Kenneth J. Noe, racing secretary for the New York Racing Association, in a discussion with the *New York Daily News'* Gene Ward about his handicapping of the 1974 Metropolitan Mile at Belmont, revealed what was perhaps the real reason why Secretariat's next race after the Triple Crown was won was in Chicago. Noe was talking about assigning Forego 134 pounds in the Metropolitan Mile. "That's the worst weight I've ever put on a horse," he said, "except for the 136 I assigned Secretariat for the 1¼-mile Dwyer last July. But Meadow Stable didn't accept the weight and it went for the match race in Chicago instead." The decision not to run him in New York recalled Samuel Riddle's decision to retire Man o' War after his third year of racing, rather than risk the expected heavy weights the colt would surely have been laden with if he participated in the 1921 handicap races.

Just prior to leaving for Chicago, Secretariat made news of another sort. It was announced that the William Morris Agency, the world's largest talent agency, would now represent him in deals for posters, statues, and other merchandising items. That brought some rather caustic comments. According to Dave Anderson:

> Up there where the William Morris Agency executives wheel and deal for Elvis Presley, Sophia Loren, Bill Cosby, Don Rickles, Pearl Bailey, and the Jackson Five, a new client has been added to, if the old clients will pardon the expression, the stable. . . . But the William Morris Agency, accustomed as it is to merchandising sex symbols, won't accompany Secretariat to stud. . . . 'The creative efforts of our clients are solely and completely their property.'

Frank Beerman, in the show-business bible *Variety*, put it another way. "Secretariat, the Triple Crown racehorse, may be in show biz up to its 17-hands-high withers now that its owner, Penny Tweedy, has signed with the William Morris Agency to represent it. But there are no *National Velvet* acting roles in its future, she says. 'The horse is an athlete,' she said, 'and anything he does will probably have to be at a race track in a setting natural to him.'" Beerman figured that in the spring Secretariat "will lightly be turned to thoughts of love and will hardly have time for extracurricular activities at those prices."

The news kept tumbling forth unabatedly from Meadow Stable. Early in July it was announced that Riva Ridge, their four-year-old star who had become the 12ᵗʰ Thoroughbred to earn $1 million, had been syndicated for $5,120,000, the 32 shares worth $160,000 each. His was the third highest deal of this sort, behind Secretariat and Nijinsky II. It seemed to be the season for these things, as Sham was also split up at $90,000 per share, or a total of approximately $3,000,000. Finally, Jack Krumpe, president of the New York Racing Association, announced that a match race between Secretariat and Riva Ridge had been set for September 15. It would be called the Marlboro Cup because Philip Morris, Inc., manufacturer of the cigarette of that name, had put up $200,000 as a purse. CBS would televise the race, and the distance would be at 1⅛ miles, with weights to be announced in the future. The story was that racing secretaries Kenny Noe of New York, Frank Kilroe of Hollywood Park, and Kenneth Lennox of Monmouth Park had been polled, and they had voted unanimously for Riva Ridge as the best opponent for Secretariat. Penny Tweedy added to this that she had always wanted to see the two run, and had agreed with her father's heirs to donate both purses to charity. The winner was to receive $200,000, and the loser $50,000, the latter to be put up by the New York Racing Association. Jack Krumpe further stated, "There will be a race, rain or shine," bearing in mind, no doubt, Riva Ridge's disdain for mud. Thus, this would be the first match race in New York since Armed beat Triple Crown winner Assault by eight lengths on September 27, 1947.

The whole idea started to blow up almost as soon as it was born. The New York Racing Association stewards put a damper on it by stating that it would have to be only an exhibition because match races involve separate interests or owners. Racing fans were unimpressed because there could not be any betting. They called it just a publicity stunt. "It's a funny situation," mused one trainer. "The winner will be whichever horse the trainer wants to win." Others asked which of the two horses Ron Turcotte would choose to ride.

Adding to the woes of the "matchmakers" was the totally unexpected defeat of Riva Ridge by a 56-1 outsider, Wichita Oil, in a 1¹⁄₁₆-mile overnight grass race at Saratoga on August 1, even though Riva Ridge had been the 1-2 choice and had broken the record in the Brooklyn Handicap in his last start. This shocking news had writer Gene Ward wondering: "What Will TV People Think If Secretariat Loses?" He was referring to the upcoming prestigious Whitney Stakes on August 4. Because CBS had bought four races for televising—the Whitney, Marlboro Cup, Woodward, and Jockey Club Gold Cup— the "network biggies are very unhappy about the Riva Ridge defeat," he wrote, "but should Secretariat get his lumps Saturday there is going to be one helluva explosion. Madison Avenue and the television folk just don't like anything or anybody to mess with their carefully plotted scripts."

It happened. The Whitney Stakes was virtually a replay of the Wood Memorial. Onion, a four-year-old gelding who had never won a stakes race and was a lightly regarded 6-1 choice, pulled off a masterful upset over the 1-10 favored Triple Crown champion. The feat left everyone gasping. He won by a length over Secretariat, who just barely made second by a half-length, and it was the first race since the Derby that Turcotte went to the whip. The second-guessing was furious. During the days preceding the race, it was reported that Laurin was worried about the distance, 1⅛ miles, the same at which they lost in the Wood. This was also Secretariat's first competition against older horses, and he had not had any real competition since his battles with Sham in the Derby and Preakness. Onion, with Jacinto Vasquez in the saddle, moved out front at the start, kept the pace slow, and had enough left to withstand a challenge by Secretariat in the stretch. Coincidentally, it was also Vasquez who had ridden Angle Light to a victory over the red colt and Sham in the Wood, eliciting from him the comment: "I'll make the Hall of Fame yet, beating these famous horses."

The historic defeat was compared to the losses by Man o' War to Upset, his only career loss, in the 1919 Sanford, and Gallant Fox to the 100-1 shot Jim Dandy, in the 1930 Travers—both at Saratoga too. It also brought out the verbal knives. "Super Horse? No. They All Get Beat," headlined William Rudy in his *New York Post* column. He claimed the horse was carrying "the incalculable burden of being a golden equine god, a running machine who could turn it on at any time, run that one fast furlong that kills the opposition." Gene Ward felt "some of the living legend label peeled away." Ed Bowen claimed there was "no horse so great as to be assured of constant success." As for the forthcoming Marlboro match race, some facetiously thought it should be between Onion and Wichita Oil instead, that because Marlboro and the New York Racing Association were left with two tarnished champions, the fans might find it more intriguing to watch the Marlboro Man race a Camel. For Secretariat, the defeat also prevented him from becoming a millionaire, his total earnings with the $11,847 second-place money reaching $982,089.

Jack Landry, group vice president of marketing for Philip Morris, is credited with having come up with the idea for the match race between Secretariat and Riva Ridge. He told of how he first admired Secretariat in 1972 when he won the Sanford Stakes, and of how the idea for the match race came to him after

The four-year-old gelding, Onion, ridden by Jacinto Vasquez, pulls off a masterful defeat of Triple Crown champion Secretariat (right) in the Whitney Stakes at Saratoga.

the Belmont. Then, before the Whitney and after Riva Ridge had lost just four days earlier, he told reporters: "If Secretariat loses, you'll see one dead man lying in the middle of the track—me."

He did not die. Rather, he went into a huddle with all of the principals involved and came up with a new idea that met with public approval. The Marlboro Cup would be an invitational affair, with the best horses in the country asked to participate. First prize would be $150,000, second $55,000, third $30,000, and fourth $15,000. It turned out, indeed, to be the greatest gathering of top horses ever. They were Secretariat, Riva Ridge, Onion, Cougar II, Key to the Mint, Kennedy Road, Tentam, and Annihilate 'Em. Together, they had won $4,544,335 in purses and 63 stakes. Riva Ridge and Cougar II had topped the million mark in earnings. The only poor relation was Onion, who had won "only" $124,657 but was the one horse who had beaten Secretariat. The red colt was the only three-year-old in the lot. The race was also the first rich venture into outside commercial sponsorship for a major New York turf event. Because the Belmont track was presenting the $100,000

Beldame Handicap on the same card, the purses for the nine races of the day came to more than $451,800, making it the richest afternoon in Thoroughbred history.

Secretariat was pronounced fit following a bout with the flu. He was found to have a virus after the Whitney, which may have contributed to his upset defeat and which caused him to miss six days and a couple of workouts before the match race. Despite this, he was assigned 124 pounds. Riva Ridge had the highest impost, 127 pounds. According to weight-for-age scales, therefore, the three-year-old in theory was carrying the top weight in the race and was giving his stablemate 2 pounds to the good. Ron Turcotte was on Secretariat, and Eddie Maple was on Riva Ridge. Lucien Laurin told them in the paddock: "I want to finish one-two, and I don't care who finishes first." Mrs. Tweedy, however, differed: "Secretariat needs to win more than Riva Ridge. He needs to prove he can give weight and win a handicap."

Secretariat started with the others, then settled into fifth place on the outside. Onion took the lead and Riva Ridge stayed with him. Going into the far turn, Riva Ridge made his move, as did Secretariat. The stablemates ran head-to-head at that point, and it became a match race between the two after all. At the 3/16 pole, Eddie Maple recalled, "I saw a big red head and body coming right at me and there was nothing I could do about it. It was a helpless feeling." Secretariat crossed the finish line in front by three and a half lengths and in a new world-record time of 1:45⅖ for a dirt track, to better the mark of 1:46⅕ set by Canonero II against Riva Ridge in the 1972 Stymie Handicap.

The crowd of 48,023 wildly embraced their hero once more. William Rudy called him a "great horse" and assumed "the doubters are satisfied now," no doubt forgetting his own doubts about the colt following the Whitney. Gene Ward summed it up best when he wrote: "Not even on Madison Avenue, where they live on dreams, could they have hoped for a dream race with the dream horse winning in record time." The win made Secretariat the 13th millionaire Thoroughbred in turf history, at $1,132,089, and the eighth on the all-time winners list.

Two weeks later, "Super Red," as some were calling him, threw his fans into another paroxysm by losing the 1½-mile Woodward Stakes to a four-year-old, who was winning only his seventh race in 32 starts. Prove Out went off at 16-1 and gave the three-year-old star 7 pounds by carrying 126. His trainer was Allen Jerkins, the same man who had sent out another outsider, Onion,

ANNIHILATE 'EM KENNEDY ROAD KEY TO THE MINT ONION COUGAR II RIVA RIDGE SECRETARIAT

Secretariat barrels home in record-breaking time to take the Marlboro Cup at Belmont. The race featured the top horses in the country, with the Triple Crown champion the only three-year-old. The time of 1:45⅗ was a new world record on a dirt track for 1⅛ miles. The purse made Secretariat the 13th millionaire Thoroughbred.

in the Whitney to clobber the red colt. Secretariat looked good down the backstretch on a sloppy track, maintaining a couple of lengths' lead. Then Prove Out moved up on him on the far turn and never quit, winning by four and a half lengths.

Lucien Laurin was furious over the slow time. Jorge Velasquez, the winner's jockey, confirmed this. He said he slowed the pace, hoping to save his horse and take second money. "When I saw Ron whipping the choochoo train," he recalled, "I thought for the first time I had a shot. I went to the whip, too. But instead of the choochoo taking off and running away from me, it was my horse who took off. He just kept on running."

To prove his point, Laurin referred to the :50 time for the ½ mile, compared to the :45⅗ of the Marlboro Cup race. It was the equivalent of 25 lengths, he fumed. Call it coincidence or oddity, but it was a fact that Secretariat apparently did not take to stakes races whose names begin with the letter *W*. His only losses in 1973 were in the Wood, Whitney, and Woodward.

New York's last glimpse of Secretariat in action was in the $100,000 Man o' War Stakes on October 8, 1973, at Belmont Park, and he left his fans on a high note. The race marked his first on turf. Tentam was the horse to beat because he had set a world record for 1⅜ miles on turf. Once more, the Laurin-Turcotte strategy after a loss that resulted from a slow pace was to keep everyone honest. Secretariat dashed to the front within ¼ of a mile and never let go. "Every time Tentam moved up, Turcotte chirped and Secretariat responded," said William Rudy. He ran smoothly and roared home ahead by five lengths in a new course record of 2:24⅘, faster by ⅗ second. There was an element of revenge in the win. Trainer Allen Jerkens, whose colts had beaten Secretariat in the Whitney and Woodward, saw his Triangular come in fourth, some 13 lengths in the rear.

The time was fast approaching for Secretariat to hang up his racing shoes. He had been given until November 15, and his 28 syndicate owners were waiting patiently, not without some trepidation. As long as he raced, there was

Prove Out, a 16-1 underdog with Jorge Vasquez up, defeats Secretariat in the Woodward Stakes. Cougar II is third. It was the third stakes race with a name beginning with the letter W—Wood, Whitney, and Woodward—that Secretariat lost.

always the possibility of injury. Fittingly enough, Lucien Laurin picked the Canadian International Championship on October 28, 1973, for his last outing. The race is held at the Woodbine Racecourse near Toronto, about 200 miles from Kenilworth Park, where Man o' War ran his last race, the match race with Triple Crown champion Sir Barton in 1920. There was a certain amount of nationalism in the choice, as well, because both Laurin and Turcotte were Canadian, and it would be the big colt's first race in the Dominion. It is run on the Marshall Course at Woodbine, which is a combination of turf, dirt, and turf strips, at 1⅝ miles, a furlong longer than the Man o' War Stakes.

Unfortunately, the plans did not gel as desired. Ron Turcotte was grounded for interference in a race on Wednesday of that week. He was slated to ride Riva Ridge in that colt's last race in the two-mile Jockey Club Gold Cup on Saturday at Aqueduct, and then fly to Canada to wind up Secretariat's career. Consequently, Eddie Maple, the Ohio farm boy who had ridden eight thousand races and won more than $7 million, was selected for the two chores. Riva Ridge's finale was a fiasco. He finished last to Prove Out, who could boast of having beaten Meadow Stable's two millionaires. Riva Ridge's record thus was 17 wins in 30 races, two classic victories, a world record for 1³⁄₁₆ miles, and earnings of $1,111,347.

Sunday at Woodbine was cold, windy, enshrouded in drizzle and mist. Despite the inclement weather, 35,117 people turned out. They were well rewarded. With stiff competition expected from Kennedy Road, who had set a track record in the Hollywood Gold Cup the previous week, Secretariat stormed home with ease after having opened a 12-length lead, in 2:41⅘, only ⅖ second off the track record. Frank Deford waxed eloquent in describing the race for *Sports Illustrated*: "Hard by the hedge, snorting steam in the raw twilight like some mythical beast running across a faded storybook, he drove home alone through the mist and almost, it seemed, out of the low lake clouds, and won at his leisure, from here to there." The last race was good for $92,775, bringing his total earnings to $1,316,808 and making him the fourth leading money-winner in turf history. It was the 16th victory in 21 starts, in only 16 months since he first started to race and barely three and a half years since he was foaled. His third year was the richest single season ever for a horse, with nine of twelve wins and $860,404 in purses, topping the mark of $817,941 set by Damascus in 1967. Secretariat established another record of sorts along the way. It was estimated that some $100,000 in uncashed pari-mutuel win tickets, including 5,617 from the Belmont Stakes worth $14,597, were being held by racing fans as mementos. A Canadian collector, in fact, ran an advertisement in the *Daily Racing Form*, offering $20 for a winning ticket from the Preakness with a face value of merely $2.60.

Secretariat paraded in regal panoply at the Aqueduct track in New York on November 6, 1973. Dressed in silks in the time-honored, traditional ritual of American turfdom reserved for Thoroughbred heroes who were retiring from the racing campaigns, with his jockey, Ron Turcotte, on his back, the chestnut colt made his last public appearance before 32,990 loudly and fervently cheering fans. His next stop would be the Claiborne Stud Farm in Kentucky, where he would live out the rest of his days as a stallion in luxurious, lazy splendor, with the appetizing thought that each year 30 of the best Thoroughbred mares would be brought to him for his favors. The mere thought of it whetted the typewriters of newsmen, and they came up with some affectionate chidings. Their copy referred to him as "the most celebrated sex symbol since Errol Flynn, or anyway, Joe Namath." Because it was also the day New Yorkers were voting for a new mayor, they joked that he would "probably win in a walkover" if he were a candidate. They even reported that his fan mail had included a postcard signed "Fiji," which read: "I can't wait." She was one of the elite broodmares who would be "dating" him in 1974. "For the big horse, it's all fun now," concluded another story. Penny Tweedy was asked for her schedule the next day, and she sadly replied: "I don't know, a hangover, I guess."

On November 11, the Meadow Stable's two equine millionaires, Secretariat and Riva Ridge, were flown to Lexington and let out on the fields of Claiborne Farm, not, however, before they were given tranquilizers. "We had to do it," said the Claiborne manager. "You just don't turn out colts who are fresh off the track like that. They're liable to run through a fence or something."

Early in December, Secretariat had his first sex experience with a test Appaloosa mare. Thereafter, he underwent a series of fertility tests, called for by the syndicate terms. By the end of the year, too, his value was enhanced with his being named Champion Three-Year-Old Colt, Champion Grass Horse, and Horse of the Year. He was only the 10th Thoroughbred of the century to win successive Horse of the Year awards. Since 1936, only Challedon (1939 and 1940), Whirlaway (1941 and 1942), and Kelso (1960 and 1961) had been so honored.

But all was not well down on the farm. Rumblings were heard that jarred the syndicate. The tests were not coming up with the desired results. It was

Secretariat, with Ron Turcotte in the saddle, parades in silks at Aqueduct in his last public appearance before retiring to stud.

hardly appropriate as a yuletide greetings telegram that Seth Hancock, manager of the syndicate, sent to the breeders on Christmas Eve. It read: "Veterinarians have requested additional 60 days to complete Secretariat [or Riva Ridge, whichever applicable] fertility tests and are unanimously optimistic about final results. Request your approval to extend time to March 1, 1974, subject to insurance underwriters' approval of similar extension. Please wire or cable your consent. Regards. Seth."

The fact was that although Secretariat exhibited a fondness for the females, according to young Hancock, like "any well-adjusted three-year-old colt," microscopic studies revealed the presence of spermatogonia, immature cells, in his semen. It was the same with Riva Ridge. By February 1974, Hancock advised the subscribers of the syndicate that the colt had failed to pass the fertility test in an unqualified manner, and that the original agreement was "forthwith terminated." Then it was announced that two of the three test mares he had been mated with were in foal. Finally, a new agreement was offered to the breeders who chose to remain in the syndicate. It was stipulated that if 60 percent of the mares were in foal by September 1, not counting mares who had been barren the last two years or were more than 16 years old, the syndicate would stand as originally formed and unpaid fees would be due.

This steady stream of news bulletins from Paris, Kentucky, was too much for television sportscaster Dick Schaap. On his *NBC-TV News* program, he said, somewhat indiscreetly, that Secretariat and Riva Ridge were "the most famous pair of stablemates since Joseph and Mary." The studio's switchboard quickly lit up with calls from irate listeners. Cardinal Cooke deplored the attack on Catholicism and Christian symbols, and Schaap was put on the air twice the following day to express his abject apologies. On top of that, Claiborne Farms faced another problem. Joe Taylor, its manager, reported that he had received so many letters from people wanting to purchase the Appaloosa mare in foal to Secretariat that he had decided to sell the mother and fetus. "I want to get her off my neck," he said. "The mare doesn't even have a name. She is called No. 24 and was chosen because she happened to be in heat at the time." Sealed bids by special-delivery letter were suggested.

As he approached the end of his racing career, Secretariat was called "the horse of the century" and, quite naturally, was being compared to Man o' War, who has worn that title since 1919. However, he was ranked No. 2 on *The Blood-Horse's* Top 100 Race Horses of the 20th Century.

When he retired, he stood in stud at the Claiborne Stud near Paris, Kentucky. He sired a Horse of the Year in Lady Secret, and a winner of the Preakness and Belmont Stakes in Risen Star. He died on October 4, 1989, but in 1992 was acclaimed the leading broodmare sire, when 135 of his get won a combined total of $6,665,507.

Seattle Slew

Seattle Slew
(dark bay or
brown colt)
{
Bold Reasoning {
Boldnesian

Reason to Earn
}

My Charmer {
Poker

Fair Charmer
}
}

| Chapter 10 |

Seattle Slew

~1977~

Foaled on February 15, 1974, at the White Horse Acres breeding farm near Lexington, Kentucky, Seattle Slew was not a "pretty baby." His head seemed large and out of proportion to his body, and his legs were awkwardly long. He had a dark brown coat, almost black, without a distinctive blaze or star or white patches. These features hardly seemed to be the makings of a champion Thoroughbred. However, he did have an impressive family tree. His sire, Bold Reasoning, was the grandson of Bold Ruler, the father of the great Secretariat. His dam was My Charmer, the offspring of Myrtle Charm, the champion filly of 1948.

Their ugly duckling was Seattle Slew.

By the time he became a yearling, he had filled out nicely to a 700-pound colt with a good disposition. Nevertheless, the horse aficionados who attended the auction sales had reservations about him. Some thought he was not graceful, that he was like "a 7' basketball player who's only 16 years old, too big and tall for his age." Others harped on the sire and dam, claiming they were unproven, this being only his third foal and her first. Therefore, he was rejected for showing at the prestigious Keeneland Sales but was entered in the Fasig-Tipton sale in Lexington. It was an auction that had been started the year prior for horses that would not generate the Keeneland prices.

Mickey and Karen Taylor were among the prospective bidders at the auction. They were only 30 years old and in their second year as horse owners. They had been high school sweethearts who had dated for seven years before they were married in 1970. Mickey worked as a logger and Karen worked as a Northwest Airlines flight attendant. They lived in a trailer on the grounds of the logging company. Two years later, the company went bankrupt. Mickey and his brother seized the opportunity and took over the company with an investment of $500. It was a fortuitous move because in 1973, Canada curtailed the shipment of paper to the West Coast, creating a shortage of paper and a dramatic spike in the price of pulpwood. It marked the end of economic woes for the Taylors. They settled in White Swan, Washington, near Seattle. Mickey had always been interested in horses, largely to bet on them. Karen simply loved them. After a successful investment, the Taylors decided that they had the means to try their hand at owning racehorses.

Their advisor and business partner was their friend Dr. Jim Hill, a noted veterinarian. Dr. Hill had to leave town before the start of the Fasig-Tipton auction, but he strongly recommended that the Taylors purchase "the Bold Reasoning colt." Mickey and Karen followed his advice. They entered the last bid of $17,500. The modest price was an indication that to most of the onlookers he was "just another yearling."

Karen and Mickey Taylor thought otherwise. Karen then insisted on giving the horse a "snappy name." She decided to create one that reflected the dual ownership. Seattle was Taylor territory. Slew referred to the alligator-filled swamps in South Florida where Dr. Hill grew up. The swamps were commonly referred to as "sloughs" or "slews." Thus, the dark bay colt was named Seattle Slew.

They sent him to a farm in Maryland run by Billy and Paula Turner. Paula broke in the young horses, and Billy trained them at Belmont Park in New York. Paula later revealed that "the Slew," as he was affectionately called by his handlers, was a very independent horse, who possessed much desire and ability to run. He was tough to settle down. After some time with Paula, Seattle Slew was shipped to Billy in New York to learn how to race.

Billy Turner was known for his patience with horses and took his time with the colt. He had learned about horses from his days as a steeplechase rider before he became a racing trainer. He brought Seattle Slew along slowly, until he was satisfied that the colt was ready for his first effort on the track.

It was the fifth race at Saratoga on September 20, 1976, for six furlongs. The *Daily Racing Form* duly recorded that Seattle Slew "begins his career today." Ten horses competed, and he broke his maiden by five lengths even though he left the gate last. After the race, a trainer sidled up and offered to buy the horse for $300,000.

Turner wasted no time and sent him out again on October 5 in a seven-furlong allowance, which he won easily by three-and-one-half lengths at

Belmont. There was no reluctance then to enter him in the prestigious Champagne Stakes for two-year-olds. It was hardly a race, for he trounced the field by nine-and-three-quarter lengths while running the fastest mile ever by a two-year-old. The turf writers buzzed with excitement over the results and voted him Two-Year-Old Horse of the Year.

Other trainers were confounded. Seattle Slew had run in only three races within a matter of weeks and still had received top honors. It was enough to make the Taylors, Hills, and Turners heady with excitement at the thought of preparing for the Kentucky Derby in 1977.

The Slew rested well over the winter and started his prep for the Derby in typical fashion. He began the campaign at Hialeah in Florida on March 20, with a nine-length romp in a seven-furlong allowance race, followed by a four-length win in the Hialeah Stakes at 1⅛ miles on March 26 to set a new track record. Less than a month later, he polished off the 1⅛-mile Wood Memorial three-and-a-quarter lengths in front. Because the Wood is one of the top stakes races before the Kentucky Derby and Seattle Slew was undefeated in all six races he ran, it was no surprise that he was the 1-2 favorite in the Run for the Roses. Despite the odds, the skeptics still claimed that he was overrated and did not have the foundation for the 1¼-mile distance.

His supporters had a different outlook. Carey Winfrey of *The New York Times* wrote: "Every once upon a time an athlete comes along whose appeal extends far beyond the borders of a particular sport to engage the imagination of those who wouldn't know an earned run from a four iron. A Babe Ruth, a Joe Louis, an Arnold Palmer. . . . In just a few short months, he has become one of the most exciting performers in sports."

Edward Bowen put it another way in *The Blood-Horse*: "He aroused the sort of fanfare routine for any returning astronaut who has just married a royal princess during a brief respite in his campaign for president—or for an unbeaten Kentucky Derby candidate."

Louisville was its usual cauldron of excitement on Derby Day. A boisterous crowd of 124,038 squeezed into the historic Churchill Downs. The ladies wore their fashionable hats; mint juleps were the favorite drink; and the noise was deafening at post time. Seattle Slew reacted to the fanfare. He sweated profusely as he walked to the starting gate, entered his fourth spot, and waited impatiently for the other horses to be loaded into the starting gate. He was not happy, which his owners, trainers, and jockey sensed.

The last horse finally entered the gate and the race went off. Seattle Slew turned his head sideways and swerved to the right while the gateman tried to

Seattle Slew leads the field into the homestretch of the Kentucky Derby.

push him out of the stall. By the time he did come out, he was two or three lengths behind a wall of straining horses. Jean Cruguet, the seasoned French jockey who had ridden him in all of his races, settled him down and then proceeded to pick holes in the wall to slip through. By the time they reached the first ¼ mile, Cruguet and Seattle Slew had left the herd behind and were challenging the leader, For the Moment.

They ran head-to-head down the backstretch to the far turn. Cruguet, who had not used the whip since the Champagne, whacked him. Russ Harris of the *New York Daily News* picked up the story: "Moving on the outside, Seattle Slew looked For the Moment in the eye and forced the overmatched son of What a Pleasure to make a retreat." Neil Milbert of the *Chicago Tribune* confirmed how the race played out: "Seattle Slew did what he had to—he ran to daylight. . . . Then, with about a quarter of a mile to go, Cruguet unleashed Seattle Slew— and For the Moment unraveled."

Although the track was fast, the time was not. The 2:02⅕ was hardly in the league of Secretariat's 1:59⅖. Nevertheless, the purse was $214,700, which raised the Slew's career earnings to $370,000—not a bad return for a $17,500 investment.

The Slew has a commanding lead over Run Dusty Run and Sanhadrin as they approach the Churchill Downs finish line.

Official Chart of the Kentucky Derby

EIGHTH RACE
CD
May 7, 1977

1¼ MILES. (1:59⅖). One hundred and third running KENTUCKY DERBY. SCALE WEIGHTS. $125,000 added. 3-year-olds. By subscription of $100 each, which covers nomination for both The Kentucky Derby and Derby Trial. All nomination fees to Derby winner, $4,000 to pass entry box Thursday, May 5; $3,500 additional to start with $125,000 added, of which $30,000 to second, $15,000 to third, $7,500 to fourth. $100,000 guaranteed to the winner (to be divided equally in the event of a dead-heat). Weight, 126 lbs. Starters to be named through the entry box Thursday, May 5, at time of closing. The maximum number of starters for The Kentucky Derby will be limited to twenty. In the event more than twenty entries pass through the entry box at the usual time of closing, the twenty starters will be determined at that time with preference given to those that have accumulated the highest lifetime earnings. For those that enter and are eliminated under this condition, the nomination fee and the fee to pass through the entry box will be refunded. The owner of the winner to receive a gold trophy. Closed with 297 nominations.

Value of race $267,200. Value to winner $214,700; second, $30,000; third, $15,000; fourth, $7,500.
Mutuel Pool, $3,655,225.

Last Raced	Horse	EqtAWt	PP	¼	½	¾	1	Str	Fin	Jockeys	Owners	Odds to $1
23 Apr77 8Aqu1	Seattle Slew	3 126	4	2¹	2⁴	2⁴	1h	1³	1¹½	JCruguet	Karen L Taylor	.50
28 Apr77 7Kee2	Run Dusty Run	3 126	8	4½	4³	4¹	3¹	2³	2nk	DGMcHargue	Golden Chance Fm	a–5.90
23 Apr77 8Aqu2	Sanhedrin	b3 126	1	12¹½	10¹	12²	8²	4¹½	3³½	JVelasquez	Darby Dan Farm	14.60
28 Apr77 7Kee4	Get the Axe	3 126	5	9²	9¹½	9h	9h	7²	4no	WShoemaker	Bwamazon Farm	27.90
17 Apr77 8Hol1	Steve's Friend	b3 126	11	7¹½	7¹½	5¹½	4²	5½	5no	RHernandez	Kinship Stable	29.20
30 Apr77 7CD2	Papelote	b3 126	14	5¹½	6²	8¹½	7¹½	6²	6²½	MARivera	M L Warner	f–42.80
28 Apr77 7Kee9	Giboulee	b3 126	13	11²	8½	10h	13¹½	9¹½	7h	JFell	J L Levesque	40.20
28 Apr77 7Kee1	For the Moment	b3 126	10	1½	1h	1¹	2³	3½	8³	ACorderoJr	G Robins	7.00
17 Apr77 8Hol2	Affiliate	b3 126	7	10½	12²	11h	6½	8½	9¹½	LPincayJr	Harbor View Farm	38.20
23 Apr77 8Spt1	Flag Officer	3 126	6	15	11½	13½	10¹	10¹½	10½	LAhrens	Nasty Stable	46.90
28 Apr77 7Kee5	Bob's Dusty	3 126	3	3³	3⁵	3²	5²	12²	11nk	JCEspinoza	R N Lehmann	a–5.90
5 Apr77 9Hia5	Sir Sir	3 126	2	6½	5¹	6²	12²	11h	12²	JSRodriguez	La Luna Stable	f–42.60
30 Apr77 7CD1	Nostalgia	b3 126	15	13¹½	14¹½	14¹	14³	13⁶	13³	LSnyder	W S Farish III	40.00
28 Apr77 7Kee3	Western Wind	3 126	9	14¹½	15	15	15	14⁷	14¹⁰	RTurcotte	J M Roebling	31.10
30 Apr77 7CD3	Best Person	b3 126	12	8³	13½	7¹	11¹	15	15	GPatterson	W C Partee	f–42.80

Coupled, a-Run Dusty Run and Bob's Dusty.   f-Mutuel field.

OFF AT 5:40 EDT. Start good. Won ridden out. Time, :23, :45⅘, 1:10⅗, 1:36, 2:02⅕. Track fast.

$2 Mutuel Prices:
3-SEATTLE SLEW	3.00	2.80	2.80
1A-RUN DUSTY RUN (a-Entry)		3.40	3.20
2-SANHEDRIN			4.60

Dk. b. or br. c, by Bold Reasoning—My Charmer, by Poker. Trainer, William H. Turner, Jr. Bred by B. S. Castleman (Ky.).

SEATTLE SLEW swerved sharply to the outside into GET THE AXE, after failing to break smartly, was rushed to the leaders early placing SIR SIR in slightly close quarters, continuing through tight quarters nearing the end of the opening quarter. SEATTLE SLEW forced his way through moving FLAG OFFICER, AFFILIATE and BOB'S DUSTY out. Continuing in full stride, SEATTLE SLEW engaged FOR THE MOMENT at that point to duel for the lead from the outside to the top of the stretch at which stage he disposed of that one when put to extreme pressure, drew off with a rush and prevailed under intermittent urging. RUN DUSTY RUN broke well to gain a forward position, rallied along the outside on the final turn, continued willingly only to lug in through the closing stages and could not reach the winner. RUN DUSTY RUN survived a claim of foul lodged by the rider of SANHEDRIN for alleged interference in the closing stages. The latter, unhurried early while racing along the inner railing, came out between horses for the drive and finished full of run. GET THE AXE closed some ground in his late bid but could not seriously threaten. STEVE'S FRIEND, unhurried early, moved up gradually along the outside on the second turn to loom boldly a furlong away but lacked a further response. PAPELOTE saved ground to no avail. FOR THE MOMENT, away sharply to make the pace, saved ground while dueling with SEATTLE SLEW to the top of the stretch at which point he succumbed suddenly. FLAG OFFICER was outrun. BOB'S DUSTY showed forwardly for three-quarters and retired. SIR SIR was caught in close quarters after the start.

Official Chart of Preakness

EIGHTH RACE Pim May 21, 1977 — $1\frac{3}{16}$ MILES. (1:54). One hundred and second running PREAKNESS STAKES. SCALE WEIGHTS. $150,000 added. 3-year-olds. By subscription of $100 each, this fee to accompany the nomination; $1,000 to pass the entry box; starters to pay $1,000 additional. All eligibility, entrance and starting fees to the winner, with $150,000 added, of which $30,000 to second, $15,000 to third and $7,500 to fourth. Weight, 126 lbs. A replica of the Woodlawn Vase will be presented to the winning owner to remain his or her personal property. Closed with 231 nominations.
Value of race $191,100. Value to winner $138,600; second, $30,000; third, $15,000; fourth, $7,500.
Mutuel Pool, $1,105,489. Exacta Pool, $266,680.

Last Raced	Horse	EqtAWt	PP	St	¼	½	¾	Str	Fin	Jockeys	Owners	Odds to $1
7 May77 ^{8}CD^{1}	Seattle Slew	3 126	8	2	2^{3}	1^{h}	2^{4}	1^{3}	$1^{1\frac{1}{2}}$	JCruguet	Karen L Taylor	.40
14 May77 ^{8}Aqu^{1}	Iron Constitution	3 126	7	8	9	$7\frac{1}{2}$	3^{2}	2^{1}	2^{2}	JVelasquez	H T Mangurian Jr	30.90
7 May77 ^{8}CD^{2}	Run Dusty Run	3 126	9	7	6^{1}	6^{h}	$4\frac{1}{2}$	5^{10}	$3^{1\frac{1}{2}}$	DMcHargue	Golden Chance Fm Inc	7.20
14 May77 ^{8}Aqu^{2}	Cormorant	3 126	1	1	1^{h}	2^{8}	$1\frac{1}{2}$	$3^{1\frac{1}{2}}$	$4\frac{1}{2}$	DRWright	C T Berry Jr	4.80
30 Apr77 ^{8}Hol^{1}	J. O. Tobin	3 126	6	9	7^{3}	8^{4}	5^{1}	4^{1}	5^{8}	WShoemaker	El Peco Ranch	6.50
7 May77 ^{8}CD^{12}	Sir Sir	3 126	3	6	$8^{1\frac{1}{2}}$	9	8^{h}	6^{6}	6^{10}	RPineda	Laluna Stable	86.00
5 May77 ^{8}Aqu^{3}	Hey Hey J. P.	b3 126	5	4	$4\frac{1}{2}$	$4^{1\frac{1}{2}}$	7^{1}	8^{2}	7^{nk}	ACorderoJr	Fast Piarina Stable	78.10
7 May77 ^{8}Pim^{2}	Counter Punch	3 126	2	5	$5^{1\frac{1}{2}}$	3^{h}	6^{2}	$7^{1\frac{1}{2}}$	8^{3}	GMcCarron	J E Hughes	75.40
14 May77 ^{7}WO^{3}	Regal Sir	3 126	4	3	3^{h}	$5^{1\frac{1}{2}}$	9	9	9	CJMcCarron	J W B Carmichael	69.60

OFF AT 5:41 EDT. Start good. Won driving. Time, :22⅗, :45⅗, 1:09⅘, 1:34⅘, 1:54⅖. Track fast.

$2 Mutuel Prices:

8-SEATTLE SLEW	2.80	2.80	2.20
7-IRON CONSTITUTION		12.20	5.00
9-RUN DUSTY RUN			2.80

$2 EXACTA (8-7) PAID $42.20.

Dk. b. or br. c, by Bold Reasoning—My Charmer, by Poker. Trainer, William H. Turner, Jr. Bred by B. S. Castleman (Ky.).

SEATTLE SLEW, forced in slightly by RUN DUSTY RUN while breaking alertly, moved up readily under strong restraint and prompted CORMORANT for the lead before the first turn. He was hard held outside that one down the backstretch and, responding to hand encouragement, took command leaving the backstretch. SEATTLE SLEW drew clear under pressure into the stretch, and relaxed in the final yards while being kept to a steady hand ride. IRON CONSTITUTION angled quickly to the inside after breaking a bit slowly, moved up well along the rail in the backstretch after having been allowed to settle early, came out for room in the drive and finished willingly to be second best. RUN DUSTY RUN broke inward, was forced wide while being reserved entering the first turn, remained wide before coming in slightly leaving the backstretch, found room along the rail in the drive and was unable to mount the needed response. CORMORANT broke in stride, was quickly taken in hand to hold a short early lead along the rail, continued willingly to the three-eighths pole, then could not stay with SEATTLE SLEW and drifted a bit in midstretch while weakening. J. O. TOBIN broke in the air slightly and was unhurried while outrun early, moved up willingly around horses on the second turn, then drifted beyond the middle of the track through the stretch run and could not sustain his bid. SIR SIR was unable to seriously menace. HEY HEY J. P., close up early, was in tight quarters leaving the backstretch and gave way readily. COUNTER PUNCH showed little. REGAL SIR, close up early, was bumped leaving the half-mile pole and stopped.

Only two of his fourteen rivals in the Kentucky Derby came out for the 102nd running of the Preakness at the Pimlico Race Course in Baltimore on May 21. They were Run Dusty Run, who finished second in the Derby, and Sir Sir, who came in twelfth. The two greatest threats in the field of nine were the speedsters, Cormorant, with Danny Wright up, and J. O. Tobin, with Willie Shoemaker in the saddle. Those horses were Seattle Slew's strongest opponents in the $1\frac{3}{16}$ mile race.

A record crowd of 77,346 was treated to a dazzling replay of the Derby. Moving out of the eight post position, the Slew quickly took the lead and was never headed. Cruguet hit him once or twice in the upper stretch to keep him focused, and hand-rode him to the finish. The Frenchman eased him in the stretch, which enabled Iron Constitution to move up and finish second one-and-a half lengths behind. It was the Slew's smallest margin of victory, but it elicited rave reviews.

Willie Shoemaker, who rode J. O. Tobin, said of Seattle Slew: "He's got to be good. He wins every time he runs."

Red Smith, in *The New York Times*, wrote: "There is a growing suspicion here that Seattle Slew will never stop running—never, at least, until he moves into the handicap division next year and racing secretaries put enough lead in his saddle pockets to overload a Greyhound bus."

Ray Kerrison offered a pointed analogy in the *New York Post*: "Seattle Slew has such powers of propulsion one is tempted to think your Aunt Gertie could ride him and win."

Saturday, June 11, 1977, was Belmont Day, and 71,026 racing fans were elbow-to-elbow in New York's venerable Belmont Park. They turned out to see the running of the 109th Belmont Stakes. More importantly, they were eagerly anticipating the crowning of a new Triple Crown Champion, the 10th in the history of American Thoroughbred racing. Of even greater significance, the winner would be the first undefeated three-year-old to accomplish the magnificent feat. In fact, the entire country was caught up in the excitement. Even Governor Dixie Lee Ray of Washington got into the act. She issued a proclamation declaring June 11 Seattle Slew Day to honor the state's heroic equine son.

Karen Taylor and Sally Hill sat excitedly in their box, ready to support their horse. They wore the same yellow dresses and black shoes—the stable colors of Seattle Slew. They had done so for each of his other races and were convinced it was a lucky charm that would ensure victory once more. They became nervous when their horse was late to reach the paddock. The excuse was that so many cars were parked in the area that another route had to be found for the horses to take from the barn. As a result, post time was delayed nine minutes, and Turner was later fined $200.

From interviews with the jockeys and trainers, the general agreement was that none of the seven challengers could beat Seattle Slew. Their only hope was that the extra ¼ mile of the race would come to their rescue, would be too much for the Slew, and he would fall apart. In that event, one of them would be able to scamper home first.

The eight colts came out on a track that was muddy from two days of rain. He had already beaten half of them. The start of the race found the Slew, a 1-5 favorite, running up front, where he remained for the rest of the 1½ miles. The pace was extremely slow. Run Dusty Run made a charge, as did Sanhedrin, but they were quickly dispatched. *The Blood-Horse* felt sorry for the rest of the field as it reported: "The others were not asking anything of him. They were just there, waiting to get smacked in the face." Jockey Cruguet smelled victory before they had even gone a half of a mile. He recalled: "Slew

Jockey Jean Cruguet stands up in the stirrups and waves to the crowd as Seattle Slew nears the finish line of the Belmont Stakes.

was practically walking, the pace was so slow. About as slow as a horse can be conned into running."

There was one scary moment at the very end. Cruguet was so exuberant over winning that he stood up in the stirrups 20 yards from the finish, four lengths in front of Run Dusty Run, and waved his arm and whip in a victory salute. Trainer Billy Turner gasped, as he had visions of the jockey falling from the mount before reaching the finish line. The time was 2:29⅘. When someone needled the trainer by pointing to Secretariat's record-busting Belmont race of 2:24, Taylor retorted that Seattle Slew was undefeated and Secretariat had lost three times.

Official Chart of Belmont

EIGHTH RACE Bel June 11, 1977 — 1½ MILES. (2:24). One hundred and ninth running BELMONT. SCALE WEIGHTS. $150,000 added. 3-year-olds. By subscription of $100 each to accompany the nomination; $1,000 to start. A supplementary nomination may be made of $2,500 on Wednesday, June 8, plus an additional $10,000 to start, with $150,000 added, of which 60% to the winner, 22% to second, 12% to third and 6% to fourth. Colts and geldings, 126 lbs.; fillies, 121 lbs. The winning owner will be presented with the August Belmont Memorial Cup to be retained for one year, as well as a trophy for permanent possession and trophies will be presented to the winning trainer and jockey. Closed with 238 nominations.
Value of race $181,800. Value to winner $109,080; second, $39,996; third, $21,816; fourth, $10,908.
Mutuel Pool, $1,446,714. Off-track betting, $1,681,726.

Last Raced	Horse	Eqt	A	Wt	PP	¼	½	1	1¼	Str	Fin	Jockeys	Owners	Odds to $1
21 May77 ^{8}Pim^{1}	Seattle Slew		3	126	5	$1^{1\frac{1}{2}}$	$1^{1\frac{1}{2}}$	$1^{1\frac{1}{2}}$	1^{4}	$1^{3\frac{1}{2}}$	1^{4}	JCruguet	K L Taylor	.40
21 May77 ^{8}Pim^{3}	Run Dusty Run		3	126	1	$3^{\frac{1}{2}}$	$3^{1\frac{1}{2}}$	2^{h}	3^{3}	2^{2}	2^{2}	SHawley	Golden Chance Farm	5.10
1 Jun77 ^{8}Bel^{2}	Sanhedrin	b	3	126	6	4^{2}	4^{4}	$4^{1\frac{1}{2}}$	2^{h}	3^{3}	$3^{2\frac{1}{4}}$	JVelasquez	Darby Dan Farm	6.50
1 Jun77 ^{8}Bel^{4}	Mr. Red Wing		3	126	7	5^{2}	5^{5}	5^{4}	4^{1}	$4^{1\frac{1}{2}}$	$4^{4\frac{3}{4}}$	JVasquez	J L Greer	69.90
30 May77 ^{8}Atl^{2}	Iron Constitution		3	126	2	8	8	6^{6}	6^{14}	$5^{\frac{1}{2}}$	5no	ACorderoJr	H T Mangurian Jr	7.40
1 Jun77 ^{8}Bel^{1}	Spirit Level		3	126	8	2^{2}	$2^{1\frac{1}{2}}$	3^{2}	$5^{\frac{1}{2}}$	6^{16}	6^{19}	AGraell	Meadow Stable	15.90
30 May77 ^{8}Atl^{7}	Sir Sir		3	126	4	6^{h}	6^{h}	7^{8}	7^{20}	7^{28}	7^{30}	RHernandez	L A Navas	94.90
28 May77 ^{7}Bel^{5}	Make Amends	b	3	126	3	7^{2}	$7^{\frac{1}{2}}$	8	8	8	8	RTurcotte	Elmendorf	57.20

OFF AT 5:47½ EDT. Start good. Won handily. Time, :24⅗, :48⅖, 1:14, 1:38⅘, 2:03⅘, 2:29⅗. Track muddy.

$2 Mutuel Prices:

5-SEATTLE SLEW	2.80	2.60	2.20
2-RUN DUSTY RUN		3.20	2.40
7-SANHEDRIN			2.60

Dk. b. or br. c, by Bold Reasoning—My Charmer, by Poker. Trainer, William H. Turner, Jr. Bred by B. S. Castleman (Ky.).

SEATTLE SLEW had speed from the start, was rated along in the lead while remaining slightly out from the rail, drew off quickly approaching the stretch and won with something left as Cruguet stood up in the saddle about twenty yards from the wire to wave victoriously. RUN DUSTY RUN, away in good order and unhurried early, was sent up between SEATTLE SLEW and SPIRIT LEVEL soon after entering the backstretch, wasn't able to stay with the winner nearing the stretch but continued on with good courge to be second best. SANHEDRIN, reserved early behind the leaders to the far turn, made a run from the outside at the three-eighths pole but weakened during the drive. MR. RED WING moved within striking distance at the far turn but lacked a further response. IRON CONSTITUTION failed to be a serious factor. SPIRIT LEVEL went right after SEATTLE SLEW, remained a factor to the far turn while racing well out in the track and tired badly. SIR SIR was never close. MAKE AMENDS wasn't able to keep up.

Scratched—Hey Hey J. P., Leading Scorer.

The Slew breezes across the finish line to become America's 10th Triple Crown champion.

Happy owner Karen Taylor holds the bridle of Seattle Slew, with Jockey Jean Cruguet up, in the Belmont Park winner's circle. Her husband, Mickey Taylor, stands behind her, partially hidden by her hat.

Unfortunately, the joy over capturing the crown devolved into discord between Seattle Slew's owners and trainer. Billy Turner was in favor of letting the horse rest after the grueling Triple Crown campaign. Steve Cady of *The New York Times* described it aptly when he wrote: "The Triple Crown is the hardest assignment in racing: three tough races against the best opposition at different distances on different surfaces during the short span of five weeks."

There were demands for appearances at major racetracks everywhere, even at the horse show in Madison Square Garden in New York, to bolster crowds. Mickey and Karen Taylor were eager to oblige. They even began a heavy promotion campaign, replete with colorful Seattle Slew jackets, T-shirts, and bumper stickers. They also accepted an invitation for him to race in the Hollywood Park Swaps Stakes in Inglewood, California, only three weeks after the Belmont, as well as an appearance in a Seattle Slew Day parade at the Longacres track near Seattle.

The Swaps race was a disaster. He came in fourth, 16 lengths back, in the 1¼-mile race. The claim was that he had been tranquilized for the plane trip to the West Coast and had appeared listless in the post parade. That was his last race as a three-year-old. He was returned to New York and then to Florida to prepare for the coming year with a new trainer, Doug Peterson. Peterson was hired because of a disagreement between Turner and the Taylors over how much racing the Slew was to do.

Another problem arose that August, when Dr. Hill was suspended for 30 days by the New York State Racing and Wagering Board because he had failed to disclose his interest in Wooden Horse Investment that Taylor had set up for his stable of horses. A state law prohibited veterinarians from practicing in New York if they owned horses that raced in the state. Despite all the turmoil, the year ended on a happy note when Seattle Slew was named Horse of the Year.

The following year began inauspiciously. In February 1978, the Slew contracted a virus that almost killed him. Fortunately, he was nursed back to health and was able to resume racing. He won an allowance by seven furlongs in May, but then had to sit out because of a leg injury. He returned to the track at Saratoga on August 12 and won another allowance by seven furlongs, only to lose by a neck in a 1⅛ mile race at the Meadowlands Racetrack in New Jersey on September 5. When Jean Cruguet claimed the horse was tired, Mickey Taylor became so infuriated that he replaced the jockey with Angel Cordero Jr. The Marlboro Cup at nine furlongs at Belmont Park on September 16, his fourth start of the year, was remarkable because it featured, for the first time, two Triple Crown winners in the same race. Affirmed had won the crown earlier in the year, ridden by Steve Cauthen. There was never any doubt about the outcome of the Marlboro Cup from the very outset—the Slew flew through the stretch and scored a decisive three-length victory over the younger champion. He competed three more times in 1978, winning two and losing one by a nose.

In his seven starts in 1978, he was the winner of five, came in second in two, earned $473,006 in purses, and was presented with the Eclipse Award as the champion older male. He also had been syndicated for $12 million and was retired to stud. Once again he was a winner, for he became one of the outstanding stallions at Three Chimneys Farm near Lexington, Kentucky. At his peak, he serviced 70 mares each year at $150,000 per live foal, and his offspring went on to earn purses amounting to $75 million. He sired 102 stakes winners, including the 1984 Kentucky Derby winner, Swale, and the 1992 Horse of the Year, A. P. Indy. In 2001 his stud fee was $300,000.

Early in 2002 he had to be moved to the nearby Hill 'n' Dale Farm because his barn at Three Chimneys was too close to the breeding shed. He was 28 years old, but he still became too agitated when the mares arrived. In March, he became severely arthritic, had difficulty walking, and underwent surgery to fuse joints in his neck.

Mickey and Karen Taylor moved to Lexington to be with Seattle Slew during his period of failing health. On May 6, he was in his stall and was visited by their pet black Labrador. The two exchanged licks, and then after the Slew lay down and went to sleep, 25 years to the day he had won the Kentucky Derby.

Seattle Slew was buried on the grounds of Three Chimneys Farm.

Affirmed

Affirmed
(chesnut colt)
{
  Exclusive Native {
    Raise a Native
    Exclusive
  }
  Won't Tell You {
    Crafty Admiral
    Scarlet Ribbon
  }
}

| Chapter 11 |

Affirmed
~1978~

The approach of the 1978 Kentucky Derby and the start of the competition for Thoroughbred racing's Triple Crown was underscored by a growing consensus. Racing fans, railbirds, and trainers were of the opinion that it would be nothing more than a two-horse match. The other entries would just be onlookers whose names would merely fill out the racing card. Jimmy Conway, who had won the 1963 Derby with Chateaugay, confessed ruefully to Steve Cady of *The New York Times*: "Let's face it, it's a race between Affirmed and Alydar. . . . They'll have to look each other in the eye somewhere along the line, and that could be your Derby."

Never before had two three-year-old colts come along at the same time so evenly matched. Both were chestnuts with burnished, copper-colored coats, and both traced their lineage to Raise a Native. Each had placid dispositions until they raced, then they became combative. Affirmed liked to run in front or near the lead, and Alydar preferred to mount a charge from behind. Also, they arrived at Churchill Downs with matching records for three-year-olds, having won all four of their prep races.

The owners of the two colts were equally distinguished figures of the racing community. Affirmed was one of Louis and Patrice Wolfson's extensive stock of Thoroughbred horses at their Harbor View Farm. Louis Wolfson entered racing in 1958 and became America's leading breeder in 1970 and 1971. In fact, he was ranked among the top 10 on the breeders list in 10 of the 11 years leading up to 1978. Tall, handsome, silver-haired, and 66 years old, Wolfson was a self-made millionaire. He left college to run his father's junk-metal business in Jacksonville, Florida, made a big success of it, and

221

subsequently became a Wall Street financier, buying and selling companies. In 1967, he even offered Walter O'Malley $5 million for the Brooklyn Dodgers to keep the baseball team from being moved to California.

In 1958, he began to buy and breed horses and opened Harbor View Farm. However, nine years later he was convicted of selling unregistered stocks and served a nine-month prison term. He was forced to get rid of the farm and disperse his horses to pay his legal debts. In 1968, he reestablished Harbor View Farm, a 438-acre spread in Ocala, Florida, and resumed buying and breeding horses. A widower for several years before 1972, he met and married Patrice Jacobs, the daughter of Hirsch Jacobs, the "winningest trainer" in racing history. Louis and Patrice Wolfson became one of the most successful and popular couples in the sport, and Harbor View its leading money winner. Their foundation sire was Raise a Native, whom Wolfson bought for $30,000. Raise a Native became the grandsire of Affirmed. He later sold the stallion to Calumet Farm.

Affirmed was foaled on the morning of February 21, 1975, at the Harbor View Farm. His sire was Exclusive Native. His dam was Won't Tell You, a daughter of Crafty Admiral. Both grandsires were champions. On the maternal side, Crafty Admiral earned $499,200 in four years of racing, and the paternal grandsire, Raise a Native, was undefeated in four races before he was injured and had to retire. Still, he was highly regarded by knowledgeable track people. As a handler of horses at the Harbor View Farm described Affirmed: "A man waits a lifetime for a horse like this."

It was a nostalgic Patrice Wolfson who gave Affirmed his name—"based on many important decisions, personal, business, and otherwise, that have been affirmed over the years." Wolfson preferred to think it was because his wife liked the combination of "Aff" in names, and he acknowledged that they had enjoyed some luck with such names for their horses. One of these was Affiliate, who ran in the 1977 Derby.

According to the farm's manager, Affirmed was a nice-looking colt who always liked to run. Even as a weanling, he was at the front most of the time when galloping with other youngsters.

The Harbor View horses had their early training with the starting gate at the farm's three-furlong track. After they were broken, they were sent to trainer Laz Barrera in New York for final preparation to race. He had been a trainer for 38 years in his native Cuba, as well as in Mexico, California, and New York. In 1976 and 1977, he saddled winners of more than $5 million in purses. He won his first Kentucky Derby with Bold Forbes in 1976.

Alydar belonged to Gene and Lucille Markey, the octogenarian owners of Calumet Farm, a Kentucky landmark dating back to the thirties. It had been established by Mrs. Markey's first husband, Warren Wright Sr., a baking-powder magnate who died in 1950. No other stable dominated racing as it did from 1941 to 1961. Among its prize horses were Triple Crown champions Citation and Whirlaway. As of 1968, Calumet had captured eight Kentucky Derbies, which gave rise to the sarcasm that the only thing it ever did was win. There was also the cry, "Break up Calumet."

Gene Markey was a former Hollywood celebrity, film producer, and novelist. He was also noted for his ex-wives, screen stars Joan Bennett, Myrna Loy, and Hedy Lamarr. He and Lucille had been married for 26 years. They lived at Calumet, and their home was festooned with 500 gold and silver trophies won by their stable. They were affectionately called the "wheelchair kids." Their purchase of Raise a Native from Louis Wolfson paid off when he sired Alydar.

Affirmed and Alydar reached the racetrack at the same time as two-year-olds. The Harbor View colt's first race was on May 24, 1977, at Belmont Park in New York. Affirmed won the race easily and followed this with a victory in the Youthful Stakes on June 15. Alydar was also entered in the race, his first time on a track. He was prepared by John Veitch, who had taken over as Calumet's trainer. Alydar found himself boxed in and wound up fifth. Their next meeting was on July 6 in the Great American Stakes at Belmont Park in New York, and that time Alydar made what became his patented rush from behind to catch and beat Affirmed by three and a half lengths. This convinced the racing buffs that Alydar was the "best youngster in the East."

The two chestnut colts then went their separate, winning ways: Affirmed at Hollywood and Saratoga, Alydar at Belmont, Saratoga, and New Jersey. Along the way, a new member was added to the Harbor View training and racing crew. He was Steve Cauthen, Affirmed's new jockey. Only 17 years old and from Walton, Kentucky, he had become the talk of the racing world because of his remarkable success as a jockey.

Affirmed and Alydar finally met for the third time in the Hopeful Stakes at Saratoga, New York, in August. They went off at even money and again galvanized the fans with a head-to-head struggle in the stretch. Alydar made his typical stretch run on the outside, but never got by Affirmed, who held on to win by half of a length.

The two colts continued to rouse racing fans in the Champagne Stakes at Belmont on October 15. John Veitch had turned over Alydar's reins to jockey

Jorge Velasquez in an effort to put a different finish on their races. It worked, for Alydar caught up to Affirmed at the 1/16 pole and won going away by one and a quarter lengths.

Their final meeting of the year was in the Laurel Futurity at the Laurel Race Course in Maryland. Only four horses started, and the juvenile title was on the line. As expected, it became a two-horse affair. Cauthen rode a strong race, held off the Calumet colt, and won by a neck. That brought the exciting two-year-old campaign to an end. Affirmed had won four of six meetings with Alydar, seven of nine races overall, and was named Best Two-Year-Old Colt. Their next encounter would be in the 1978 Kentucky Derby.

Affirmed rode out the winter in sunny California. At least, it was supposed to be sunny. There was so much rain that the Santa Anita backstretch was deep in mud, and Laz Barrera had to improvise some exercise for the colt under the shedrow instead of on the track. Still, Affirmed won the four prep races between March 8 and April 16, even though he ran unimpressively in the Hollywood Derby. Steve Cauthen had to whip him 12 times in the stretch to keep him focused.

Alydar spent the winter in Florida and also won four prep races. He had everyone in awe when he captured the Blue Grass Stakes by 13½ lengths. On the other hand, doubts were raised about Steve Cauthen riding Affirmed in the Derby. Cauthen, or "the Kid," as he was tagged by the press, would be celebrating only his 18th birthday before the race, and might be uptight to ride in so big and important an event. His record suggested otherwise, however. In 1977, the earnings of his mounts had exceeded $6 million; he had won 487 races and three Eclipse Awards and had been named Sportsman of the Year by *Sports Illustrated*. The magazine reckoned that Cauthen's year was better than "hitting three home runs in one game to help win the World Series."

The 104th running of the Derby drew a crowd of 131,004 that made Alydar the 6-5 favorite in the field of 11. Even though Affirmed had taken top honors among two-year-olds, the Kentucky fans showed their partiality to a native foaled and bred horse. Although Affirmed had also been foaled in Kentucky, he still was Florida bred.

Affirmed broke like a flash, took the lead at the second turn of the Churchill Downs track, and was never headed. Alydar appeared to have trouble holding the track and dropped off the pack. He was 17 lengths behind before he ratcheted up his charge. Cauthen said that on the backstretch Affirmed "started to prick his ears once clear like he always does, so I started hitting him and he won

Affirmed, with Jockey Steve Cauthen in the saddle, wins the Kentucky Derby by 1½ lengths over Alydar, ridden by Jorge Velasquez.

Official Chart of the Kentucky Derby

EIGHTH RACE
Churchill
MAY 6, 1978

1 ¼ MILES. (1.59⅖) 104th running THE KENTUCKY DERBY. $125,000 Added 3-year-olds. By subscription of $100 which covers nomination for both The Kentucky Derby and Derby Trial. All nomination fees to Derby Winner. $4,000 to pass the entry box Thursday, May 4, $3,500 additional to start, $125,000 added, of which $30,000 to second, $15,000 to third, $7,500 to fourth, $100,000 guaranteed to winner (to be divided euqally in the event of a dead heat.) Weight 126 lbs. Starters to be named through the entry box Thursday, May 4, at time of closing. The maximum number of starters for The Kentucky Derby will be limited to twenty. In the event more than twenty entries pass through the entry box at the usual time of closing, the twenty starters will be determined at that time with preference given to those that have accumulated the highest lifetime earnings. For those that enter and are eliminated under this condition, the nomination fee and the fee to pass through the entry box, will be refunded. The owner of the winner to receive a gold trophy. Closed with 319 nominations.

Value of race $239,400, value to winner $186,900, second $30,000, third $15,000, fourth $7,500. Mutuel pool $4,425,828.

Last Raced	Horse	Eqt.	A.	Wt	PP	¼	½	¾	1	Str	Fin	Jockey	Odds $1
16Apr78 ^{8}Hol^{1}	Affirmed		3	126	2	2^{hd}	$3^{2\frac{1}{2}}$	$3^{1\frac{1}{2}}$	2^{3}	1^{2}	$1^{1\frac{1}{2}}$	Cauthen S	1.80
27Apr78 ^{7}Kee^{1}	Alydar	b	3	126	10	9^{hd}	9^{5}	8^{hd}	4^{hd}	3^{3}	$2^{1\frac{1}{4}}$	Velasquez J	1.20
22Apr78 ^{8}Aqu^{1}	Believe It		3	126	9	$4^{\frac{1}{2}}$	$4^{\frac{1}{2}}$	5^{3}	1^{hd}	2^{2}	$3^{4\frac{1}{4}}$	Maple E	7.40
22Apr78 ^{8}Aqu^{2}	Darby Creek Road	b	3	126	7	$7^{\frac{1}{2}}$	7^{2}	7^{2}	$5^{\frac{1}{2}}$	4^{2}	$4^{2\frac{1}{4}}$	Brumfield D	33.00
29Apr78 ^{7}CD^{2}	Esops Foibles	b	3	126	3	$5^{1\frac{1}{2}}$	5^{4}	4^{1}	6^{3}	5^{3}	$5^{5\frac{1}{4}}$	McCarron C J	49.70
18Apr78 ^{7}Kee^{1}	Sensitive Prince		3	126	11	$3^{2\frac{1}{2}}$	$1^{1\frac{1}{2}}$	1^{2}	$3^{1\frac{1}{2}}$	6^{3}	$6^{\frac{1}{2}}$	Solomone M	4.50
22Apr78 ^{9}GP^{6}	Dr. Valeri	b	3	126	8	11	11	10^{4}	10^{5}	$7^{1\frac{1}{2}}$	$7^{3\frac{1}{4}}$	Riera R Jr	96.10
29Apr78 ^{7}CD^{3}	Hoist the Silver		3	126	5	8^{2}	$8^{\frac{1}{2}}$	9^{5}	7^{3}	8^{5}	8^{7}	Depass R	123.70
19Apr78 ^{8}Kee^{1}	Chief of Dixieland	b	3	126	6	6^{3}	6^{2}	$6^{\frac{1}{2}}$	9^{1}	9^{1}	9^{1}	Rini A	121.70
27Apr78 ^{7}Kee^{2}	Raymond Earl		3	126	1	1^{2}	2^{4}	2^{2}	8^{1}	10^{2}	10^{2}	Baird R L	117.10
27Apr78 ^{7}Kee^{6}	Special Honor	b	3	126	4	10^{3}	$10^{\frac{1}{2}}$	11	11	11	11	Nicolo P	177.10

OFF AT 5:41 EDT. Start good for all but SPECIAL HONOR, Won driving. Time, :22⅗, :45⅗, 1:10⅘, 1:35⅘, 2:01⅕ Track fast.

$2 Mutuel Prices:			
2-AFFIRMED	5.60	2.80	2.60
10-ALYDAR		2.60	2.40
9-BELIEVE IT			2.80

Ch. c, by Exclusive Native—Won't Tell You, by Crafty Admiral. Trainer Barrera Lazaro S. Bred by Harbor View Farm (Fla).

AFFIRMED away alertly but held in reserve for six furlongs, moved up boldly along outside thereafter to take command on second turn, relinquished the lead momentarily a quarter mile out but responded to a rousing ride to regain command in upper stretch and was fully extended to hold ALYDAR safe. The latter, under snug restraint early, commenced to advance from the outside after six furlongs, continued wide into the stretch, swerved in to bump with BELIEVE IT in closing sixteenth and finished strongly when straightened.BELIEVE IT reserved off the early pace, moved up with a bold rush while bearing out on second turn to gain command momentarily a quarter mile away, continued wide while lacking a further response and was bumped by ALYDAR in the closing stages. DARBY CREEK ROAD lacked speed and hung after making a rally on the final bend. ESOPS FOIBLES faltered after making a mild bid on the second turn. SENSITIVE PRINCE sent to the fore on rounding the first turn, continued to make a swift pace while along the inside to final bend where he gave way suddenly. DR. VALERI was without speed. CHIEF OF DIXIELAND was bumped about before going a quarter mile. RAYMOND EARL showed brief early speed and tired badly. SPECIAL HONOR reared at the start.

Owners— 1, Harbor View Farm; 2, Calumet Farm; 3, Hickory Tree Stable; 4, Phillips J W; 5, Frankel J; 6, Top the Marc Stable; 7, Renzi V & R; 8, Dasso-Golob-Levinson-Solomon; 9, Dixie Jake Inc; 10, Lehmann R N; 11, Gaston Linda T & Haynes A D.

Trainers— 1, Barrera Lazaro S; 2, Veitch John M; 3, Stephens Woodford C; 4, Rondinello Thomas L; 5, Rettele Loren; 6, Jerkens H Allen; 7, Perez Aurelio M; 8, Fischer Richard J; 9, Morreale Jake; 10, Adams W E Smiley; 11, McCann Edward T.

Affirmed (6) and jockey Steve Cauthen lead Alydar (3) and Jorge Velasquez over the finish line to win the Preakness, the second leg of the Triple Crown.

like he always does." They crossed the finish line one and a half lengths in front of Alydar, who had staged a remarkable finishing drive.

It was the 12th win in 14 starts for the Wolfson colt, who had earned purses that totaled $186,900, which boosted his earnings to a phenomenal $887,027. However, the approach of the Preakness two weeks later on May 20 raised more questions about his ability than answers. Racing fans wondered if Affirmed would continue his unbeaten streak of five and capture the second leg of the Triple Crown races. Would he have the needed speed to contend with the shorter race of 1³⁄₁₆ miles on the sharp turns of the Pimlico track? With only six other horses in the field, it was unlikely that any of the horses would have to be concerned about being boxed in and prevented from running a strong race. Finally, would Alydar prove he was the best three-year-old most people had thought he was before the Derby?

After the race in Louisville, Laz Bearrera had crowed: "We are waiting to find a horse that really makes Affirmed run." He voiced little concern over whatever competition they would face. John Veitch, on the other hand, supported jockey Jorge Velasquez' claim that Alydar had shown a dislike for the track and vowed "to hang much closer to the lead horse this time."

Veitch was particularly bitter over some of the comments in the press over the way Alydar had been ridden. Dick Young of the *New York Daily News* wrote: "Jorge rode him in the first mile as though he was on a Sunday canter in Central Park." Someone else had wired the Markeys to suggest that they "send Velasquez back to Panama and keep the canal."

A record crowd of 81,261 filled the Pimlico Race Course outside of Baltimore to witness the running of the 103ʳᵈ Preakness. Even the painter perched atop the pole in the infield was filled with anticipation. He was next to the metal weather vane with the figure of a jockey astride a racehorse. It had been scrubbed clean and was waiting for the racing colors of the winning stable to be painted on it—a Pimlico tradition. Would it be the flamingo pink and black of Harbor View, or the devil's red and blue of Calumet? Almost everyone in the park was convinced it would be one or the other.

"Affirmed's and Alydar's Preakness battle was pure art," wrote Edward Bowen in *The Blood-Horse*. The two golden chestnut colts dueled in the backstretch, and the Calumet colt was only a head behind at the top of the stretch. What followed was a furious charge to the finish line, with Alydar on the outside and Affirmed on the inside. Whenever Alydar inched up, Affirmed inched away. The ultimate winner was in doubt to the delirious crowd and the nationwide television audience even after they had cleared the finish line. There was an agonizing wait for the formal announcement of the winner after the stewards studied the photos of the finish. It finally came. It was a victory by a neck—Affirmed's neck.

A trainer of one of the also-rans later commented dryly on what it was like to run against Affirmed. "You've run into an iron wall when you get up to him." It was also apparent that Affirmed was the only horse Alydar could not beat.

The winner's purse was $136,200, which pushed Affirmed's total bankroll to $1,023,227. Although 20 other horses had earned $1 million or more, none had accomplished it so early in their racing careers.

The Belmont Stakes is the defining race of the three that make up the Triple Crown. At 1½ miles it is the longest of them. A three-year-old Thoroughbred must possess speed, stamina, and endurance to have a chance to win. That is why breeders of racehorses yearn the most for a winner of the Test of the Champions, as it is familiarly called.

A crowd of more than 65,417 people showed up at Belmont Park in New York on June 10 for the running of the 110ᵗʰ Belmont Stakes. They came to see another classic duel between Affirmed and Alydar and, perhaps, the crowning of a new Triple Crown Champion. Only five horses paraded to the starting gate.

Affirmed rushed for the lead at the very outset but was caught up to by Alydar in the backstretch. After that the two ran as if chained together like a team, without daylight between them, the lead never more than the tip of Affirmed's nose. They ran so close to each other that Cauthen, on the inside,

227

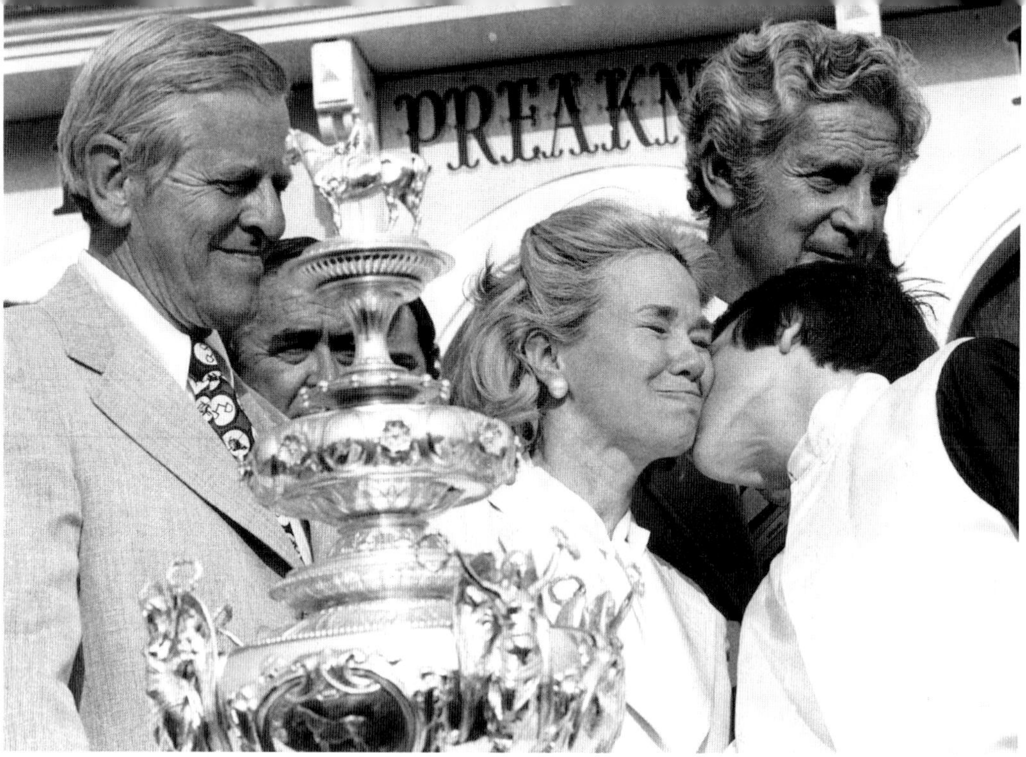

Jockey Steve Cauthen busses the cheek of owner Patrice Wolfson after the Preakness victory. Her husband, Louis Wolfson, is in the rear (right). Maryland Governor Blair Lee waits to present the Preakness trophy to the owners.

Official Chart of Preakness

EIGHTH RACE
Pimlico
MAY 20, 1978

$1\frac{3}{16}$ MILES. (1.54) 103rd Running PREAKNESS. $150,000 Added. 3-year-olds by subscription of $100 each, this fee to accompany the nomination. $1,000 to pass the entry box, starters to pay $1,000 additional. All eligibility, entrance and starting fees to the winner, with $150,000 added, of which $30,000 to second, $15,000 to third and $7,500 to fourth. Weight 126 lbs. Starters to be named through the entry box Thursday, May 18, two days before the race by the usual time of closing. A replica of the Woodlawn Vase will be presented to the winning owner to remain his or her personal property. Closed Wednesday, February 15, 1978 with 247 nominations.
Value of race $188,700, value to winner $136,200, second $30,000, third $15,000, fourth $7,500. Mutuel pool $1,335,965, Minus place pool $17,998.60, Minus show pool $17,914.65. Exacta Pool $262,946.

Last Raced	Horse	Eqt.	A.	Wt	PP	St	¼	½	¾	Str	Fin	Jockey	Odds $1
6May78 ^{8}CD^{1}	Affirmed		3	126	6	1	2^{1}	1^{1}	1^{1}	$1^{\frac{1}{2}}$	1^{nk}	Cauthen S	.50
6May78 ^{8}CD^{2}	Alydar	b	3	126	3	2	6^{2}	6^{4}	$4^{1\frac{1}{2}}$	$2^{1\frac{1}{2}}$	$2^{7\frac{1}{2}}$	Velasquez J	1.80
6May78 ^{8}CD^{3}	Believe It		3	126	2	5	3^{1}	3^{2}	3^{hd}	$3^{3\frac{1}{2}}$	$3^{2\frac{1}{2}}$	Maple E	6.70
6May78 ^{8}Pim^{8}	Noon Time Spender	b	3	126	1	7	$5^{2\frac{1}{2}}$	$4^{\frac{1}{2}}$	2^{1}	4^{5}	4^{8}	Hinojosa H	80.80
6May78 ^{8}Pim^{5}	Indigo Star	b	3	126	7	3	$4^{\frac{1}{2}}$	5^{1}	$6^{2\frac{1}{2}}$	5^{6}	5^{6}	Fitzgerald R	89.80
12May78 ^{5}Pim^{1}	Dax S.	b	3	126	5	4	7	7	7	6^{1}	6^{4}	Kurtz J	93.30
14May78 ^{8}Aqu^{5}	Track Reward		3	126	4	6	1^{hd}	2^{1}	5^{2}	7	7	Gonzalez B	88.70

OFF AT 5:41 EDT. Start good, Won driving. Time, $:23\frac{3}{5}$, $:47\frac{3}{5}$, $1:11\frac{4}{5}$, $1:36\frac{1}{5}$, $1:54\frac{2}{5}$ Track fast.

$2 Mutuel Prices:

	Win	Place	Show
6–AFFIRMED	3.00	2.10	2.10
3–ALYDAR		2.10	2.10
2–BELIEVE IT			2.10

$2 EXACTA 6–3 PAID $4.00.

Ch. c, by Exclusive Native—Won't Tell You, by Crafty Admiral. Trainer Barrera Lazaro S. Bred by Harbor View Farm (Fla).

AFFIRMED, taken under light restraint after breaking alertly, quickly joined TRACK REWARD from the outside, gained the advantage leaving the first turn, made the pace under clever rating, responded gamely to rousing when challenged by ALYDAR in the upper stretch and turned back that rival under brisk handling. ALYDAR, under restraint and allowed to settle early, advanced willingly outside of horses in backstretch, engaged AFFIRMED well out from the rail approaching the stretch to nearly reach even terms then couldn't get to that rival when set down in a steady drive. BELIEVE IT saved ground under a snug hold while maintaining a good striking position, came around TRACK REWARD when that rival began to retire on the final turn then quickly regained the rail and couldn't stay with the top pair when the real test came. NOON TIME SPENDER, saving ground while not far back, eased outside of horses in backstretch and steadily gained ground, loomed boldly on the final turn and weakened in the drive. INDIGO STAR had good early speed and gave way readily on the final turn. DAX S. showed little. TRACK REWARD was quickly sent up to join for the lead soon after the start, saved ground while prompting the pace into the last bend and gave way readily.

Owners— 1, Harbor View Farm; 2, Calumet Farm; 3, Hickory Tree Stable; 4, Miami Lakes Ranch; 5, Procopio R F; 6, Scherr N; 7, Aisquith Stable.

Trainers— 1, Barrera Lazaro S; 2, Veitch John M; 3, Stephens Woodford C; 4, Arcodia Antonio; 5, Leatherbury King T; 6, Gross Mel W; 7, Barrera Albert S.

Affirmed, with Steve Cauthen up (right). battles Alydar, with Jorge Valasquez up, down the stretch of the Stakes at Belmont Park.

Affirmed (on the rail) wins the Belmont Stakes by a nose over Alydar to become America's 11th Triple Crown champion. Turf writers said it was perhaps the fiercest struggle ever seen on a racetrack.

Official Chart of Belmont Stakes

EIGHTH RACE
Belmont
JUNE 10, 1978

1 ½ MILES. (2.24) 110th running THE BELMONT. $150,000 Added. 3–year–olds. By subscription of $100 each to accompany the nominations; $500 to pass the entry box; $1,000 to start. A supplementary nomination may be made of $2,500 on Wednesday, June 7 plus an additional $10,000 to start, with $150,000 added, of which 60% to the winner, 22% to second, 12% to third and 6% to fourth. Colts and Geldings, weights, 126 lbs. Fillies, 121 lbs. Starters to be named at the closing time of entries. Thursday, June 8. The winning owner will be presented with the August Belmont Memorial Cup to be retained for one year, as well as a trophy for permanent possession and trophies will be presented to the winning trainer and jockey. (Closed Wednesday, February 15, 1978 with 268 nomina-tons.)

Value of race $184,300, value to winner $110,580, second $40,546, third $22,116, fourth $11,058. Mutuel pool $1,186,662, OTB pool $1,389,646.

Last Raced	Horse	Eqt.A.Wt PP	¼	½	1	1¼	Str	Fin	Jockey	Odds $1
20May78 ⁸Pim¹	Affirmed	3 126 3	1¹	1¹	1½	1hd	1hd	1hd	Cauthen S	.60
20May78 ⁸Pim²	Alydar	3 126 2	3¹½	2¹	2⁵	2⁸	2¹²	2¹³	Velasquez J	1.10
28May78 ⁸Bel²	Darby Creek Road	3 126 1	5	5	5	3¹½	3⁴	3⁷¾	Cordero A Jr	9.90
22May78 ⁵Aqu⁹	Judge Advocate	3 126 4	2¹½	3²½	4³	5	4hd	4¹¼	Fell J	30.10
29May78 ⁸Mth²	Noon Time Spender	b 3 126 5	4¹	4³	3½	4hd	5	5	Hernandez R	38.40

OFF AT 5:43, EDT. Start good, Won driving. Time, :25, :50, 1:14, 1:37⅖, 2:01⅗, 2:26⅘, Track fast.

$2 Mutuel Prices:

3–(C)–AFFIRMED	3.20	2.10	—
2–(B)–ALYDAR		2.20	—
1–(A)–DARBY CREEK ROAD	—	—	—

(No Show Wagering)

Ch. c, by Exclusive Native—Won't Tell You, by Crafty Admiral. Trainer Barrera Lazaro S. Bred by Harbor View Farm (Fla).

AFFIRMED went right to the front and was rated along on the lead while remaining well out from the rail. He responded readily when challenged by ALYDAR soon after entering the backstretch, held a narrow advantage into the stretch while continuing to save ground and was under left-handed urging to prevail in a determined effort. ALYDAR, away in good order, saved ground to the first turn. He came out to go after AFFIRMED with seven furlongs remaining, raced with that rival to the stretch, reached almost even terms with AFFIRMED near the three-sixteenths pole but wasn't good enough in a stiff drive. DARBY CREEK ROAD, unhurried while being outrun early, moved around horses while rallying on the far turn but lacked a further response. JUDGE ADVOCATE broke through before the start and was finished at the far turn. NOON TIME SPENDER raced within striking distance for a mile and gave way.

Owners— 1, Harbor View Farm; 2, Calumet Farm; 3, Phillips J W; 4, Phipps O; 5, Miami Lakes Ranch.
Trainers— 1, Barrera Lazaro S; 2, Veitch John M; 3, Rondinello Thomas L; 4, Russell John W; 5, Arcodia Antonio.

could only use the whip with his left hand, while Valesquez had to spur on Alydar with the whip in his right hand. Affirmed managed to push his head in front across the finish line in what was, perhaps, the fiercest struggle ever seen on a racetrack to become America's 11th Triple Crown champion.

The racing scribes of the press were hard-pressed to find enough superlatives for their stories of the race. Ed Comerford of *Newsday* put it well when he wrote: "One of these days an inventive racing secretary is going to write a race for around the world, 25,000 miles on the equator. Affirmed will win it. But Alydar will be at his throat all the way, and it will take a photo to separate them at the finish."

Of the 1978 Triple Crown, someone pointed out that for the first time the same horse had come in second in all three races. Furthermore, it was the ninth meeting and fifth photo finish together. The two horses met once more in Saratoga's Travers Stakes on August 19. Although Affirmed led the Calumet colt across the finish line, he was disqualified for interference and Alydar was declared the winner. Despite the victory, the chestnut colt still had not passed his nemesis at the wire.

Affirmed ran in three other races before the end of the year. He won the Jim Dandy Stakes at Saratoga, came in second to Seattle Slew in the Marlboro Cup at Belmont—the first time two Triple Crown Champions had run against each other, and lost the Jockey Club Gold Cup, in which he lost because his saddle slipped and jockey Steve Cauthen barely survived being thrown. Nevertheless, he still was named Horse of the Year. In the following year, he had nine starts, won seven of them, and was named Horse of the Year for the third consecutive time.

Affirmed was retired at the end of 1979 after winning 22 of his 29 career races and earning purses totaling a record $2,393,818. Syndicated for $14.4 million, he stood in stud at the Jonabell Farm near Lexington, Kentucky. He lived until 2001, when he was euthanized for humane reasons at the age of 26. Complications from surgery on a leg had made it too painful for him to walk. He was buried with the flamingo pink and black racing silks of Harbor View Farm next to the stallion complex at Jonabell Farm.

Of more than 700 Affirmed foals, 75 won stakes races. As a group, his foals earned some $40 million.

Chapter 12

Near Misses

On 17 different occasions, the owners of 17 Thoroughbreds might have been impelled to utter to themselves: "There, but for the grace of God go I," as they witnessed, in abject disappointment, the unfolding of the ceremonies in the winner's circle following the running of the Belmont Stakes. These were the 17 years in which high-flying hopes and expectations for capturing the Triple Crown were smashed to smithereens, as each of the promising candidates failed the 1½-mile torture test, the test of the champion. Each of the 17 horses had won the Kentucky Derby and the Preakness Stakes only to flunk out at Belmont Park. They were the near misses since Sir Barton won the Triple Crown in 1919. So close, yet so far.

1944—Pensive

Pensive was bred on the Calumet Farm in Lexington, Kentucky, and owned by Chicago industrialist Warren Wright Sr. The farm was known for the quality of its Thoroughbreds, including Whirlaway and Citation, who both won the Triple Crown. Pensive was turned over to the noted trainer Ben Jones, who had handled Whirlaway. Although the chestnut colt was the son of Hyperion, winner of the English Derby, his training progress was slow. In fact, he almost never made it to the Kentucky Derby because Jones did not consider him to be of Derby caliber after unimpressive winter and spring races. However, when 15 horses were entered in the Derby—a signal that the race would be wide open—he became the 16th starter at 8-5.

Jockey Eddie Arcaro rode Stir Up, Johnny Longden was on Platter, and Conn McCreary was in the saddle on Pensive. The Calumet colt chased the pacesetters until they swung wide at the top of the stretch, when he was able to move inside and wear down the leader, Broadcloth, to win by four and a half lengths.

Pensive

At that time, the Preakness was raced only a week later, and Pensive was at 8-5 odds. Seven horses made up the field. The Calumet chestnut colt was within sight of the front-runners until the top of the stretch, when he made his move. Although slammed on the way down to the finish line, he was able to keep in stride and flash by the leader, Platter, for the win by three-quarters of a length. Stir Up was third.

Pensive became only the ninth winner of the Preakness and Derby and was hailed as the "stretch-running fool." Once again, only seven horses made up the field for the Belmont Stakes. Pensive was favored at 1-2. The race went off as expected, and Conn McCreary figured he had everything in hand until he caught a glimpse of Bounding Home coming up on his right. The 16-1 long shot surged on, despite all McCreary's urging of Pensive, and made it across the finish line ahead by half a length. McCreary later bemoaned what had happened. He had been criticized in the past for keeping his mounts too far off the pace too long. He claimed he did everything right that time, yet came up short. Bounding Home had won only twice in 13 previous starts.

1958—Tim Tam

Tim Tam was a promising two-year-old Calumet Farm bay colt. He matured slowly and began to fulfill expectations only in his third year. By late April, he had won 10 out of 12 starts, including six stakes races. He won the Derby Trial on a muddy track, which made him an easy choice for his owner and trainer to represent Calumet in the 1958 Kentucky Derby, when their preferred stablemate, Kentucky Pride, became ill.

Tim Tam

Tim Tam and Silky Sullivan, the California colt that drew the most public attention because of a strong publicity campaign that focused on his intriguing name and reputation for staging spectacular stretch dashes, went off at 15-1. Willie Shoemaker rode Silky Sullivan, Eddie Arcaro was on Jewel's Reward, and Ismael Valenzuela guided Tim Tam. It rained before race day and the track was heavy. Sixteen horses made up the field. Tim Tam settled into fifth place until he was ready to challenge the leaders at the top of the stretch. He finally took the lead at about 15 yards from the wire and won by half a length. Silky Sullivan had been 25 lengths off the pace, moved up to 12th, but flattened out.

Twelve horses challenged Tim Tam in the Preakness—seven whose trainers wanted to prove that the Derby victory was a fluke. The bay colt proceeded to convince them that it was not. He moved effortlessly along the rail in the stretch and won by one and a half lengths. Warren Schweder wrote in *The Blood-Horse*: "Tim Tam appeared to have been out for a Sunday afternoon spin in the park."

The win convinced doubters that he was the best three-year-old in training, and he approached the starting gate of the Belmont Stakes as the 3-20 favorite. He had a winning streak of eight, had won 10 times in 13 starts overall, and was considered to have a real shot at being voted the best Thoroughbred of 1958. He also had earned $444,280 in purses.

There were eight horses in the field at Belmont, including four newcomers. Eddie Arcaro was aboard Cavan, his 20th mount in the classic. It was the first Belmont for Valenzuela. He and Tim Tam moved behind the Irish-bred Cavan in the homestretch and prepared to start their drive. The crowd erupted with an encouraging roar. The jockey whacked the horse with his whip on the right flank and the colt swerved out. Valenzuela quickly switched to his left hand but failed to get the expected response. He sensed something was wrong and did not punish the horse anymore. Tim Tam finished the race in second place, five and a half lengths behind the winner, Cavan. It was revealed later that Tim Tam had shattered a bone in his right fore ankle yet had gamely run the last ¼ mile despite the broken leg.

1961—Carry Back

Carry Back was a colt with a less-than-fashionable lineage. His dam was Joppy, who was banned from racing because of a nasty temper and her refusal to leave the starting gates. She was sold to Jack Price, a retired general manager of a Cleveland machine-tool company, who had turned to breeding and training. The deal was for $150 plus the cancellation of a $150 debt. Price next obtained the stud services of a stallion, Saggy, for $400. The result was Carry Back.

As a three-year-old he was an unattractive, scrawny-looking little colt weighing less than one thousand pounds. He had a long tail that almost touched the ground, reminiscent of Whirlaway. Price thought so little of him that he raced him early and often to get the most out of him before he faded. Still, by the end of his first year on the track, he had been in 21 races and had earned $612,868. He had polished off such reputable stakes races as the Florida Derby, Flamingo Stakes,

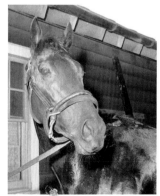

Carry Back

and Everglades Stakes. He had also shown an ability to handle a muddy track. Therefore, he was entered in the Kentucky Derby.

Two days of torrential rain had turned Churchill Downs into a quagmire. That, plus Carry Back's record and reputation as a "mudder," saw him bet down to the 5-2 favorite in a field of 15. His jockey, Johnny Sellers, found himself and the colt in a scramble of horses early on and sent Carry Back to the outside, where he had room to put his speed to work. He ran down the opposition with a spectacular burst in the homestretch to score a three-quarters-of-a-length victory. Joe Nichols of *The New York Times* reported a sardonic comment from a proper Bostonian on Carry Back's accomplishment: "Tonight the bluegrass breeding book will be burned."

The Preakness had an even more startling ending. Carry Back went up against eight Thoroughbreds as the 7-4 favorite and blew them away. He left the gate 15 lengths off the pace but put on an unbelievable performance that carried him to a three-quarters-of-a-length win over Globemaster.

Racing fans responded by making him the Belmont Stakes 2-5 favorite in a field of nine, as they eagerly anticipated another of his thrilling stretch drives and the crowning of a new Triple Crown Champion. Going into the stretch turn, he moved up to sixth place and was on the verge of over-whelming the front-runners in his usual way. However, when Sellers called on him to start his spurt, he "spit out the bit," to use the common racing expres-sion to indicate that the horse did not feel like running. He wound up seventh. The winner was Sherluck, a 65-1 outsider who had won only once in 10 starts in 1961. The Belmont Stakes Trophy was presented by former President Dwight D. Eisenhower.

1964—Northern Dancer

Northern Dancer

Northern Dancer was bred on the Oshawa, Ontario, farm of his owner, E. P. Taylor, one of Canada's wealthiest men and the chair-man of the Ontario Jockey Club. The colt, as a two-year-old, won seven of nine races and had a winning streak of eight leading up to the 1964 Kentucky Derby. Taylor hoped he would emulate another Canadian-owned horse, Sir Barton, America's first Triple Crown champion in 1919. Despite Northern Dancer's record, the oddsmaker of the Derby had him at 5-2, second to the California-bred Hill Rise, who was at 6-5 and also on an eight-straight victory streak.

Bill Hartack, winner of more than three thousand races, was Northern Dancer's jockey, and Willie Shoemaker, with five thousand wins, was on Hill Rise. The Derby became a scorching match race between the two colts as they dueled down the homestretch. Northern Dancer prevailed, but only by a neck in the record time of two minutes flat. He was the first Canadian-born horse to win the Kentucky Derby. (Sir Barton, although Canadian-owned, had been foaled in Kentucky.)

A field of only six went out for the Preakness, and once again Hill Rise was the favorite at 7-5. Northern Dancer was the second choice at 8-5. This time, the Dancer won handily by two and a half lengths over Hill Rise.

The Belmont Stakes was run at the Aqueduct Race Track in New York because repairs were being made at Belmont Park. It drew a record attendance of 61,215, the largest ever to witness the famous race. Northern Dancer was decisively defeated, finishing third some six lengths behind the winner, Quadrangle, who had won only three of eight races that year. Steve Cady of *The New York Times* reported jockey Bill Hartack's appraisal of the race: "You don't get given a Belmont Stakes. You have to take it."

1966—Kauai King

Kauai King was bred in Maryland, raised in Virginia, owned by a Nebraskan businessman, and named for a Hawaiian island. In the native tongue, Kauai supposedly meant "unconquerable island." That hardly applied to the colt when he was two. He won only once in four races and earned a total of $6,120. The following year was something else. With the approach of the Kentucky Derby, he had a record of seven wins out of nine, total earnings of $240,027, and was the top choice in the Run for the Roses. Not everyone agreed, however, and 14 horses were sent out to prove otherwise. When the race was over, a lot of minds were changed as he lived up to his "speed horse" reputation.

He took the lead at the start, was never headed, and won by half a length. He was the first Maryland-bred horse to win the Derby, and it was the first Derby victory for his jockey, Don Brumfield; his trainer, Henry Forrest; and his owner, Michael Ford.

Two weeks later at Pimlico for the Preakness, it was a field of only nine, and it became strictly a two-horse race, as the King engaged in a battle with Stupendous in the stretch. Kauai King prevailed by one and a half lengths.

Kauai King

The win in the Preakness wiped out the doubts about him. Confidence in the horse was so high that he was made the 3-5 favorite to capture the Belmont Stakes and the Triple Crown. Nevertheless, nine mounts showed up to challenge him. Their trainers were hoping that Kauai King would have an off day. He did. By the first turn he was rank. He tried to run faster than his jockey wanted at that stage of the race. According to Steve Cady, "He was wobbling like a drunken acrobat on a high wire," and wound up fourth, eight lengths behind the winner, Amberoid. A footnote to the race is that Kauai King's sire, the great Native Dancer, also failed in his quest for the Triple Crown, except that he lost the Kentucky Derby by a nose because his jockey misjudged when to begin the big push to the finish line.

1969—Majestic Prince

Majestic Prince was first observed as a yearling by Frank McMahon on the Kentucky farm where he was foaled. The wealthy Canadian oil utilities executive was so taken with the chestnut colt that he warned the breeder he would not be outbid for him at the 1967 Keeneland Yearling Sales. He was not, and paid $250,000 for the young horse, a record price at the time. The new owner was a graduate of Gonzaga University in Spokane, Washington, and did much of his business in the Northwest, so it was no surprise that he sent the horse to California for training. The trainer was Johnny Longdon, at age 59, who had been Count Fleet's jockey when he won the Triple Crown. Longdon had retired from riding in 1966 with 6,026 victories.

The Prince did most of his racing in California and won his first six events, including the Santa Anita Derby, before he was sent east to vie for the Triple Crown. He was undefeated in seven races by Kentucky Derby time. Still, there were serious doubts about how he would fare against eastern horses, which were considered to be far superior to the competition from the West.

Although the general public made him their Kentucky Derby favorite, the knowledgeable turf writers, the commentators, and the racing establishment placed him second to Arts and Letters. Despite a field of only eight, the race hinged on which of the two favored horses would come out on top of a blistering stretch drive staged by them. It was Majestic Prince by a neck. An interested onlooker in the stands was President Richard Nixon, the first president to witness the Derby while in office. It was the fifth Derby

Majestic Prince

victory in ten for jockey Bill Hartack, which tied him with Eddie Arcaro. Longdon became the only person to win the classic as both a jockey and trainer, and the value of the colt zoomed to $2.5 million.

The Preakness was a replay of the Derby, as Bill Hartack whipped Majestic Prince and Braulio Baeza did the same to Arts and Letters in a stirring stretch drive that Majestic Prince, again, won by a neck. Baeza's claim of interference was disallowed. After the race, Longdon startled everyone with his announcement that Majestic Prince was tired, 50–100 pounds underweight, deserved a rest, and would pass up the Belmont Stakes rather than risk possible injury. Longdon recalled how Count Fleet had torn a ligament in the Belmont, finished the race on three legs, and had to be retired. The owner agreed with his trainer but suddenly found himself confronted by a storm of public protests. Never before had an owner, with two-thirds of the Triple Crown in hand, failed to complete the racing triad. McMahon finally relented, admitting that the odds were 15 million-to-1 that he would ever again be so close to winning the crown.

A record crowd of 66,115 showed up for the Belmont Stakes. It was a field of six. The pace was slow, and Arts and Letters went into the lead after a mile. Caught in a traffic jam, Hartack moved Majestic Prince to the outside and drove around horses to catch up with the front-runner. Arts and Letters meant business, fought off the challenge, and won by five and a half lengths. It was Majestic Prince's first defeat in 10 starts. Bitter criticism was launched at Hartack for moving too late in the homestretch.

1971—Canonero II

Canonero II was purchased as a yearling for $1,200 and then resold as part of a three-horse package to Pedro Baptista, a pipe manufacturer in Caracas, Venezuela. The colt went cheaply because one foot was not straight and he had a big belly. Baptista, in turn, gave the horse to his son-in-law, Edgar Caibett, as a wedding present. The English translation of the colt's name was "canoneer," and nobody would say if there was a Canonero I. He was shipped to Venezuela, where he did most of his racing.

Canonero II

In 1971, Hoist the Flag was the star three-year-old Thoroughbred and everyone's choice to win the Triple Crown until he broke a leg during a normal workout. That opened up the Kentucky Derby, and 20 horses were entered, including Canonero II. He barely made it in time to Louisville, for he was held in quarantine in Miami for four days. He arrived at Churchill Downs on the Monday before the Saturday of the race. That year's Derby was ridiculed as a race by a lot of "nothing" horses, but it had one of the most surprising endings in its history. Canonero II was in 18th place at the far turn, when his jockey, Gustavo Avila, one of South America's leading riders, let him loose. He galloped past the field to a three-and-a-half-length victory over jockey Jim French aboard the Pacific Coast champion, Unconscious. The usual discounting of the result followed.

Ten horses were entered in the Preakness, including five that ran in the Derby. Avila kept his mount up front all the way. The stretch run became a hot duel with Eastern Fleet, but it ended when the South American rider and colt finally pulled away and reached the wire in front by one and a half lengths.

That win brought about a decided change of attitude toward the colt. Canonero II was finally recognized as the most important three-year-old in North and South America, and his name became as important as that of Simon Bolivar. Not to be overlooked were his 1971 earnings, which soared to $303,212. The colt's name was on everyone's lips, in the press, and on the radio. He literally was the "talk of the town," as people debated his chances to win the Triple Crown. A thousand Venezuelans flew directly to New York from Caracas on special flights, and others desperately sought passage to New York via New Orleans, Miami, and Puerto Rico. The Harry M. Stevens Company, the caterer for Belmont Park, promised to have Spanish-speaking bartenders and waiters in the clubhouse—even Spanish delicacies.

Twelve horses went to the post with Canonero II and fought him all the way to the stretch, where he seemed to wilt and gave way to Pass Catcher, the eventual winner. Canonero II finished fourth, nearly five lengths behind. That ended the exciting adventure of a South American Thoroughbred horse.

1979—Spectacular Bid

Spectacular Bid was purchased by Tom Meyerhoff, a wealthy Baltimore construction executive, for $37,000 after the charcoal gray yearling was shunned at the 1977 Keeneland Sales because of a slightly turned leg. Two years later, he arrived in Louisville for the Kentucky Derby with a record of 12 wins in 14 races, one second-place finish, and one loss.

He had won all five of his three-year-old races, and the racing community regarded him as a sure bet to become the third consecutive winner of the

Triple Crown, in the footsteps of Seattle Slew and Affirmed. His trainer, Grover "Buddy" Delp, loudly boasted, "Only an act of God can stop us from winning the Triple Crown."

Spectacular Bid went off a 3-5 favorite in a field of 10 in the Derby. His chief opponents included Flying Paster, the top horse in the West, and General Assembly, the son of Secretariat who was hailed as the best two-year-old in the country the year prior. The Bid had little trouble with each. He took control in the backstretch and won by nearly two lengths. General Assembly was second, and Flying Paster was fifth for his first time out of the money.

Spectacular Bid

The smallest crowd since 1948, when Citation charged toward the Triple Crown, showed up for the Preakness. The running gag with the bettors was who would come in second, first place having been conceded to Spectacular Bid. He lived up to their prediction by trouncing the other colts in 1:54⅖, faster than the times of Seattle Slew and Affirmed.

Although he had raced 16 times on 12 different tracks since June 1978, had won 14 straight stakes races, and raised his earnings to $1,123,586, eight fearless steeds still challenged him in the Belmont. One of them was a newcomer, Coastal, a chestnut son of Majestic Prince, lightly raced and in only three starts as a three-year-old. His owner and trainer weighed the pros and cons: although it was a long race, their horse was fresh, and Spectacular Bid had been through a very demanding campaign. Furthermore, the potential rewards were tempting. The winner's purse was $161,400, plus a victory would enhance tremendously the colt's stud value. Even second and third would be profitable. Therefore, four hours before post time, they added the $15,000 late fee to the $5,000 supplementary fee they had already posted to allow Coastal to run in the race. It was a gamble they were willing to take.

Spectacular Bid went off at 4-5 in a race that was considered to be little more than a 1½-mile walkover for him. At the outset, his 19-year-old jockey, Ron Franklin, had him running close to the lead at a fast pace. With 1¼ miles to go, he took the lead away from the rail. Ruben Hernandez, Coastal's jockey, saw the opening and guided his colt through it on the inside of Spectacular Bid, and Golden Act came up on the outside. Coastal never let up on his charge to the wire, and finished three and a quarter lengths ahead of second-place Golden Act, who was second by a neck over Spectacular Bid. Trainer Buddy Delp had an answer for the loss: "Last half-mile is what counts."

Pleasant Colony

1981—Pleasant Colony

Pleasant Colony, at the outset, was not the stuff of champions. His sire, His Majesty, and dam, Sun Colony, were moderately successful on the track and in the mating shed. He was foaled on the Virginia farm of his owner, Thomas M. Evans, a New York industrialist and financier. As a yearling, the colt was awkward, leggy, and thin of body. He was also difficult to handle and won only two starts in five during his first year at the track. After he lost the first two races in his third year, he was shipped to New York to trainer John Campo. Campo detected immediately two qualities that he liked. The colt had speed and stamina. The further he ran, the stronger he became.

That encouraged trainer and owner to enter him in the Wood Memorial, the prestigious New York prep race before the Kentucky Derby. The result was an eye-opener. He charged from 13 lengths off the pace to victory with such speed that it looked like the other horses had stopped running. The performance convinced his owner and trainer to enter him in the Derby, where he met up with 20 other horses.

Pleasant Colony went off at 7-2, with Jorge Velasquez up. He again dawdled at the start, 17 lengths off the pace, before he went into gear and raced through the field until the final turn. Then the jockey moved him away from the rail to the outside, whipped him a couple of times, and hand-rode to the finish, easing up to win by three-quarters of a length.

Only 13 horses made up the field at the Preakness, where he was the 3-2 favorite. Bold Ego, second at 7-2, took command at the start and dictated the pace, not slow but not fast. Pleasant Colony remained in the middle of the track, passing horses until the top of the stretch. Velasquez then applied the whip and let him go. Pleasant Colony stormed down the track, caught up to and passed Bold Ego 70 yards from the finish, and was hand-ridden to a one-length victory.

At the Belmont Stakes, Pleasant Colony went off at 4-5 in a field of 11. He appeared reluctant to leave the barn and was sweaty in the paddock area. Reportedly, someone threw a firecracker at his feet. Then, he was spooked by a cameraman perched on the gate and would not move into his stall until the man left. He was last as usual at the start of the race, but caught up with the leaders at the turn into the stretch. Velasquez urged him to begin his run, and he responded but seemed to flatten out. Summing won the race by a neck over Highland Blade, who finished a length and a half in front of Pleasant Colony. John Campo offered no excuses. He simply said: "We got beat."

1987—Alysheba

Alysheba was purchased as a yearling in 1985 by Clarence and Dorothy Scharbauer of Midland, Texas, for $500,000. The price was somewhat of a bargain because he was the son of Alydar, who had dueled furiously with Affirmed in the 1978 Triple Crown races. Some of Alydar's offspring that year had sold at public auctions for an average of $600,304. Also, Alysheba's pedigree traced back to Native Dancer and War Admiral.

Alysheba

Alysheba approached the Kentucky Derby with only one win in 10 starts. His trainer, Jack Van Berg, had previously detected an obstruction in the colt's throat that interfered with his breathing and recommended surgery. The Derby was his first race after that. Despite being caught up in close quarters among the 16 other horses at the start and nearly knocked over at the approach to the stretch, he managed to eke out a three-quarters-of-a-length victory. The time was the slowest for the race in 13 years. It was the first Derby win for jockey Chris McCarron.

Alysheba was made the 7-5 favorite for the Preakness in a field of nine. The race was a virtual duplicate of the Derby. Alysheba challenged Bet Twice at the top of the stretch, inched ahead, and won by half a length. Once again the time was slow, the slowest since 1975, but it was the first one-two finish in the Derby and Preakness since Affirmed and Alydar hooked up.

Alysheba was made the 8-5 favorite in the Belmont Stakes, but raced poorly. Bet Twice took the lead before a mile had been run, increased it to five lengths at the top of the stretch, and finished ahead by fourteen. Alysheba came in a sorry fourth. Bet Twice, a great grandson of Northern Dancer, had won the first five races of his career, then went one for seven until the Belmont. Van Berg blamed McCarron for holding back too long.

1989—Sunday Silence

Sunday Silence was spurned twice in auctions, first as a yearling and then as a two-year-old, by buyers who refused to pay the minimum bid set by his owner and breeder, Arthur B. Hancock, III. Hancock then sold a half interest in the colt to his trainer, the venerable, 78-year-old Charles Whittingham, and placed him in his care in California. The trainer, noted for giving a horse time to develop, delayed racing him until October. Later, as a three-year-old, the colt ran off four wins in as many starts before the Kentucky Derby. One of the wins was in the Santa Anita Derby, which he

243

Sunday Silence

won by 11 lengths. That convinced his handlers to enter him in the Kentucky Derby.

The Derby favorite was the 4-5 Easy Goer, a son of Alydar, who was the two-year-old champion, had won all three of his 1989 races, had matched the world record in the Gotham Mile, and had earned $1,240,900. Sunday Silence went off at 3-1. Fifteen horses started; there was bumping, and Sunday Silence ducked sharply when his jockey, Pat Valenzuela, whipped him in the stretch. Easy Goer also had trouble with the muddy track and the slow pace, the slowest in 31 years. Those problems notwithstanding, Sunday Silence scored a major upset, winning by two and a half lengths over Easy Goer.

The two colts wrestled with each other once more in the Preakness. Easy Goer was the 3-5 favorite, and Sunday Silence went off at 2-1. They raced neck and neck until the final few yards, when the Hancock colt, in a dramatic last effort, won by a nose. Sunday Silence then came out at the Belmont Stakes the 9-10 favorite in a field of 10. He raced close to the pace but was shadowed by Easy Goer, who had jockey Pat Day in the irons. As Sunday Silence started to inch up to take over the lead at the top of the homestretch, Easy Goer flashed by with a powerful burst of speed and raced off to an eight-length victory.

244

1997—Silver Charm

Silver Charm was foaled in Florida and purchased by trainer Bob Baffert for $85,000 on behalf of Bob Lewis, the owner of the biggest beer distributorship in California. Baffert, whose specialty was converting bargain-priced horses with moderate pedigrees into high-class runners, prepped Silver Charm for the Kentucky Derby.

Silver Charm

He went off at 4-1, second to 3-1 Captain Bodgit. Also in the field of 13 was Free House, who had already beaten Silver Charm twice. It boiled down to a race between the Captain and the Charm, and the Baffert colt won in a photo finish by a nose. Free House trailed closely behind. It was the smallest Derby field since 1985, and the result marked the 18th year in a row that the favorite had lost.

The Preakness had 12 in the field, four of whom had not been in the Derby, including Touch Gold. Once again there was a close finish. The photo finish showed Silver Charm ahead of Free House by a head and Captain Bodgit by one and a quarter lengths. Touch Gold stumbled at the start, almost unseated his jockey, kicked and cut his left front foot, but still managed to come in fourth.

Captain Bodgit was not entered in the Belmont. Silver Charm was favored at 6-5, with Touch Gold second at 2-1 because of his gallant effort in the Preakness. A speed horse, he was fitted with a fiberglass patch over his injured foot. Silver Charm seemed to have the long Belmont Stakes and the Triple Crown won, then he was caught and passed by Free House in the stretch. However, the pace had been slow and Touch Gold, with jockey Chris McCarron up, also went into high gear. Touch Gold stormed down the middle of the track, blew by Free House, and mowed down Silver Charm to win by three-quarters of a length in the final strides.

1998—Real Quiet

Real Quiet was called a bargain-basement colt. He was bought for only $17,000 by Mike Pegram, owner of 22 McDonald's restaurants in Washington State and a stable of 70 horses. His trainer, Bob Baffert, recommended the buy despite the colt's crooked legs, narrow frame, and moderate lineage. Baffert said he liked the way the colt moved, like an athlete. Still, it took seven races before he broke his maiden. He was two for twelve by Kentucky Derby time, but he showed closing speed, so the trainer figured he might come in second. Baffert was more interested in Indian Charlie, a colt he was handling for another patron.

Fifteen horses started at Churchill Downs, with Indian Charlie the favorite and Real Quiet at 8-1. Indian Charlie was set to make his move to the finish line at the turn into the stretch, but Real Quiet had other ideas. He had stayed close then made a sudden move into the lead to finish by half a length in front of Victory Gallop, who had also mounted a relentless drive. Indian Charlie was third. The win was worth $700,000 for "the Fish," as Real Quiet was nicknamed because he was so skinny. It was the first win for him in four races as a three-year-old.

The Preakness found him up against 10 horses and in another furious stretch duel with Victory Gallop. Real Quiet won by two and a quarter lengths. Baffert was beside himself with excitement. The Triple Crown was his for the taking a second year in a row. He was also the only trainer to win the Derby and Preakness in two consecutive years.

Real Quiet

Eleven horses came out for the Belmont Stakes, with Real Quiet favored at 4-5 and Victory Gallop at 9-2. The finish was another excruciating battle by the same two horses, a graphic reminder of the struggles between Affirmed and Alydar 20 years prior. With a furlong to go, Real Quiet was tiring and Victory Gallop was mounting a devastating charge. The two horses hit the finish line as one, and it took an agonizing while before the racing stewards could determine the winner, even with the photo of the finish line. Their final decision was in favor of Victory Gallop. It was another year without a Triple Crown winner.

1999—Charismatic

Charismatic was a $200,000 disappointment. That was how much Beverly and Bob Lewis of Los Angeles paid for him. He had raced 13 times as a two-year-old and until March 1999, when he was on a seven-race losing streak. He had been offered twice as a $62,500 claimer without any takers. His trainer, D. Wayne Lukas, often referred to him as excess baggage in his barn. In spite of the negatives, he improved slowly and finally came up with an impressive win in the Lexington Stakes at Keeneland. The win was sufficient to convince everyone involved with him that he should be entered in the Kentucky Derby. Besides, the classic would be run by 19 nondescript colts and two fillies, and it was wide open for any of them to win.

Charismatic went off at 30-1 in the Derby and ran on the outside to stay clear of the cavalry charge. He made a late spurt in the homestretch for a dramatic win by a neck over Menifee. The victory was worth $1.1 million, but few were ready to place the colt on a special pedestal. In fact, two weeks later at the Preakness his odds dropped to 8-1.

The Preakness was a close replica of the Derby. The difference was that Menifee chased Charismatic but again lost by one and a half lengths. Charismatic's earnings grew to $1.9 million.

Charismatic was honored as the 2-1 favorite at the Belmont Stakes. With a ¼ mile to go in the race, Charismatic took the lead from Silverbulletday, the only filly running, and battled two long shots, 29-1 Lemon Drop Kid and 54-1 Vision and Verse. Jockey Chris Antley whipped him but got no response. He then felt the colt suddenly dip underneath him and realized Charismatic was in pain. Still, the game colt managed to finish third behind Vision and Verse. Antley jumped off as soon as Charismatic

Charismatic

stopped running and held the colt's left hoof in his hands to keep the weight off it until help arrived. An ambulance was rushed out on the track to take the colt back to the barn, where X-rays showed that he had fractured two bones in his left front leg. He underwent surgery on the following day. The prognosis was that he would recover and be sound for stud duty.

2002—War Emblem

War Emblem played an unwitting role in a bizarre drama against the backdrop of the Triple Crown Races. Kentucky-bred, his owner was a Chicago businessman, Russell Reineman, who paid only $20,000 for him because he had bone chips in his front ankles. Despite them, he could run with speed. On April 6, 2002, he demolished the field of the Illinois Derby by six and a quarter lengths. Saudi Arabian prince Ahmed bin Salman, a media mogul who also bred, bought, and raced Thoroughbred horses, saw the race on television. He was so impressed with the colt's performance that he called his agents in America and told them to explore the possibility of purchasing the colt. A sale was negotiated for a price of $900.000. This was three weeks before the Kentucky Derby.

Bob Baffert, who trained some of the prince's horses and helped with the purchase, was asked to enter the colt in the classic race and prepare him for it. Baffert managed to enter him and then began an urgent training program. War Emblem's odds were at 20-1. By the ½-mile pole, it was obvious that no horse would catch him. He led the Derby wire to wire. Many wrote off the win with the usual criticism that it was a fluke because he was allowed to set the pace unchallenged.

At the Preakness, he was the 5-2 favorite and ran a different race. He stayed off the pace until the middle of the far turn, when he displayed his speed capability once more. He made up four lengths and charged to a three-fourths-length lead across the finish line.

The Belmont was another story. His odds were 6-5 in a field of 11, and everything looked positive. But, he stumbled coming out of the gate, almost went to his knees, was bunched in behind the lead horses, and began to tire from his effort to catch up to them. The race was over for him. He came in eighth. Sarava won at 70-1 for a payoff of $142.50 for a $2 bet.

War Emblem

2003—Funny Cide

Funny Cide

Funny Cide was the hero of a rags to riches fairy tale that touched the emotions of the entire country. Six buddies in the tiny village of Sackets Harbor, New York, decided to do something about the approach of their midlife crises. They were five small businessmen and a teacher.

Because they enjoyed going to the racetrack, they formed a partnership in 1995 and bought a horse to race in Saratoga for the fun of it. Their equine advisor was Barclay Tagg, aged 65, a respected New York trainer. The group had a modicum of success and built up its investment to $130,000. The group next bought a New York–bred chestnut gelding for $75,000. He was Funny Cide. He progressed slowly in his training until his third year, when he displayed good speed in the Louisiana Derby and New York's Wood Memorial. That convinced "the hicks from the sticks," as they liked to call themselves, to go on a real fling and enter the colt in the Kentucky Derby.

The owners of the field of horses included a sheik from Dubai, a prince from Saudi Arabia, wealthy horsemen from Ireland, and Hollywood partners that included Steven Spielberg, the motion picture director and producer. The favorite of the field was Empire Maker, who had beaten Funny Cide in the Wood. Funny Cide's odds were 12-1, and he proceeded to shake up everyone by racing through the pack to a length-and-three-quarters win over Empire Maker. The victory was dismissed in Kentucky racing circles because the colt was New York–bred and Tagg had not raced horses in Louisville. That did not dampen the delirious joy of "the hicks" and their families, all of whom traveled to Churchill Downs in a school bus festooned with the colors of the local high school.

At Pimlico, two weeks later, the colt was tabbed the favorite at 9-5 odds in a field of 10. Peace Rules, who was second in the Derby, was set at 2-1. Empire Maker was not entered. The outcome of the race was never in doubt. Funny Cide blew away the opposition by nine and three-quarter lengths, the second-largest winning margin in the history of the race. It was also the first time that a New York–bred gelding had reached the doorsteps of the Triple Crown. New York went wild over their hero, as did all of America. Newspapers published editorials, and schoolchildren sent fan letters to the horse.

The track was muddy for the Belmont Stakes, and Funny Cide was made the even-money favorite. Empire Maker came back to try him again and was the second choice at 2-1. It was a clean start by the six-horse field, and the New York colt bounded into the lead. However, he appeared to be fighting the jockey, who desperately tried to slow him down. It was obvious that he was rank. The end for him came at the top of the stretch. Empire Maker, who had been tailing him, drew alongside then swooped ahead to finish in front by three-quarters of a length over Ten Most Wanted. Funny Cide came in third. The crowd throughout Belmont Park grew silent. In a last salute to their hero, they booed the winner.

2004—Smarty Jones

Smarty Jones became an American equine icon despite a less-than-glamorous pedigree and a quirky name that endeared him to the public. He was foaled at Roy and Patricia Chapman's 100-acre Someday Farm in Chester County, Pennsylvania. The successful automobile dealer and his wife bred second-tier Thoroughbreds, which they turned over to John Servis to train and race at nearby Philadelphia Park and on the surrounding racing circuit.

Servis had had good results with such horses. While being schooled at a starting gate, however, the colt suddenly reared up, banged his head against a bar, and fractured his skull. He almost lost an eye, too. Surgery and good medical care saved him, and he was able to resume his training. He won his first race handily by seven and three-quarter lengths and followed it with a win in the Pennsylvania Nursery Stakes by 15 lengths. Servis was so impressed that he talked the owners into allowing him to prepare the horse for the Kentucky Derby.

The colt was sent to Arkansas Oaklawn Park to do his racing. Shortly after his arrival, the track's management offered a bonus of $5 million to any three-year-old that won the Rebel Stakes, Arkansas Derby, and Kentucky Derby. Smarty Jones won the two Arkansas races, and the prospect of his earning the large bonus made him the pride of Pennsylvania.

His Derby jockey was Stewart Elliot, who had never raced in a classic but had won more than three thousand races with cheap claimers. Because the colt was undefeated, he was made the 4-1 favorite in the Derby. Second was 5-1 Lion Heart, a Kentucky-bred horse that had been purchased as a two-year-old for $1.4 million. The track was sloppy, and Smarty Jones was hemmed in between horses up to the first turn. He managed to catch up to the pacemaker, Lion Heart, after which

Smarty Jones

249

the two got into a match race down the stretch. He finally spurted ahead and won by two and three-quarters lengths.

At Pimlico, 1,706 media people covered the Preakness, and a record 113,668 people crammed into the racetrack to make Smarty Jones their favorite at 7-10. Once again, Lion Heart held the lead down the backstretch then was passed by Smarty Jones, who won by an incredible 11½ lengths. It was the largest Preakness victory margin. Racing fans throughout Pimlico wept openly for joy over the accomplishment of their newfound hero. In fact, all of America was suddenly caught up in the Smarty Jones fever, as he approached the final leg of the Triple Crown. People lined the roadways, and Pennsylvania Turnpike workers applauded when his caravan traveled to Belmont Park. One billboard proclaimed: "Look Out New York, Smarty's Coming."

He was favored at 3-10 in a field of nine at Belmont and took the lead right away. He had to fight off draining challenges by Rock Hard Ten, Eddington, and Prado until the top of the stretch, by which time he had opened a lead of three and a half lengths. But he showed signs that he was tiring. Suddenly, 36-1 Birdstone began to creep up on him in the middle of the track with a ¼ mile to go. Smarty Jones held on, but there was no stopping the challenger, who swept by and raced to victory by a length. The crowd became absolutely silent when it was obvious that Smarty Jones would be beaten. Later, Marylou Whitney, the winner's owner, summed up everyone's sentiment. She sobbed, "I feel so awful, Smarty Jones. We were hoping we'd be second. I love Smarty."

Epilogue

The most glorious crown is set with false diamonds.

—Corneille: *Héraclius*, I (1647)

They Were Only Human

Adulation of heroes has been the fancy of sports fans from time immemorial. Physical attributes, prowess, and noble achievements have provided fodder for endless debate, argument, and comparison. With it all, however, none of these heroic figures ever could be deemed to be the ultimate paragon. Each in his own way and time exhibited some flaw that marred an otherwise perfect image. So it could be said of the 11 super horses who make up the elite Triple Crown club. While these equine giants represented the finest of their breed and fully deserved the accolades they accumulated, the truth is that some failings manifested themselves in each which, to stretch the application of the phrase, may be excused by the simple fact that, after all, "they were only human."

There is an old axiom that says in effect that anyone who reaches the top of the heap is fair game to those who would like to climb to the pinnacle. If reaching the summit is impossible, then the next best thing is to embarrass the champ, or best him in one fashion or another. Of the handsome 11, for example, four were directly challenged to match races, and all four lost in head-to-head duels—Sir Barton to Man o' War, War Admiral to Seabiscuit, Whirlaway to Alsab, Assault to Armed.

When Hollywood was grinding out horse-racing sagas in years gone by, the film moguls' image of the Thoroughbred was one of rugged mien, unexcelled beauty, and tremendous will and stamina. Very often, he was raised under the most difficult of conditions, by poor owners and amateur trainers. Despite these shortcomings, he was strong as iron, met all competitors head-on and unflinchingly, never missed a race, and prevailed over all adversities.

With the exception of two, the Triple Crown winners would have flunked any screen test for one of these roles. They had their problems. Sir Barton's feet constantly hurt, causing him to be irascible. Omaha went lame within a few months after he captured the crown and never again raced in the United States. War Admiral sheared off a piece of his forefoot in the Belmont Stakes and was out of action from June to October. Whirlaway hurt his leg at the end of his third year of racing, which rushed his retirement the following spring. The great Count Fleet struck himself in the left fore ankle, which created a splint and abruptly ended his racing career. Assault injured a foot as a yearling and walked as though he were about to fall down. He also suffered a kidney ailment in his third year and a leg splint in his fourth year. Citation had tendon trouble, which kept him from racing during his entire fourth year.

However, in the business of breeding Thoroughbred horses, a fine stallion obviously is a desirable commodity. Should he be a top stallion, then he is an extremely valuable asset to the breeding farm. The measure of a stallion's potential at the outset is twofold: his lineage and his racing record. Thoroughbreds, for the most part, have respectable family trees. It is when one reaches stardom as a champion that he becomes sorely in demand as a stallion when he is retired. Because matings can involve between 30 and 40 mares per year per stallion and his ability in stud may continue for more than 20 years, a little simple arithmetic will produce a rather staggering figure on his earning potential long after his racing days are over. For example, in 2001 at the age of 27, Seattle Slew's stud fee was $300,000 per mating.

They Had Charisma

The Sultan of Swat, Broadway Joe, the Brown Bomber, the Golden Jet, Wilt the Stilt. Ask any sports fan to identify these individuals, and the chances are he will answer unhesitatingly, from left to right: baseball's Babe Ruth, football's Joe Namath, boxing's Joe Louis, hockey's Bobby Hull, and basketball's Wilt Chamberlain. It is commonplace for imaginative sportswriters, with a flair for turning a phrase, to create special monikers for heroic athletes by which, in time, they are almost more identifiable than by their legal names. Usually, the appellations reflect the hero's special prowess, physical mien, or personality.

The Triple Crown champions were equally honored. While their names may not be as easily identifiable as the ones above, as far as the general public is concerned, they have special significance for racing buffs:

Gallant Fox—the Fox of Belair
Omaha—the Belair Bullet
War Admiral—the Mighty Atom
Whirlaway—Mr. Longtail
Count Fleet—the Fleet
Assault—the Clubfooted Comet
Citation—Big Cy
Secretariat—Super Red
Seattle Slew—the Slew
Affirmed—the Streetfighter or the Barroom Bully

Sir Barton never made the list with a special name. He was not a particularly endearing colt, being rather irascible and aloof, refusing to allow people or pets to cotton up to him. This may very well have been due to his constantly aching feet. However, it would appear to be an unkind cut of fate that the Thoroughbred who began this whole business of America's Triple Crown should not be dignified with some sort of special identification. He is assuredly deserving of it. So, to America's first Triple Crown champion, we herewith dub him:

Sir Barton—the Tender-Toed Typhoon

Dearth of Triple Crown Champions

Actually, until 1948 and the heroics of Citation, the American Triple Crown winners were coming along at a fairly steady clip. However, there followed a 25-year wait for the arrival of Secretariat in 1973. Things picked up then, as Seattle Slew, in 1977, and Affirmed, in 1978, stirred up racing fans in quick order by capturing the celebrated equine crown. Unfortunately, another dry spell set in from 1978 to 2004 when an American Thoroughbred failed to capture the Triple Crown. By the same token, England did not fare better. No British Triple Crown Champion has shown up since Nijinsky II in 1970, a 34-year void through 2004. He was their 15th winner dating back to 1853. By comparison, American has not done too poorly. Affirmed was its 11th since Sir Barton in 1919.

The following are the respective winners of the British and American Triple Crowns:

England

1853—West Australian

1865—Gladiateur

1866—Lord Lyon

1886—Ormonde

1891—Common

1893— Isinglass

1897—Galtee More

1899—Flying Fox

1900—Diamond Jubilee

1903—Rock Sand

1915—Pommern

1917—Gay Crusader

1918—Gainsborough

1935—Bahram

1970—Nijinsky II

America

1919—Sir Barton

1930—Gallant Fox

1935—Omaha

1937—War Admiral

1941—Whirlaway

1943—Count Fleet

1946—Assault

1948—Citation

1973—Secretariat

1977—Seattle Slew

1978—Affirmed

The answer to the question of why so few is simple. There is just too much competition these days. A Triple Crown champion today has to be that much better than were his predecessors if he is to prevail over the field in the three "jewel" races. This state of affairs is due largely to the fantastic growth of Thoroughbred racing in America since early in the 20th century.

For example, in 1920 there were a total of 4,032 horses of all ages who were starters in races throughout the country. By 1970, this figure had risen to 49,087. In 1920, too, there were 1,022 racing days in the year, and in 1970 the number had reached the 6,242 mark. Concomitant with this tremendous expansion was the constantly growing demand for more and more Thoroughbreds to fill out the racing programs. Needless to say, the breeding farms answered the call. In 1916, the year Sir Barton was born, 2,128 foals were dropped. In 1970, approximately twenty-five thousand foals entered the world.

The number kept growing so that by the year 2001 it had reached thirty-two thousand. Every horse from this crop was potentially a racer that could qualify for the Triple Crown. Therefore, with the greater mix of steeds, the keener competition, and the grueling schedule of races, capturing the holy grail of American Thoroughbred racing has become much more difficult and infrequent.

The following chart indicates the number of foals that were dropped in the years when America's Triple Crown champions were born:

Triple Crown Year	Colts in Crop	Total Crop
1919 Sir Barton	1,036	2,128 in 1916
1930 Gallant Fox	2,046	4,182 in 1927
1935 Omaha	2,567	5,256 in 1932
1937 War Admiral	2,424	4,924 in 1934
1941 Whirlaway	2,761	5,696 in 1938
1943 Count Fleet	2,991	6,003 in 1940
1946 Assault	2,940	5,923 in 1943
1948 Citation	2,860	5,819 in 1945
1973 Secretariat	10,683	25,056 in 1970
1974 Seattle Slew	13,586	27,586 in 1971
1975 Affirmed	14,008	28,271 in 1972

Records and Earnings of Triple Crown Champions

Nobody can gainsay that the Triple Crown champions of America earned their keep. For the most part, they had reasonable total earnings by the time they reached the end of their racing days, although some were at more heady plateaus than others. The reasons for this disparity are twofold and make it well-nigh impossible to attempt to rate one horse against another on the basis of how much money they garnered. First, not all of the horses campaigned the same number of years. Second, the value of stakes purses leaped enormously through the years from 1918 to 2004.

None of the owners fared poorly. In some respects, the earlier earnings could be compared favorably with the larger, later takes simply because the dollar was worth a great deal more then. Of all the owners involved, three split honors for the greatest success. Samuel Doyle Riddle had the unique pleasure of experiencing victory and defeat on two sides of the fence. In 1920, his Man o' War toppled the Triple Crown champion Sir Barton in their match race. Then, in 1937, he enjoyed the thrill of owning a Triple Crown winner, War Admiral. The following year, he found himself on the short end, when his horse was defeated by Seabiscuit in their match race. William Woodward became the first double winner, with Gallant Fox and Omaha. Warren Wright Sr. matched this record with Whirlaway and Citation.

The following are the campaign records of each of the Triple Crown champions:

	Year	Age	Starts	1st	2nd	3rd	Unplaced	Earnings
Sir Barton	1918	2	6	0	1	0	5	$4,113
	1919	3	13	8	3	2	0	$88,250
	1920	4	12	5	2	3	2	$24,494
			31	13	6	5	7	$116,857
Gallant Fox	1929	2	7	2	2	2	1	$19,890
	1930	3	10	9	1	0	0	$308,275
			17	11	3	2	1	$328,165
Omaha	1934	2	9	1	4	0	4	$3,850
	1935	3	9	6	1	2	0	$142,255
	1936	4	4	2	2	0	0	$8,650
			22	9	7	2	4	$154,755

War Admiral	1936	2	6	3	2	1	0	$14,800
	1937	3	8	8	0	0	0	$166,500
	1938	4	11	9	1	0	1	$90,840
	1939	5	1	1	0	0	0	$1,100
			26	21	3	1	1	$273,240
Whirlaway	1940	2	16	7	2	4	3	$77,275
	1941	3	20	13	5	2	0	$272,386
	1942	4	22	12	8	2	0	$211,250
	1943	5	2	0	0	1	1	$250
			60	32	15	9	4	$561,161
Count Fleet	1942	2	15	10	4	1	0	$76,245
	1943	3	6	6	0	0	0	$174,055
			21	16	4	1	0	$250,300
Assault	1945	2	9	2	2	1	4	$17,250
	1946	3	15	8	2	3	2	$424,195
	1947	4	7	5	1	1	0	$181,925
	1948	5	2	1	0	0	1	$3,250
	1949	6	6	1	1	1	3	$45,900
	1950	7	3	1	0	1	1	$2,950
			42	18	6	7	11	$675,470
Citation	1947	2	9	8	1	0	0	$155,680
	1948	3	20	19	1	0	0	$709,470
	1949	4	0	0	0	0	0	$000,000
	1950	5	9	2	7	0	0	$73,480
	1951	6	7	3	1	2	1	$147,130
			45	32	10	2	1	$1,085,760
Secretariat	1972	2	9	7	1*	0	1	$456,404
	1973	3	12	9	2	1	0	$860,404
			21	16	3	1	1	$1,316,808

*Champagne Stakes—penalized from first to second for interference.

Seattle Slew	1976	2	3	3	0	0	0	$94,350
	1977	3	7	6	0	0	0	$641,370
	1978	4	7	5	2	0	0	$473,006
			17	14	2	0	0	$1,208,726
Affirmed	1977	2	9	7	2	0	0	$343,477
	1978	3	11	8	2	0	1	$901,541
	1979	4	9	7	1	1	0	$1,148,800
			29	22	5	1	1	$2,393,818

Purses of Triple Crown Races

In 2004 it cost an owner $70,000 in entry fees to run a horse in the Triple Crown races. However, the potential returns were equally high. The winning purses were $854,800 for the Kentucky Derby, $650,000 for the Preakness, and $600,000 for the Belmont. Had there been a Triple Crown winner, he would have received a bonus of $5 million from the television sponsor of the races. In contrast, the entry fees in 1918 were approximately $800, with a return of $57,275. The following chart details are the purses won by each of the 11 Triple Crown champions, from Sir Barton to Affirmed:

	Kentucky Derby	Preakness	Belmont Stakes	Total
Sir Barton	$20,825	$24,500	$11,950	$57,275
Gallant Fox	$50,725	$51,925	$66,040	$168,690
Omaha	$39,525	$25,325	$35,480	$100,330
War Admiral	$52,050	$45,600	$38,020	$135,670
Whirlaway	$61,275	$49,365	$39,770	$150,410
Count Fleet	$60,725	$43,190	$35,340	$139,255
Assault	$96,400	$96,620	$75,400	$268,420
Citation	$83,400	$91,870	$77,700	$252,970
Secretariat	$155,050	$129,900	$90,120	$375,070
Seattle Slew	$214,700	$138,600	$109,080	$462,380
Affirmed	$186,900	$136,200	$110,580	$433,680

Times of Triple Crown Victories

	Kentucky Derby	Preakness	Belmont Stakes
Sir Barton	2:09⅘	1:53*	2:17⅖**
Gallant Fox	2:07⅗	2:00⅗	2:31⅗
Omaha	2:05	1:58⅖	2:30⅗
War Admiral	2:03⅕	1:58⅖	2:28⅗
Whirlaway	2:01⅖	1:58⅘	2:31
Count Fleet	2:04	1:57⅖	2:28⅕
Assault	2:06⅗	2:01⅖	2:30⅘
Citation	2:05⅖	2:02⅖	2:28⅕
Secretariat	1:59⅖	1:54⅖	2:24
Seattle Slew	2:02⅕	1:54⅖	2:29⅗
Affirmed	2:01⅕	1:54⅖	2:26⅘

*The Preakness was raced at 1⅛ miles from 1911 to 1925.

**The Belmont Stakes was raced at 1⅜ miles from 1906 to 1925.

Other Misses

Twenty-eight horses won two out of the three Triple Crown "jewels," but they lost either the Kentucky Derby of the Preakness or failed to start in all three races, and so, were never really in the running for the crown. They were:

1877—Cloverbrook	did not start in Kentucky Derby
1878—Duke of Magenta	did not start in Kentucky Derby
1880—Grenada	did not start in Kentucky Derby
1881—Saunterer	did not start in Kentucky Derby
1895—Belmar	did not start in Kentucky Derby
1920—Man o' War	did not start in Kentucky Derby
1922—Pillory	did not start in Kentucky Derby
1923—Zev	twelfth to Virgil, Preakness
1931—Twenty Grand	second to Mate, Preakness
1939—Johnstown	fifth to Challedon, Preakness
1940—Bimelech	second to Gallahadion, Kentucky Derby
1942—Shut Out	fifth to Alsab, Kentucky Derby
1949—Capot	second to Ponder, Kentucky Derby
1950—Middleground	second to Hill Prince, Preakness

1953—Native Dancer	second to Dark Star, Kentucky Derby
1955—Nashua	second to Swaps, Kentucky Derby
1956—Needles	second to Fabius, Preakness
1963—Chateaugay	second to Candy Spots, Preakness
1967—Damascus	third to Proud Clarion, Kentucky Derby
1972—Riva Ridge	fourth to Bee Bee Bee, Preakness
1974—Little Current	second to Cannonade, Kentucky Derby
1976—Bold Forbes	third to Elocutionist, Preakness
1988—Risen Star	third to Winning Colors, Kentucky Derby
1991—Hansel	tenth to Strike the Gold, Kentucky Derby
1994—Tabasco Cat	sixth to Go for Gin, Kentucky Derby
1995—Thunder Gulch	third to Timber Country, Preakness
2001—Point Given	fifth to Monarchos, Kentucky Derby

Glossary

Throughout this narration, various terms and phrases, commonly used in Thoroughbred racing circles, have been employed to describe situations, conditions, or events. Some of the terms may be rather remote in meaning for the unindoctrinated. It is for their benefit, through the courtesy of the Thoroughbred Racing Associations, that the following definitions and explanations are offered:

The Thoroughbred

HORSE: Among Thoroughbreds, a male animal five years old or more.

COLT: A male Thoroughbred through his fourth year.

FILLY: A female Thoroughbred until the age of five.

MARE: A female Thoroughbred five years old or more.

BROODMARE: A mare who becomes a mother.

FOAL: A Thoroughbred prior to his first birthday. For the sake of uniformity and to avoid confusion, the birthdays of all foals are established as of January 1 of each year.

WEANLING: The foal, when he is separated from his mother in the fall of his first year.

YEARLING: The Thoroughbred after he celebrates his first New Year's Day.

TWO-YEAR-OLD: The Thoroughbred on January 1 of his second year, when he becomes eligible to race.

JUVENILE: A two-year-old horse.

SOPHOMORE: A three-year-old horse.

STALLION: A male horse not castrated.

GELDING: A castrated male horse.

STUD: A stallion used for breeding. Also a breeding farm.

SIRE: A Thoroughbred's father.

DAM: A Thoroughbred's mother.

PRODUCE: A dam's collective offspring.

GET: The collective offspring of a sire, or stallion.

PRODUCER: The term applied to a mare when one of her sons or daughters has won a race. On the other hand, a stallion is not officially a sire until one of his get has won.

FAMILY: The female side of a Thoroughbred pedigree.

LINE: Horses traceable to a common paternal ancestor are said to form a particular line.

Color

BAY: This color varies from a light, yellowish tan (light bay) to a dark, rich shade, almost brown, and between these a bright mahogany. Although occasionally a horse is listed as "dark bay or brown," the bay can usually be distinguished by black points—a black mane and tail and shadings of black low on the legs.

BROWN: Sometimes difficult to separate from black or dark bay, this color usually can be distinguished by noting fine tan or brown hairs on the muzzles or flanks.

CHESTNUT: This varies from light, washy yellow to a dark liver color, between which will come brilliant red, gold, and copper shades. A chestnut never has black points, mane, or tail.

BLACK: Doubt between a dark brown or black can usually be resolved by noting fine black hair on the muzzle.

GRAY: A mixture of white hairs and black. A gray foal will sometimes appear to be black at birth but will lighten with age. To produce a gray, one or both of the parents must be gray. However, a gray parent does not necessarily mean the offspring will be gray.

ROAN: This is a mixture of white hairs and chestnut or white bay. It is considered a variation of gray. Depending on their color, such horses are sometimes referred to as "strawberry roan" or "blue roan"; for registration purposes they are listed as roan.

DUN: A rare color among Thoroughbreds, varying from mouse color to a golden dun, and generally accompanied by black points and a black stripe down the spine.

WHITE: Perhaps the rarest color among Thoroughbreds. The first white to be registered by the Jockey Club was in 1963, a filly by Kentucky Colonel—Filly O'Mine, appropriately named White Beauty.

Although black shows up with the hero's horse in fables, the color is rare among Thoroughbreds. There is also no indication that color has any bearing on a Thoroughbred's racing ability. Bay is predominant among Thoroughbreds, followed by chestnut and brown, the last frequently appearing to be black. About 90 percent of registered Thoroughbreds are bay, brown, or chestnut, with the remainder as gray, roan, or black.

Races

STAKES RACE: Originally a "sweepstakes," in which the owners put up "stakes," such as a nominating fee, entry fee, and starting fee—all of which went to the winner. Today, the racetrack adds money to these stakes. This is called added money and can range from a few thousand dollars to more than $100,000. In most stakes races today, the original fees paid by the various owners still go to the winner along with the major share of the added money. The second, third, and fourth horses (and in some cases horses finishing farther back) earn a portion of the added money.

HANDICAP RACE: A race in which the racing secretary assigns the weight to be carried by each horse according to his evaluation of the horse's potential. In theory, these weight assignments put all the contestants on an equal basis. Some of the major stakes races are run under handicap conditions.

ALLOWANCE RACE: While some stakes races are run under allowance conditions, the allowance race usually refers to an event in which the weight carried is determined by the amount of money and/or the number of races won by a horse during a specified time.

CLAIMING RACE: Any horse entered in a claiming race is subject to purchase for the amount for which the horse is entered by any owner who has started a horse at that particular race meeting. In some such races, the claiming price will have a range of $1,000 or $2,000, with weight allowances made for horses entered at the lower price. The claiming race is a method of classifying horses in order to produce races involving competition of equal ability. When a horse wins easily while running among $3,000 claimers, he is usually moved up in value to avoid his being claimed. Many good stakes horses have evolved from the claiming ranks, the most notable perhaps being Stymie, a $1,500 claim who went on to win $918,425.

MAIDEN RACE: A race for horses that have never won. When they do win their first, they are said to have "broken their maiden."

FUTURITY: A stakes event for two-year-olds for which they are entered as foals.

PRODUCE RACE: One to be contested by the produce of horses named at the time nominations for the race are closed. (With the exception of the early closing of stakes events, and a few special races in which specific horses are invited to compete, entries for races are usually made the morning of the day prior to the race.)

OVERNIGHT RACE: A race in which entries close 72 hours (exclusive of Sundays) or less before the post time for the first race on the day the race is to be run.

OAKS: A stakes event for three-year-old fillies named for the ancestral estate of England's Lord Derby.

At the Track

ALSO-RAN: A horse that does not finish among the first three.

BACKSTRETCH: The straightaway on the far side of the racetrack.

BANDAGES: Bandages or cloth wrappings on a horse's legs, not necessarily denoting lameness or infirmity. Many trainers keep their horses in standing bandages at all times as protection. They are also used in racing for protection and support.

BARRIER: The starting gate is sometimes referred to as the barrier. Before the invention of the starting gate, the horses stood behind several ropes stretched across the track, which, when raised with the ringing of a bell and the dropping of a flag, started the race.

BLINKERS: Once called the "rogue's badge," blinkers are a common piece of racing equipment today. The eye cups on the blinkers, depending on modifications, block side and rear vision in either or both eyes. The use or disuse of blinkers must be approved by the stewards and the change reported on the official program.

CLUBHOUSE TURN: The turn to the right of the grandstand, so called because the clubhouse is usually to the right of the general stands.

COLORS: The jockey's silk or nylon jacket and cap provided by the owner. Distinctive colors are registered by the owner with the Jockey Club and with the state racing authority. The practice of using individually registered colors was introduced at Newmarket, England, in 1762.

DEAD HEAT: Where the photo-finish camera shows two horses inseparable at the finish, the race is declared a "dead heat" or tie.

EIGHTH POLE: The pole ⅛ of a mile before the finish line.

ENTRY: Two or more horses in a race owned by the same stable or trained by the same trainer are termed an "entry" and coupled as a single betting unit, a bet on one being a bet on both.

FAR TURN: The turn off the backstretch.

FAST: A racetrack at its best condition is said to be fast.

FIELD: This word has two meanings in racing. The entire group of starters in a race is known collectively as the "field." However, a "field horse" is one of a group designated by the racing secretary in a case where there are more starters than there are betting units provided by the pari-mutuel equipment. Rightly called the "pari-mutuel field," this group runs as a single betting unit. For example, in the Kentucky Derby of 1971, while there were only 12 betting units, actually there were 22 horses running. Therefore, the horses 12 through 22 were paired and were the "field horses."

FURLONG: One-eighth of a mile. Originally a "furrow long" or the length of a plowed field.

HAND: A unit of four inches by which a horse's height is measured, placing one hand above the other from the ground to the withers, or the point where the saddle sits. A horse that measures 16 hands is five feet, four inches tall at the withers.

HANDICAPPER: One who assigns the weights to be carried in a handicap race.

HANDILY: A horse working or racing with ease and without urging is said to be going handily.

HOMESTRETCH: The straightaway leading to the finish.

IN THE MONEY: A horse finishing first, second, or third is "in the money."

INFIELD: The area within the inner rail of a racetrack.

IRONS: The stirrups are referred to as irons.

ODDS ON: Odds of less than even money ($1 to $1). A winner at a payoff of under $4 is "odds-on."

PADDOCK: The area at the racetrack where the horses are saddled and viewed prior to a race. A fenced-off field on a farm.

POST: The starting point of a race.

POST POSITION: A horse's position in the starting gate from the inner rail outward, which is decided by a drawing at the close of entries the day prior to the race.

POST TIME: The time at which all horses are required to be at the post and ready to start.

PURSE: Technically, a race to which the owners do not contribute to the prize. There was a time when the prize money was contained in a purse and hung on a wire that crossed the finish line. The terms "taking down a purse" and "going under the wire" once had literal meanings.

QUARTER POLE: On a one-mile track, the pole at the turn into the stretch ¼ of a mile before the finish.

RACING SECRETARY: The official who makes up the conditions for the races and assigns the weights for handicap races.

SCALE OF WEIGHTS: An arbitrary set of weights to be carried by horses of a certain age at a certain time of year at a certain distance.

SCRATCH: To withdraw a horse from a race. There is a deadline for scratches, after which permission must be obtained from the stewards.

SEX ALLOWANCE: In all races other than handicaps, or where conditions state otherwise, fillies and mares are allowed weight below the scale, usually three pounds for two-year-old fillies and five pounds for fillies and mares three years and up, prior to September 1, and three pounds thereafter.

STAYER: A horse that can run well at longer distances.

WALKOVER: A rare occurrence in which only one starter goes to the post and is required only to gallop the distance of the race to be declared the winner and collect the purse, or a prescribed portion thereof, depending on the rules in effect.

WEIGHT-FOR-AGE: A type of race in which horses carry scale weight, or weight assigned arbitrarily according to age, distance, and month of year.

WIN BY A NOSE: The expression "win by a nose" became official in 1937, when the New York Racing Commission made the nose the official part of a horse in a photo finish, to end any dispute which might occur over outstretched legs or hooves.

Horse Ailments

BLEEDER: A horse suffering a nasal hemorrhage resulting from a ruptured throat vein.

BOWED TENDON: A rupture of tendon fibers due to strain of one or both flexor tendons, which extend down the back of the cannon and pastern bones. Bowed tendons become inflamed, sore, and swollen.

BREAKING DOWN: A general term for going lame in a workout or in a race, due to any ailment or injury causing a horse to go lame while running, most often a bowed tendon.

FILLED: A swelling accompanied by heat usually in the limb area.

FIRING: An operation in which a hot metal tip is inserted many times under the skin in the area of the trouble, such as bowed tendons, splints, osselets, or arthritic conditions. It is done under local anesthesia.

OSSELETS: Arthritic growths in and around the fetlock joint (ankle). When acute, the fetlock joint becomes visibly inflamed and swollen. The condition usually affects both front ankles.

SPLINT: An inflamed, oval enlargement on the splint bone, located along the sides of the cannon bone, just below the knee of the foreleg, and the hock of the hind leg.

267

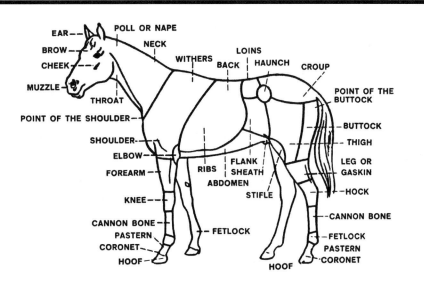

Conformation of Horse

Bibliography

Books

Alexander, David. *The History and Romance of the Horse*. New York: Cooper Square Publishers, 1963.

The American Racing Manual. Compiled and published by Daily Racing Form, Triangle Publications, Inc.

Anderson, C. W. *Thoroughbreds*. New York: The Macmillan Co., 1942.

Beckwith, B. K. *Seabiscuit: The Saga of a Great Champion*. San Francisco: Wilfred Crowell, Inc., 1940.

Cady, Steve, and Barton Silverman. *Seattle Slew*. New York: Viking Press, 1977.

Corum, Bill. *Off and Running*, edited by Arthur Mann. New York: Henry Holt & Co., 1959.

Craig, Davis. *Horse-Racing: The Breeding of Thoroughbreds and a Short History of the English Turf*. London: J. A. Allen & Co., Ltd., 1963.

Encyclopaedia Britannica (1959).

Hervey, John. *Racing in America: 1922–1936*. Written for the Jockey Club, printed privately. New York: the Jockey Club, 1937.

Hervey, John. *American Race Horses: 1936*. New York: Sagamore Press, 1936.

Hervey, John. *American Race Horses: 1937*. New York: Sagamore Press, 1937.

Hervey, John. *American Race Horses: 1938*. New York: Sagamore Press, 1938.

Kelley, Robert F. *Racing in America: 1937–1959*. Written for the Jockey Club. New York: North Press, 1960.

Newman, Neil. *Famous Horses of the American Turf, Vol. 1: 1930*. New York: The Derrydale Press, 1931.

New York Times Encyclopedic Almanac (1970).

Palmer, Joe H. *American Race Horses: 1946*. New York: Sagamore Press, 1947.

Palmer, Joe H. *American Race Horses: 1947.* New York: Sagamore Press, 1948.

Palmer, Joe H. *American Race Horses: 1948.* New York: Sagamore Press, 1949.

Palmer, Joe H. *American Race Horses: 1950.* New York: Sagamore Press, 1951.

Palmer, Joe H. *American Race Horses: 1951.* New York: Sagamore Press, 1952.

Parmer, Charles B. *For Gold and Glory: The Story of Thoroughbred Racing in America.* New York: Carrick and Evans, Inc., 1939.

Rice, Grantland. *The Tumult and the Shouting: My Life in Sport.* New York: A. S. Barnes & Co., 1954.

Robertson, H. P. *The History of Thoroughbred Racing in America.* Englewood Cliffs, N. J.: Prentice-Hall, Inc., 1964.

Rogrigo, R. *The Racing Game: A History of Flat Racing.* London: Phoenix Sports Books, 1958.

Ross, J. K. M. *Boots and Saddles: The Story of the Fabulous Ross Stable in the Golden Days of Racing.* New York: E. P. Dutton & Co., Inc., 1956.

Rudy, William H. *Racing in America—1960–1979.* New York: The Jockey Club, 1980.

Russell, George B. *Hoofprints in Time.* South Brunswick, N. J.: A. S. Barnes and Co., 1966.

Summerhays, R. S. *Summerhays' Encyclopedia for Horsemen.* London, New York: Frederick Warne & Co., Ltd., 1962, 1966.

Underwood, Tom R., and Day, John I. *Call Me Horse: Interesting Humorous and Informative Notes and Anecdotes About Horse Racing and Breeding.* New York: Coward-McCann, Inc., 1946.

Vesey-Fitzgerald, Brian Seymour. *The Book of the Horse.* London: Nicholson & Watson, 1946, 1947.

Vosburgh, W. S. *Racing in America: 1866–1921.* Written for the Jockey Club, printed privately. New York: The Jockey Club, 1937.

Newspapers and Periodicals

American Horseman
    1974—Mar.
Baltimore Sun
    1938—Nov. 2
    1973—May 17, 20
Blood-Horse
    1936—July 25; Nov. 28

1938—Jan. 1, 8, 15, 22; Feb. 5, 12, 16; Mar. 5, 12, 26; Apr. 2, 9, 16, 30; May 7, 14, 21, 28; June 4,18; July 9, 23, 30; Aug. 6, 20, 27; Sept. 3, 24; Oct. 8, 22, 29; Nov. 5

1940—Aug. 17; Oct. 5, 12, 26; Nov. 23

1941—Feb. 15; May 3, 9, 10, 17; June 14, 28; July 26; Aug. 2, 16, 23, 30; Sept. 20, 27; Dec. 13, 20

1942—Mar. 14; Apr. 18; May 2, 16, 23; June 6, 20, 27; July 4, 11, 25; Aug. 8, 15; Sept. 5, 19, 26; Oct. 3, 10, 17, 31; Nov. 7, 14, 21, 28; Dec. 19

1943—Jan. 9; Mar. 6; Apr. 24; May 8, 15; June 12; July 3, 10, 17; Aug. 7

1944—Jan. 22; July 29

1947—May 31; July 29

1950—July 15, 29; Aug. 5

1951—Jan. 6; July 14; Oct. 20; Nov. 3; Dec. 22

1953—Apr. 11

1954—Nov. 20

1969—Mar. 29; July 2, 12

1970—Apr. 15, 25; Oct. 24

1971—June 7; Sept. 27

1972—Mar. 20; May 8, 15; Aug. 28; Sept. 4, 16, 17, 25; Oct. 14, 23; Nov. 6, 27

1973— Jan 1, 15; Mar. 5, 12, 26; Apr. 16, 30; May 14, 28; June 4, 18, 25; July 2, 9; Aug. 6, 13, 20; Sept. 24; Oct. 8, 15; Nov. 5; Dec. 10, 24

1974—Jan. 7, 16; Feb. 11, 18, 25

Daily Racing Form

1973—Apr. 19, 20, 21, 23; June 11

Horsemen's Journal

1971—June

Louisville Courier-Journal

1973—May 2, 6

Morning Telegraph

1938—Mar. 16, 30; Apr. 7, 9, 10, 12, 15, 18, 26; May 21, 25, 29; Oct. 7, 30; Nov. 1, 2, 3

1950—July 13

New York American

1930—May 18; June 8

New York Daily Mirror

1941—May 8, 11, 12

New Yorker
    1940—Sept. 28
New York Daily News
    1972—Jul. 31; Aug. 1, 17, 26; Sept. 15, 16, 17; Oct. 14, 15, 26, 29; Nov. 19, 22
    1973—Mar. 17, 18, 19; Apr. 8, 16, 22, 23; May 5, 6, 7, 20; June 7, 8, 9, 10, 11, 28; July 1; Aug. 4, 5, 6; Sept. 16, 30; Oct. 9, 27, 28
    1974—Feb. 15; May 24
New York Herald Tribune
    1938—Apr. 6, 9, 12, 13, 15, 16, 17, 26; May 8, 24, 25, 26, 28; Oct. 6, 23, 28, 30, 31; Nov. 1, 2
New York Journal
    1930—May 10, 17
New York Journal-American
    1938—Mar. 16, 30; Apr. 7, 9, 10, 12, 15, 18, 26; May 21, 25, 29; Oct. 7, 30; Nov. 1, 23
    1945—Aug. 6
    1953—Apr. 7, 9; May 3, 9, 11; June 8
New York Post
    1972—Sept. 18; Oct. 14, 25, 30; Nov. 20
    1973—Mar. 16, 19; Apr. 4, 9, 21; May 1, 3, 5, 7, 21; June 6, 9, 11, 28; July 27; Aug. 6; Sept. 17; Oct. 1
    1974—Feb. 14, 19, 20
The New York Times
    1920—Oct. 10, 13, 15
    1930—Mar. 20; Apr. 4, 27, 29; May 10, 12, 17 , 18, 19; June 7, 8, 28, 29; July 12, 13; Aug. 10, 16, 17 ,18; Oct. 2, 28
    1938—Apr. 6, 7, 8, 9, 10, 13, 14, 15, 17, 18, 19, 26, 29; May 12, 23, 25, 26, 29; Sept. 20, 21; Oct. 6, 16, 28; Nov. 1, 2
    1941—Aug. 10
    1942—Oct. 4, 10, 11
    1943—Apr. 14, 16, 18, 19, 20; May 1, 2, 3, 5, 9, 11, 23; June 6; Dec. 19
    1944—May 7, 8, 13, 14
    1950—July 14
    1953—Apr. 8
    1958—May 3, 7, 17
    1972—July 5; Aug. 17, 27; Oct. 15, 29; Nov. 19; Dec. 27

1973—Jan. 5, 12; Feb. 16, 27, 28; Mar. 18; Apr. 1, 8, 21, 22, 23, 24; May 2, 3, 4, 5, 6, 7, 8, 15, 19, 20, 21, 22; June 2, 3, 8, 9, 10, 11, 21, 26, 29, 30; July 1, 8, 10, 23, 27, 28; Aug. 2, 5; Sept. 11, 12, 15, 16, 29, 30; Oct. 2, 9, 26, 27, 29, 30, 31; Nov. 4, 7, 12; Dec. 4
1974—Feb. 19, 25; Mar. 4, 8, 11

New York World-Telegram
1938—Apr. 7; May 10, 21, 25, 31; Oct. 6, 31; Nov. 1, 2, 3

Newsweek
1938—May 30; June 6, 11; Nov. 14
1973—Apr. 2; May 7, 14; June 11, 18
1974—Jan. 7

Sports Illustrated
1972—Oct. 23
1973—Jan. 8; Apr. 30; May 7, 28; June 11, 18; Aug. 13; Sept. 24; Oct. 8; Nov. 5
1974—Feb. 18

Spur of Virginia
1971—Summer

Time
1973—May 7; June 11, 18

Turf and Sport Digest
1938—Feb., May
1952—Sept.

Variety
1973—July 4

Western Horseman
1971—Jan.

Photo Credits

AP/Wide World Photos: 17, 35, 37, 53, 96 (top), 106, 115, 163, 208–36, 238–49

Bert Clark Thayer: 21, 22, 44, 84, 108, 146

Bert Morgan: 131, 136

Casper (Wyoming) *Star-Tribune*: 19, 20

Caufield & Shook: 6, 28, 33, 59, 92, 117

Churchill Downs: xi, 4

Hollywood Park: 162 (bottom)

Keeneland Library: xx, 3, 9, 11, 12, 14 (all), 35, 36, 41, 64, 78 (top), 79 (bottom), 89, 96 (bottom), 99, 108, 119, 120, 122 (all), 123, 130, 133, 134, 139, 154, 156, 158, 159, 237

King Ranch: 128, 144

Knights of Ak-Sar-Ben: 54

Narragansett Park: 104 (all)

New York Racing Association: xvi, xvii

Pimlico: xiv, xv, 82, 189, 190

Santa Anita: 70, 162 (top, center)

Thoroughbred Racing Associations: 56, 100

United Press International: xii, 16, 25, 30, 32, 40, 47, 48, 49, 50, 51, 52, 61, 63 (all), 78 (center), 79 (top left, top right), 94, 112, 142, 151, 160, 164, 167, 183, 186, 194 (all), 200, 202, 206

Index